WITHDRAWN

Published with the support of
the Société des Auteurs et Compositeurs Dramatiques

sacd

*The publication of this book was also made possible, in part, by a grant
from the Cultural Services of the French Embassy, New York*

UBU REPERTORY THEATER PUBLICATIONS

Individual plays:

Swimming Pools at War by Yves Navarre, 1982.
Night Just Before the Forest and *Struggle of the Dogs and the Black*, by Bernard–Marie Koltès, 1982.
The Fetishist by Michel Tournier, 1983.
The Office by Jean–Paul Aron, 1983.
Far From Hagondange and *Vater Land, the Country of Our Fathers* by Jean–Paul Wenzel, 1984.
Deck Chairs by Madeleine Laik, 1984.
The Passport and *The Door* by Pierre Bourgeade, 1984.
The Showman by Andrée Chedid, 1984.
Madame Knipper's Journey to Eastern Prussia by Jean–Luc Lagarce, 1984.
Family Portrait by Denise Bonal, 1985; new edition, 1992.
Passengers by Daniel Besnehard, 1985.
Cabale by Enzo Cormann, 1985.
Enough Is Enough by Protais Asseng, 1986.
Monsieur Thôgô–gnigni by Bernard Dadié, 1985.
The Glorious Destiny of Marshal Nnikon Nniku by Tchicaya U Tam'si, 1986.
Parentheses of Blood by Sony Labou Tansi, 1986.
Intelligence Powder by Kateb Yacine, 1986.
The Sea Between Us by Denise Chalem, 1986.
Country Landscapes by Jacques–Pierre Amette, 1986.
Nowhere and *A Man with Women* by Reine Bartève, 1987.
The White Bear by Daniel Besnehard, 1992.
The Best of Schools by Jean–Marie Besset, 1992.
Jock by Jean–Louis Bourdon, 1992.
A Tempest by Aimé Césaire, 1993 (new edition).
The Free Zone and *The Workroom* by Jean–Claude Grumberg, preface by Michael R. Marrus, 1993.
A Modest Proposal by Tilly, preface by Tom Bishop, 1994.
The Case of Kaspar Mayer by Jean-Yves Picq, 1995.

Ubu Repertory Theater:1982–1992, A bilingual illustrated history with personal statements by various playwrights and theater personalities, 1992.

*Distributed by Ubu Repertory Theater, 15 West 28th Street, New York, NY 10001. All other titles distributed by Theatre Communications Group, 355 Lexington Avenue, New York, NY 10017.

Anthologies:

Afrique I: New plays from the Congo, Ivory Coast, Senegal and Zaire, including *The Daughter of the Gods* by Abdou Anta Kâ, *Equatorium* by Maxime N'Debeka, *Lost Voices* by Diur N'Tumb, *The Second Ark* by Sony Labou Tansi, and *The Eye* by Bernard Zadi Zaourou. Preface by George C. Wolfe. 1987. (Out of print).

The Paris Stage: Recent Plays: *A Birthday Present for Stalin* by Jean Bouchaud, *The Rest Have Got It Wrong* by Jean–Michel Ribes, *The Sleepless City* by Jean Tardieu, *Trumpets of Death* by Tilly, and *The Neighbors* by Michel Vinaver. Preface by Catherine Temerson and Françoise Kourilsky. 1988.

Plays by Women: An International Anthology: *A Picture Perfect Sky* by Denise Bonal, *Jocasta* by Michèle Fabien, *The Girls from the Five and Ten* by Abla Farhoud, *You Have Come Back* by Fatima Gallaire–Bourega, and *Your Handsome Captain* by Simone Schwarz–Bart. Preface by Catherine Temerson and Françoise Kourilsky. 1988, 1991. (Out of print).

Gay Plays: An International Anthology: *The Function* by Jean–Marie Besset, *A Tower Near Paris* and *Grand Finale* by Copi, *Return of the Young Hippolytus* by Hervé Dupuis, *Ancient Boys* by Jean–Claude van Itallie, and *The Lives and Deaths of Miss Shakespeare* by Liliane Wouters. Preface by Catherine Temerson and Françoise Kourilsky. 1989, 1991.

Theater and Politics: An International Anthology: *Black Wedding Candles for Blessed Antigone* by Sylvain Bemba, *A Season in the Congo* by Aimé Césaire, *Burn River Burn* by Jean–Pol Fargeau, *Olympe and the Executioner* by Wendy Kesselman and *Mephisto*, adapted from Klaus Mann by Ariane Mnouchkine. Preface by Erika Munk. 1990.

Afrique II: New Plays from Madagascar, Mauritania and Togo including *The Legend of Wagadu as Seen by Sia Yatabere* by Moussa Diagana, *The Crossroads* by Josué Kossi Efoui, *The Herd* by Charlotte–Arrisoa Rafenomanjato, *The Prophet and the President* by Jean–Luc Raharimanana and *The Singing Tortoise* and *Yevi's Adventures in Monsterland* by Sénouvo Agbota Zinsou. Preface by Henry Louis Gates, Jr. 1991.

New French–Language Plays: *The Orphan Muses* by Michel Marc Bouchard (Quebec), *Fire's Daughters* by Ina Césaire (Martinique), *The Ship* by Michèle Césaire (Martinique), *Talk About Love!* by Paul Emond (Belgium), *That Old Black Magic* by Koffi Kwahulé (Ivory Coast). Preface by Rosette C. Lamont. 1993.

Plays by Women: An International Anthology. Book 2: *The Orphanage* by Reine Bartève (France), *Game of Patience* by Abla Farhoud (Quebec/Liban), *The Widow Dylemma* by Werewere Liking (Cameroon), *The Tropical Breeze Hotel* by Maryse Condé (Guadeloupe), *Beware the Heart* by Denise Bonal (France). Preface by Ntozake Shange. 1994, 1995.

Monologues: Plays from Martinique, France, Algeria, Quebec: *Another Story* by Julius Amédée Laou (Martinique), *Night Just Before The Forest* by Bernard-Marie Koltès (France), *The Sifter* by Michel Azama (France), *All It Takes Is Something Small* by Martine Drai (France), *Madame Bertin's Testimony* by Fatima Gallaire (Algeria), *Anatomy Lesson* by Larry Tremblay (Quebec). 1995.

Plays by Women: An International Anthology. Book 3: *Always Together* by Anca Visdei (Romania), *Bonds of Affection* by Loleh Bellon (France), *Lapin Lapin* by Coline Serreau (France), *A Country Wedding* by Denise Bonal (France), *Your Handsome Captain* by Simone Schwarz-Bart (Guadeloupe), *You Have Come Back* by Fatima Gallaire (Algeria). Preface by Ntozake Shange. 1996.

AN INTERNATIONAL ANTHOLOGY

plays by

women

BOOK THREE

UBU REPERTORY THEATER PUBLICATIONS
NEW YORK

CAUTION

Ubu Repertory Theater Publications
General Editor: Françoise Kourilsky
Assistant Editor: Valérie Vidal
Distributed by Theatre Communications Group, 355 Lexington Avenue, New York, NY 10017

Printed in the United States of America, 1996
Library of Congress Catalog Card Number: 89-142722
ISBN 0-913745-46-4

Price: $19.95

CONTENTS

PREFACE ix
Françoise Kourilsky

ALWAYS TOGETHER 1
Anca Visdei
Translated by Stephen J. Vogel

BONDS OF AFFECTION 77
Loleh Bellon
Translated by Barbara Bray

LAPIN LAPIN 159
Coline Serreau
Translated by Barbara Wright

A COUNTRY WEDDING 237
Denise Bonal
Translated by Timothy Johns

YOUR HANDSOME CAPTAIN 339
Simone Schwarz-Bart
Translated by Jessica Harris *and* Catherine Temerson

YOU HAVE COME BACK 365
Fatima Gallaire
Translated by Jill Mac Dougall

PREFACE

This is our third volume of plays by women who all write in French but are from different countries, different cultural backgrounds, different generations. Six voices of women, six violently contemporary plays, raising issues, whether political, social, personal, which remain deeply relevant today.

Two of the plays had previously been published in the first Ubu anthology of plays by women in 1988 (reprinted in 1991, and out of print for quite a while). These are *You Have Come Back* by Algerian-born Fatima Gallaire and *Your Handsome Captain* by Guadeloupean writer Simone Schwarz-Bart. Both plays had successful runs at Ubu Rep and elsewhere, and are very much in demand at various universities and theaters here and abroad. They are tragically pertinent today: *You Have Come Back* treats the theme of religious intolerance, and more specifically of women fighting Islamic fundamentalism; *Your Handsome Captain* deals with the poignancy of economic exile and explores the trials of separation and isolation experienced by many Caribbean workers who must migrate abroad to get work, leaving their wives who must survive alone in the homeland.

The theme of exile is also at the heart of *Always Together* by Romanian playwright Anca Visdei who, already a well-known writer at 19, was forced to emigrate to Switzerland and resumed her writing in her adopted language, French, which she struggled to make her own. Her play, the story of two sisters, a playwright and an actress, separated by the Iron Curtain, is based on her own experience as a "displaced refugee". It is a tale of endurance and survival. The two women have to make a life for themselves and find their voices in a world where men are "absent", either destroyed by the regime, or busy being part of it, or just plain husbands.

In Loleh Bellon's *Bonds of Affection*, women also take center stage. As J.B. Pontalis points out in his introduction to the play, "Men appear and disappear even when they remain: they don't really understand this story without a beginning or an end... They keep it at a distance, preferring to live their own lives." The play is the passionate "inner history" of a mother-daughter relationship, as time reverses their roles, from the thirties to well into the sixties. World War II is present and images of genocide—the mother is Jewish—but in *Bonds of Affection* as in *Always Together,* a strong sense of humor prevails, probably one of the keys to survival for women facing a society vitiated by war.

Mama, who is the central character in Coline Serreau's sharp comedy, *Lapin Lapin,* certainly needs a solid and earthy sense of humor to keep her wild family together. They are flat-broke, Papa has been fired, one daughter is getting a divorce, the other changes her mind at the altar, one son is working for a terrorist organization, another has been expelled from school, and the eldest, his mother's hope, turns out to be a gun smuggler. They all come to Mama who succeeds in keeping the family from total collapse, and calls for a new era where women won't "allow men to continue with their murders."

Bonds of Affection and *Lapin Lapin* are both urban plays. The set of Denise Bonal's latest play, *A Country Wedding,* is a large field with a large tree, and the presence of nature throughout the play—wind, sun, clouds, flowers, grass—gives the play a breath of sensuality, a kind of lightness suggesting that in the country nothing is as serious as in the city. And the large cast of characters of all ages, coming and going, criss–crossing the space, give the work an effervescent pace.

A Country Wedding is the only play in the volume which has not been produced and will not be produced on the small stage of Ubu Rep. I decided to commission a translation and to publish it, in the hope that a bigger theater would take up the challenge of staging this very unusual 40-character play which combines the elusive quality of a dream and a harsh realism.

FRANCOISE KOURILSKY

ANCA VISDEI

ALWAYS TOGETHER

Translated from the French by

STEPHEN J. VOGEL

UBU REPERTORY THEATER PUBLICATIONS
NEW YORK

Anca Visdei was born in Bucharest, Romania in 1954. She began writing at the age of 14 and later, at the University of Bucharest, studied to be a stage director. At 18 her first play, *La revedere, Florentina,* was performed and published in her native city. The following year she emigrated to Switzerland. There she studied law and criminology at the university of Lausanne, obtaining a doctorate before finding employment in the Swiss court system. But having decided to resume her original vocation, she began writing again, and soon newspaper articles, stories and plays followed in rapid succession. Since 1979, all her creative writing has been done in her adopted language, French. She is the author of a novel, *L'éternelle amoureuse* ("Woman Forever in Love"), two collections of short stories, and over a dozen plays, including *L'atroce fin d'un séducteur* ("A Seducer's Ghastly Fate"), *Doña Juana* and *René and Juliette.* Her plays have been performed throughout Europe, and, for production in Romania, she herself adapts them into her native language. She currently resides in France. *Toujours ensemble,* originally produced in 1994, is being revived this year and will be performed at the Bouffon Théâtre in Paris concurrently with the run of *Always Together,* its English-language translation, at the Ubu Repertory Theater.

Stephen J. Vogel has previously translated Daniel Besnehard's *Passengers* and *The White Bear,* both published by Ubu, as well as *A Simple Death (Arromanches)* and *The Child in Obock. The White Bear* was produced by Ubu Repertory Theater in 1992. Other translations for Ubu Repertory Theater include *All It Takes Is Something Small* by Martine Drai (France), published in Ubu's Anthology *Monologues, The Prophet and the President* by Jean-Luc Raharimanana (Madagascar), published in *Afrique II, Intelligence Powder* by Kateb Yacine (Algeria), and *The Daughter of the Gods* by Abdou Anta Kâ (Senegal), included in the first *Afrique* anthology now out of print. He is co-translator of Raymond Queneau's *En Passant* presented at the French Institute/Alliance Française as part of Théâtre de la Cabriole's *Be-Bop at Saint Germain-des-Prés.*

Always Together, in Stephen J. Vogel's translation, had its American premiere at Ubu Repertory Theater, 15 West 28th Street, New York, NY 10001, on February 13, 1996.

Director .... **Françoise Kourilsky**
Set Designer .... **Watoku Ueno**
Lighting Designer .... **Greg MacPherson**
Costume Designer .... **Carol Ann Pelletier**
Music composed and performed by .... **Genji Ito**

CAST

Alexandra .... **Maria Deasy**
Ioana .... **Thea Mercouffer**

Produced by **Ubu Repertory Theater**
Françoise Kourilsky, *Artistic Director*

If there is anything good to be said for oppression, it is that it breeds subversion. And it gives the world fine plays like Anca Visdei's *Always Together*. [...] Ms. Visdei's thoughtful two-character play manages the remarkable feat of peopling the stage with vivid individuals and multitudes and raising moral issues that transcend particular nationhood and time.
—Lawrence Van Gelder, *The New York Times,* February 22, 1996

Alexandra and Ioana, two sisters coming of age in the Eastern bloc, vow they'll be together always. Communist politics, however, makes them soon forswear themselves, as Alexandra is forced to seek exile in Switzerland to pursue her career as a writer. Their correspondence from different sides of the Iron Curtain makes up the bulk of Romanian-born playwright Anca Visdei's historically intimate,[...] epistolary drama, *Always Together.* [...] It's the characters' divergent fates that are most compelling. [...]
—Charles McNulty, *The Village Voice,* March 5, 1996

AUTHOR'S NOTE

This is the story of two sisters and, to a lesser extent, of two worlds: parallel universes as politically, socially and culturally different as possible. These two sisters were born in an Eastern Bloc country. In my mind, that country is Romania, but this is a small detail. Any country with a repressive dictatorship and a brilliant cultural elite, facing a struggle for social and economic survival, will do as well.

These two sisters, therefore, were born into a world where culture is the only escape from the stifling lack of privacy, mental and physical. And culture, especially in the form of its more fragile outgrowth, creativity, will prove to be their escape.

Alexandra wants to become a playwright. Ioana, an actress. They share a close, mutual understanding, one which is both deep and pure, arising from their twin bonds of sisterhood and friendship.

After writing a book with a "questionable" ideological slant, Alexandra is obliged to seek exile in the West. She is eighteen years old. Ioana stays behind. Both are aware that they are at a "point of no return." Alexandra, by seeking to become a political refugee, can never again set foot in her homeland. And Ioana, now stigmatized as the sister of a "deserter," sees her chances of receiving an exit visa forever destroyed.

Over the course of nearly twenty years, the only contact these two will have is through their letters, punctuated by infrequent phone calls back and forth. Separately, they will go on trying to live the same kind of life, trying to meet the same challenge: how to combine the roles of woman and artist.

Living in different environments, facing the same trials (marriage, divorce, motherhood, professional plans either successful or unrealized), they find themselves one day at the same juncture: the locus known to all women of thirty when their ambitions are of a spiritual, a personal and a social nature. The view from this juncture may be breathtaking, yet the winds that blow about it are so strong that one must hang on desperately to whatever scarce and scrawny shrubs happen to be at hand...

Alexandra, whose humor is invariably linked to cynicism and clear-sightedness, refers to an anti-Archimedean principle at work in the lives of the two sisters. Its one unshakable constant is this: a pretty body, endowed moreover with a lively mind, when plunged into adult life, will be thrust down, head first, with a force equal to the weight of her illusions. As for Ioana, she prefers to speak of fate, when writing her letters.

This umbilico-epistolary cord seems destined to remain their only link until suddenly fate takes a hand. An historical knife-thrust through the social and political fabric. The Berlin Wall comes down, the borders open up, leading to reunions and assessments. And in this new landscape, an old question, a trick question: Which is heavier, a pound of lead or a pound of feathers? Which fate weighs more heavily upon us? And of which is grace the attribute, solidity or lightness?

ANCA VISDEI

For Ion Luca and Jaroslav Caratchek

The events in the play take place between December, 1971 and December, 1989. After leaving her country in December, 1973, Alexandra Popesco will exchange letters with her sister for a few years.

CHARACTERS

ALEXANDRA POPESCO: *a writer, 18 years old at the beginning of the play, 36 at the end.*

IOANA POPESCO: *her younger sister, an actress, 17 at the beginning, 35 at the end.*

SETTING

At the beginning: the two sisters' bedroom, with twin beds, typewriter, telephone, books, clothes closet, record player and television set. Each time the TV is supposedly on, a bluish light from the cathode tube will spill over the stage. Downstage right there is a public phone. The set will undergo gradual modifications later on. New props (e.g. a telephone and a typewriter for Alexandra) will eventually appear.

1

DECEMBER 31, 1971

Alexandra enters at top speed, carrying a leather briefcase and a bag made of ugly gray paper. She closes the door quickly behind her, shivering with cold. She's out of breath, having run too much. Covering her head is a beautiful white fur toque and she has on a navy blue coat, on the sleeve of which is sewn the ID number 1067. Under the coat is a schoolgirl's uniform: sky blue blouse and navy smock. Ioana, her sister, wearing a short evening dress, is parading in front of a mirror.

ALEXANDRA: *(panting)* Greetings, Number 2001! *(Seeing the TV is turned off)* Did I miss it?

IOANA: Greetings, Number 1067! Your program just ended.

ALEXANDRA: *(vexed but resigned)* Damn. I went over to Veritas. The publishing house. To see the editor. The one who's apparently never in. At least I got to swipe a few copies of my play. *(She dumps the contents of her briefcase on the floor.)*

IOANA: Now will you sign one for me?

ALEXANDRA: *(as if she didn't care)* Was the show any good?

IOANA: Terrific! You spoke so well...

ALEXANDRA: They didn't cut out the part about self-censorship?

IOANA: No, in fact it was a little too...

ALEXANDRA: Amazing! Sorry, a phone call I've gotta make. *(Handing her the paper bag)* Martini Bianco.

IOANA: You're a genius.

ALEXANDRA: No, just patient. Two hours to buy the dollars on the black market and an hour in line for the *Martini Bianco...* Happy New Year! *(She kisses Ioana.)*

IOANA: Happy New Year!

> *Alexandra removes her coat, she also puts on some music: it's Beethoven's* Ode to Joy. *As she gets her appointment book out, the phone rings.*

ALEXANDRA: *(signaling to Ioana)* Go ahead!

IOANA: Hello. This is Ioana Popesco... Yes, she's here. I'll put her on right away. *(Covering the speaker with her hand; to Alexandra)* It's the Institute. Your professor, Gina.

ALEXANDRA: *(taking the receiver)* Hello? Yes... You saw the program?... Thanks... No, I didn't see it... but my sister did. Thank you... of course, it was only natural that I'd mention you. You've always been a help to me. To show you my thanks, I'll do extra well on my scene for the final. It's about a bride who gets left at the altar. It won't cost that much. We've just dug out Mama's old wedding dress... No, it doesn't exactly follow "the straight and narrow." But, coming from me, that's nothing new. The commission? I'll watch out, I promise. Thanks for everything... *(She hangs up.)*

IOANA: So? What was that about?

ALEXANDRA: *(wanting to drop the subject as soon as possible)* Congratulations, the program went very well, but I've upset the commission that was keeping an eye on me... Isn't anybody going to open that damn bottle?

IOANA: *(opening it)* You're not careful enough . . .

ALEXANDRA: *(dialing a number, as she takes off her boots)* Just one phone call...

IOANA: That's right, it's the last one of the year!

ALEXANDRA: To Veritas. Super-extra important!

IOANA: *(shocked)* But it's New Year's Eve!

ALEXANDRA: *(dialing the number as she continues to undress)* Hello?
I'd like to speak to the literary editor... I know it's New Year's Eve,
I'm celebrating, too, like every other human being... Alexandra
Popesco... Thank you, that's very kind of you; I'm glad you liked
the program, thank you. He's not in? I'm very sorry to hear that.
The play is being performed in February. The book has to come
out at the same time or all these fights we've had over the last two
years will have been for nothing. The commission? I know, I'll take
care of that. At least send me the contract. I'll believe it when I see
the signed contract. Yes, I know. I come across as very romantic
and ethereal on TV... I know, but a contract is a contract and the
play is being put on in February. It's not your fault, but it's certainly not mine either. You just give your boss the message, I'll take
the consequences. Thank you. Happy New Year. *(She hangs up.)*

> *During the call, Ioana has been putting on her makeup and
> getting ready. She is really very pretty. She looks at Alexandra,
> who is simmering inside as she continues to undress. By now
> Alexandra is down to her satin slip and a pair of socks.*

IOANA: You're not even dressed. We're going to be late. *(She
calmly applies more makeup. Alexandra hums the* Ode to Joy, *pours
herself a glass of* Martini Bianco *and looks at her appointment book
as she paces about, angrily.)* What about your book?

ALEXANDRA: They're making me wait and I don't know why...
There's been some kind of a fuck-up.

IOANA: *(pretending to be shocked)* A... what?

ALEXANDRA: *(pacing furiously now)* So it's come to this. I have
to wait...

IOANA: And when you're an Amazon warrior, doing nothing is
the hardest thing to do.

ALEXANDRA: I may be bowed, I may be bent, but at least I'm not broken. *(Changing the subject)* By the way, I've finished working on the script, so you can play the role of Puck for your exam.

IOANA: Great!

ALEXANDRA: *(toasting her sister with her glass)* Don't forget: always together!

IOANA: Cheers! Always together!

ALEXANDRA: I've cooked up a translation for you that's a cross between the salacious and the sublime. When they're judging our performances, those horny teachers at the Institute are in for quite a thrill, hearing those Elizabethan horrors flow from your pretty lips. Men are such fools. *(The phone rings. Ioana indicated to Alexandra that she should answer it because it's always for her. Alexandra picks up the receiver, in a hurry.)* Hello...? *(Her face lights up, birds sing, the month is June, and torrents of honey flow in her voice.)* Andrei, is that you? *(She sits down, smiling broadly and crosses her legs as if the person at the other end of the line could see her.)* Not at all, I'm so glad you called...

IOANA: *(mimicking her)* So glad you called.

ALEXANDRA: *(pantomimes spanking her sister)* I'm listening, Andrei... Tonight? We're going to the party at the Theater Institute... You'll stop by? *(She indicates to her sister that this is something wonderful, and, beside herself with barely-contained, muted joy, has trouble restraining her enthusiasm.)* We'll see each other later then? Did you see the program? No, I missed it. Was it good? At Veritas. I waited two hours to see the editor. Still nothing. Somebody up there doesn't like me. You'll take care of it? But it's not up to you... I'm a big girl now. *(Ioana gestures for her to shut up.)* No, of course, I have complete faith in you! Well, if you insist... Thanks, Andrei. Happy New Year!... You'll be there at midnight to wish me the same? I'd better run then. See you soon.

All the while this conversation has been going on, Ioana and Alexandra have been gesturing to each other: Alexandra, overcome with a feeling she tries to disguise, Ioana sometimes encouraging and sometimes mocking her sister.

IOANA: What did he promise you about the book?

ALEXANDRA: *(hanging up, looking horrified)* The book, who cares about that? I need a dress. Andrei is coming to the New Year's Eve party. A gorgeous dress, a sublime dress... My literary output for a dress. *(She appears desperate.)*

IOANA: *(opening the closet)* Quick! *(She helps her sister get undressed.)*

The closet is open in front of the two sisters, and a magnificent wedding dress is sticking out, next to two or three limp, gray outfits. Alexandra, nearly naked, her back to the audience, goes to the closet and takes down the dress.

IOANA: *(horrified)* You wouldn't dare...

Alexandra turns around, the dress pressed up in front of her and nods her head, silent, determined and smiling.

2

JANUARY 27, 1973

Ioana and Alexandra enter. Alexandra takes off her beautiful white fur toque. The two sisters have white ribbons around their heads, their ID numbers are sewn on the sleeves of their coats, and their shoes are wet. Freezing and silent, they take off their shoes and put on thick woolen socks, all the while rubbing their feet to warm them up. Ioana turns on the TV and the stage is bathed in the light of the cathode tube.

VOICE OF THE TV ANNOUNCER: Today, January 27th, 1973, tens of thousands of high school and university students, workers and intellectuals came to give a spontaneous hand to the greatest son of the people. The entire University of our capital, all the cultural elite of the nation were overjoyed on this historic day when, because of his numerous intellectual attributes, the First Among Us, the Coordinator General of the Party's Central Committee, received an honorary doctorate from the University of this, our greatest city. Having come of their own free will, in spite of the cold, tens of thousands of citizens, with tears in their eyes....

ALEXANDRA: *(nervously turning down the TV)* Okay, we know, we were there... No need to draw us a picture!

IOANA: "Of their own free will!" *(She takes off the white ribbon and puts it in her briefcase.)* Finita la... mascherata!

ALEXANDRA: *(also removing her ribbon, which she stuffs in a pocket of her uniform)* Ten times we got counted, at the start and when the motorcade arrived. Our IDs could've been taken away, if we hadn't showed up. People got off their sick beds to be there.

IOANA: So many of them were coughing. Maybe Mr. Big will catch his death. If you want to talk about it...

ALEXANDRA: Not now...

IOANA: Not even to me? *(She goes toward her sister, who throws herself into Ioana's arms and begins to sob.)* It must have been hard for you. I was watching you when Andrei started speaking. I could see you from the side. I thought you were going to start crying...

ALEXANDRA: *(crying)* Me, cry? You don't know me.

IOANA: Oh, yes I do.

ALEXANDRA: *(jokingly)* Well, maybe one tear of joy at hearing the Coordinator General... that great intellectual. *(Furiously, without any transition)* Andrei, that jerk, what got into him?

IOANA: Are you going to see him again?

ALEXANDRA: Never.

IOANA: He'll be calling you again...

ALEXANDRA: Andrei no longer exists for me. As of today. Seeing him, hearing him stumble through that speech of his, just like a flunkey. And singing the intellectual praises of the Coordinator General, recalling the man's epistemological studies, what a farce that was! Who knows if the man can even write his name.

IOANA: Well, maybe he's good at penmanship.

ALEXANDRA: Oh, the shame of it all, the shame...

IOANA: You're in love with him!

ALEXANDRA: You idiot! That has nothing to do with it.

IOANA: *(stubbornly)* Just as I thought, you're in love with him. *(After a long silence)* He may have his reasons.

ALEXANDRA: That's right, I should go ahead and forgive that little bootlicker, who, on top of everything else, knows exactly what he's doing, intelligent man that he is. Meet him for tea, talk things over like nothing's wrong, then figure out the twisted logic of a coward. All the time knowing that our father died in a forced labor camp, being "re-educated" through construction work, building the so-called dam, his recognition for the real work he did, in philosophy.

IOANA: Have you been to bed with him?

ALEXANDRA: What?

IOANA: With Andrei, not with the Coordinator General!

ALEXANDRA: *(laughing through her tears)* Ha ha!

IOANA: So my question...

ALEXANDRA: What question?

IOANA: Andrei.

ALEXANDRA: Which Andrei is that?

IOANA: *(pretending to give her a slap)* You're trying my patience, sister dear.

ALEXANDRA: But we haven't done anything.

IOANA: But a kiss, at least...

ALEXANDRA: One. It went down in history.

IOANA: Well, if that's all that went down...

ALEXANDRA: *(bristling a bit)* But it was a good one...

IOANA: There'll be plenty of others.

ALEXANDRA: Not a one. As far as I'm concerned, men are all

rotten to the core. I'm fed up with them.

IOANA: A virgin widow.

ALEXANDRA: If you want me to drop Gideon on your head, just say the word.

IOANA: You'll never do that. You'd have to give up clattering away on that thing all night just to keep me awake.

ALEXANDRA: I'll have you know that last night I was typing up the final version of your scene as Puck.

IOANA: *(dreamily)* I don't get it. All those afternoons and evenings that you were with him... and nothing happened?

ALEXANDRA: We were talking.

IOANA: About literature!

ALEXANDRA: Why not?

IOANA: Because he's fifty years old.

ALEXANDRA: Forty!

IOANA: Same difference, close to the century mark.

ALEXANDRA: The only one who wasn't a member of the Party... and the most talented...

IOANA: One little kiss! I can't understand how he can be as dumb as you are.

ALEXANDRA: As you saw for yourself today, he's now even dumber than me.

IOANA: He's looking out for his future—I mean, his old age.

3

NOVEMBER, 1973

ALEXANDRA: They're never going to publish my book... Ever since I stopped seeing Andrei, he's been out to sabotage my career. They're putting pressure on me to join the Party... The way things are going, pretty soon I'll be sent off to the boondocks to help the toiling masses get a good cultural education, at one of their arts centers.

IOANA: You've got to go abroad... That invitation to join the cultural exchange program with the Swiss, it's heaven-sent.

ALEXANDRA: Like being sent to hell, you mean, for me. Me, writing in a foreign language... No, you have no idea what you're saying. It's like telling a man when the wife he adores has just left him, "Don't worry, just marry another one, you'll get used to her."

IOANA: But that's exactly how people mend their broken hearts. Since the beginning of time.

ALEXANDRA: You can just forget it. You don't give up your own language at nineteen when you want to be a writer! I might as well cut off my tongue.

IOANA: If you stay here, somebody else will be cutting it off. They've already started.

ALEXANDRA: It's running away, it's too easy, that's not my way and you know it.

IOANA: Leaving is what takes courage.

ALEXANDRA: That's right. Go where it's safe and warm. In search of metaphysical comfort.

IOANA: For a writer, staying here would be the comfortable thing to do.

ALEXANDRA: *(shouting)* Running away is the easy way out.

IOANA: *(screaming)* Don't shout. In eighteen years we've never had a real argument. *(She screams, beside herself.)* We're not going to start shouting now that everything's going wrong. Don't worry, your so-called easy way out will cost you plenty. You'll go crazy, almost, when you can't talk or write. You, especially, who can make words do whatever you want. You, who make people cry with one sentence, and laugh with another. You'll be in despair, feeling so helpless. I'm not talking to you like a sister now, I'm talking to you like an enemy. You who're always writing, you're going to find yourself useless, mute, deaf. You'll have to learn everything over again, every word, every turn of phrase. You'll be lost, like a baby who can't even talk.

ALEXANDRA: Oh words, words, words...

IOANA: *(starting to cry)* You just can't worm your way out of this. Go and tell them we're alive...

ALEXANDRA: *(softly)* I'm frightened. I'm frightened of another language. I won't get used to it. I'm too small or too old, too lazy... I don't have the courage. You're the strong one...

IOANA: I'm not a genius.

ALEXANDRA: *(hastily)* Well, don't worry, neither am I. What about Mama?... What about you?

IOANA: We'll have each other. *(The telephone rings.)* Hello? *(For a moment she is speechless.)* Yes, I recognize you, Andrei. Yes, she's here. It's unusual, indeed. I'll put her on.

ALEXANDRA: *(looking flabbergasted, with panicky, uncomprehending gestures)* But...

IOANA: Even if it's the last time you ever speak to him, even if you plan to shoot a bullet through his belly, give him one more chance.

ALEXANDRA: *(going to the phone)* Hello... yes, it's me... My voice sounds different? Maybe... hmmm... hmmm... hmmm. *(She listens for a long time.)* Hmmm... I'm not being too quiet... I'm listening to you... Hmmm... yes... That's all you have to say to me?... That's a question. That's all you have to say to me? *(She hangs the receiver up, gently.)*

IOANA: *(looking at her sister, pleadingly)* So?

ALEXANDRA: He says he's always defending me against the old guard, the ones who don't understand my talent, that he's always fighting on my behalf. I might as well go.

4

DECEMBER, 1973

The two sisters are seated on Alexandra's bed. Patiently, each of them takes up piles of manuscripts on the floor and tears the pages out. Two garbage bags sit in front of them. Each rips a sheaf of papers into quarters and drops the remains into the bags.

ALEXANDRA: We have to tear up all these manuscripts. I'm sorry now I wrote so much... You promise me you'll be careful?

IOANA: I promise.

ALEXANDRA: You can never be too cautious.

IOANA: I will be.

ALEXANDRA: If something happens to you, it'll be my fault and I'll never forgive myself.

IOANA: You can rest easy.

ALEXANDRA: By going away like this, I'm drawing attention to you.

IOANA: *(ironically, pointing to all that remains to be destroyed)* Oh, don't leave me all alone with your complete works.

ALEXANDRA: *(sitting down, tearing up more pages; there follows a long silence)* As far as the letters, we need a code; otherwise, nothing will get by the censor. We'll write Ubu for the Coordinator General...

IOANA: What if we happen to get a censor who knows literature; then we're out of luck. No, we'd better be more discreet... Ubu... Jarry? Alfred!

ALEXANDRA: Alfred, that's brilliant! They'll never figure it out.

IOANA: We'll write "the pioneers" for our friends. That way they'll pay no attention... *(Feeling inspired)* The "brain-damaged" for the Communist Youth League... No, make that "the brain-damaged children!"

ALEXANDRA: "Aunt Prudence" for the secret police.

IOANA: "The chosen few" for the Passport Bureau... And what name should I give Andrei in my letters?

ALEXANDRA: That won't be necessary.

IOANA: Oh, but it will. I'm sure his progress will be meteoric... I'll call him Oberon.

ALEXANDRA: Oberon! I suppose that makes me Titania in your eyes.

IOANA: Of course, you two make a godlike couple... Otherwise, how could I be Puck, chosen to be your messenger? And this? *(She shows her sister the wedding dress.)*

ALEXANDRA: *(upset)* The exam is in a month. My poor scene... I'm not going to be doing it.

IOANA: Don't you want to do it, just for me?

ALEXANDRA: *(stubbornly)* No!

IOANA: Well, I'll keep the dress anyway... Who knows? Maybe I'll be performing it someday.

ALEXANDRA: *(visibly moved, falling into her sister's arms)* When I think that a year ago we swore we'd always be together...

IOANA: We will always be together.

5

THE FIRST LETTERS

The layout of the set has changed somewhat. The two beds are now as far apart as possible, one being to the far side of stage left, the other at stage right. As of this point, the setting represents two rooms separated by an invisible wall. All the contents of what used to be the two girls' room are now compressed into Ioana's room. At stage right, in what is now Alexandra's room, there is only a bed and a closet. The two sisters have also changed their clothing: during the reading of the first letters, Ioana slips on a black pullover and a black pair of slacks, and this is how she will be dressed when playing Puck. Alexandra, who starts the scene wearing an overcoat, one without an ID number on the back, later removes it to reveal a bathrobe, under which, it will soon be seen, she's wearing an attractive, short black dress.

ALEXANDRA: *(carrying a heavy suitcase into what will be her new space)* My dear little sister, this is my first letter. I'm starting it on the airplane that's taking me to Geneva. Just to let you know that my deathless literary works are here beside me. *(She puts the suitcase down on the floor, and looks at her sore hand which the handle of her suitcase has been biting into.)* Never before has the sheer gravity of the written word so impressed itself on me. As you see, I have been spewn out, along with my works. Strange to tell, I've just found out that, though of legal age when I left our country, I arrived here a minor. In Switzerland, the legal age is set at twenty and not at eighteen as it is for us. So you see, I'm off to a good start, I'm getting younger and younger.

IOANA: *(lying down, softly caressing the typewriter)* Dear Alexandra, my fairy queen, Gideon is silent, that seems so strange to me... especially at night. I was so accustomed to drifting asleep to his clacking sound. That music used to last all night long. I miss it, just as I miss everything connected with you. A lot of your classmates have been telephoning us. For now, we tell them that you're exhausted and that you've gone to stay with Grandmother and get some rest. That gives us some extra time. We already miss you... a lot. Mother is very brave; we think of you every moment, but try not to let it show too much. If we let ourselves go, we'd spend all day talking about you and sobbing in each other's arms. With tender hugs and kisses. Your sister who loves you.

ALEXANDRA: *(during Ioana's letter, she has taken off her coat, placed it on the bed, opened her suitcase and taken out a notebook and a pen. Then she curls up on the bed and begins to write to her sister.)* Dear little sister, so-far-away-and-yet-closer-than-ever, your letter filled me with delight. I'm writing at once in answer to it. I've gotten out of the habit of writing by hand. As soon as I get a little money together, I'm buying myself a typewriter. But I hope that you can at least read my handwriting. As for me, I'm sleeping, darling. You should be glad, you who used to find fault with me for staying up all night, typing on my faithful Gideon. There are some days when I sleep sixteen hours straight. Yesterday was Christmas. I celebrated by sleeping in my hotel room, with the shutters closed. Happy New Year! I haven't got a single franc, and all I ask is to be able to hibernate. I only leave my room to see if the mail has arrived. I haven't the strength to even get dressed. Down at the reception desk, they think I'm either sick in the head or else sick at heart, waiting to hear from my fiancé, and they view me with pity. 1974 is starting out with a case of chronic somnolence. Instead of waking up to my new life, I'm falling asleep over it. And still not the slightest laurel wreath to place on my fevered brow. At this point I'd even settle for one that's brown and withered. *(She takes a new sheet of paper.)* Lausanne, January 4, 1974. You write, "Gabriela and the others phoned to invite you to celebrate with them, as in the past. Think it over, come back, everything will be like before." Too late. Yesterday, I applied for refugee status. I think of all of you, of all the fun you're having. Enjoy the party and think of me now and then. *(She takes another sheet of paper.)* Lausanne again, January 4 again... and me again. This is the third letter I've written you today. Except for you, I have no one to talk to. A bit like before. I went to the Foreigners Police Service. I filled out the forms. I left them my passport. The clerk told me that as of that moment I'd broken all ties with my homeland... They're starting to give me trouble in the little hotel where I'm staying. I was complaining about not being able to phone to my country. They said, "Oh, we know all about you political refugees... Where you come from, in your country, you probably had a telephone in your bedroom..." I said of course but that aside from that we all crawled around on our hands and knees wearing animal hides. I quit when I realized that they were taking me seriously. They must have a different sense of humor. In fact, they talk to me very loud, as if I was deaf. Sometimes they emphasize their words with certain hand gestures, *(As she enumerates them, she demonstrates each gesture, as if for a simpleton.)* for "eating," "sleeping," "working," "you," "me." Today I went to the Social Services Office. They gave me two hundred Swiss Francs so I could buy myself some warm clothes. They're being nice; that's a regular fortune and I was starting to look like a bag lady. Having stuffed my suitcase with manuscripts, I only had the clothes on my back when I got here. It may just have been the smell I gave off that caused the Social Service people to be so charitable. I'm also buying some eye makeup and some lipstick... which I don't use. I feel so plain, so gray... Oh, I almost forgot, I also bought a Swiss watch. Strangely enough, my old one stopped running on the day I got to the West. *(She takes from her suitcase a typewriter which she carefully unwraps.)* I've finally rented a typewriter. To my despair I find it has a French keyboard.

IOANA: *(carefully wrapping the typewriter that belonged to Alexandra)* Dear Alexandra, your letter took two weeks to get here. You seem so sad and so fragile that, if I could, I'd come immediately to be with you. Forgive the moment of weakness in my last letter when I told you to come back. I was longing for you so... but you need a little sister who's strong, who encourages you and who backs you up. You should know that we partied very late at Liviu's, we danced, chitchatted, listened to music. I didn't get home until six o'clock in the morning.

ALEXANDRA: Ioana, my sweetie, I spent a New Year's Eve that was way beyond gloomy in my hotel room. So you danced and danced and came home late. You're quite right to do so! Take advantage of life, have fun! One never knows what tomorrow will bring. When will I go dancing again? It seems centuries since I last had the chance.

IOANA: *(unwrapping the typewriter)* I tried to mail Gideon to you. But I got turned down at customs. Very rudely. They told me that if I insisted they would confiscate him. And yet, Gideon more than fulfills the criteria for family reunification set by the Red Cross. Considering the number of nights you spent staring at each other, he's obviously become one of your nearest and dearest. More than that, even, a member of the family. Poor Gideon, I fear that, being a lover scorned, he may decide to break down on us.

ALEXANDRA: I'm starting to take French classes—advanced level, I'll have you know!—at the Ecole Migros. With my warped mind, and because it's all I ever think about, I suppose I chose it because of the name: Migros, migrate, emigrate... During the break period yesterday, the teacher invited us, his four advanced-level students, to join him for coffee. When the check arrived we all understood that we were expected to pay our own share. I barely managed, by spending my last centime, to come up with the money, which was supposed to go for my bread that evening. I remember the celebrations which our teachers, the ones who really liked us, used to invite us to... Relationships must be very different here. I'll try to understand this better. Still, the teachers here have so much more to spend than those in our country... I feel it's not simply a question of money... *(Changing her tone)* You're marvelous to have thought of sending Gideon. It's not so serious if you couldn't do it. I'm starting to get used to the new machine. Please put a date on your letters. Most of the time they cross mine in the mail and it would make reading them that much easier...

IOANA: *(gossipy)* Lidia has gotten married to a German. She expects to get her passport any day now. She came to see us yesterday, dressed head to foot like a foreigner. She did her little number for us: the glamorous star bidding farewell to her native village, before flying off to the glorious life that awaits her in the Wide World Beyond. Her husband is thirty years older than she, has only one eye, is immensely fat, and sells coldcuts in a supermarket. But of course these are minor considerations. The girls here are ready to do anything at this point. They'd gladly marry a potted palm if that would make it possible to leave. What's more, if they leave to get married, they have the right to return. When I think that they have that right and you don't, it makes my blood boil. And to think that Lidia will have her passport and not you and I... God only knows when we'll see each other again. There's no question of you coming back here, and as for me, I was told quite clearly at Aunt Prudence's what we already knew: no possible departure, even to another Eastern Bloc country, while I have a sister living abroad... Are you writing anything?

ALEXANDRA: *(typing on her machine, after a long pause, almost aggressively)* I'm writing... I'm writing... Only my journal and even at that... I put down all the important events such as my verbal sketches of the students at the Ecole Migros. Dammit all, you could at least date your letters!

IOANA: I'm getting ready for my exam. Only five months to go. I'm going to play Puck, as you suggested. The text is brilliant, your adaptation marvelous, I want so much to be worthy of it... *(She begins to rehearse, with a pencil in her mouth.)*

> "Through the forests have I gone
> But Athenian found I none
> On whose eyes I might approve
> This flower's force in stirring Love.
> Night and silence! Who is here?"

(She repeats, frightened.) "Who is here?" *(Crying out)* "Who is here?" *(Laughing riotously)* "Who is here?" *(Troubled)* "Who is he?" *(Suddenly changing her tone)* Andrei comes looking for you every day. *(Getting back into her role of Puck)*

> "Princely clothing doth he wear
> This is he (my master said)
> Despisèd the Athenian maid
> And here the virgin, sleeping sound
> On the dank and dirty ground."

(Looking tenderly at Gideon)

> "Pretty soul, she durst not lie
> Near this liar, this kill-courtesy."

Andrei even put a bouquet of white lilacs in front of your door, two days ago... Naturally, I'm the one that got to take it... I hope the next time he'll leave a diamond necklace. I really do need one. I have absolutely nothing to wear to the next weekly meeting of the Communist Youth League. *(Once again in character)*

> "Churl upon thy eyes I throw
> All the power this charm doth owe."

(She makes a vague gesture, scattering the whole room with white confetti.) You were the most talented of your generation... Everyone at the Institute thinks so...

ALEXANDRA: Dear little mischievous sister, you are really the one and only person who can still make me laugh. The Institute of Theatrical Art. To think you go there every day. How lucky you are! As for me, every day I go to the Employment Bureau of the Canton. They congratulated me on the excellence of my French. The social worker there told me I have a rich vocabulary, and an impressive fluency. She therefore advised me to try and find a job... as a sales clerk in a department store.

IOANA: Dear sad-but-incomparable older sister, don't think you're the only one who's down-in-the-dumps. Our pioneers are very depressed these days, they're wondering what good life really is, and if we've all made a hideous mistake by being born... here. Alfred is up to his old tricks. He spends his time having his picture taken and then wherever we go we run smack into his portrait, rejuvenated and retouched, printed on the glossy covers of his all-too-numerous publications. Don't let yourself get depressed, have fun, hang in there, and, oh I don't know, smoke some Kents, drink some *Martini Bianco*...

ALEXANDRA: Here, there's too much, too much in the way of Kents, as well as *Martini Bianco*. All of a sudden, I've lost all desire... they make me sick to my stomach. Maybe it's just because they're everywhere. You remember that foreign tourist who was flirting with us in front one of the big hotels, inviting us up to his room, and waving a pack of Kents under our noses? When we turned and walked away, he even said, "Two Kents, two for you two." You see how much we're worth on the Foreign Exchange? Here I'm sick to my stomach all the time: morning, evening, on the bus, in a car, going up all the hills there are in Lausanne. The people are very nice, it's true, the air is pure, the countryside is lovely... But I feel sick all over and I can't seem to throw up. Throw up what? Bile? Memories? Homesickness... I must be carrying Romania in my womb. A little bit must have gotten inside me, by mistake. A little bit of the country which must be going through the first months of gestation, the ones that give you morning sickness...

IOANA: You had the courage to leave. Now we're counting on you. You have to let them know over there that we exist and what it costs us just to survive. They mustn't forget us...

ALEXANDRA: *(From the middle of her bed, Alexandra, surrounded by her books and notebooks, throws a dictionary to the floor, in a rage.)* Oh, God. French. What a language! I've set myself the task of translating my plays. To think I chose French to make it easier for me. As soon as I have an idea to express, no problem: the words are right there, crystal clear and precise. But as soon as I go after even the least of my feelings, the vocabulary slips away. In order to translate our expression "dor de tara," all I can come up with is "homesickness." And if it isn't exactly sickness that one feels... If it's more insidious than that, what we call "dor"? Nostalgia, melancholy, that's part of it, but for "dor," that sadness of the soul that's languishing, beyond suffering, even, how do you say that? You'd think this were a language of scholarly essayists with no innards and no heart that breaks. We, on the other hand, have a language of sinews, of guts, of raw nerves... French is a language of the brain. Will I have to amputate all the rest of me just to hear my own voice again?

6
FIRST PHONE CALL

Alexandra crosses to a phone booth, down stage right. During the whole conversation that follows, she will constantly be stuffing coins into the phone, all the while keeping a nervous and a watchful eye on the "meter." As soon as she hears her sister's voice, she is so stunned that she leans back gingerly against the wall of booth.

ALEXANDRA: Hello?

IOANA: Hello!

ALEXANDRA: It's me.

IOANA: I know.

ALEXANDRA: Do you hear me?

IOANA: Like you were in the same room...

ALEXANDRA: Is everything alright?

IOANA: Same as usual. What about you?

ALEXANDRA: The same.

IOANA: Are you getting used to things?

ALEXANDRA: How's Mama doing?

IOANA: Fine. Just little aches and pains.

ALEXANDRA: Serious?

IOANA: No. Must be the start of the flu.

ALEXANDRA: *(coughing)* She's got to take care of herself.

IOANA: You, too. Have you seen a doctor? They say the ones in Switzerland are very good.

ALEXANDRA: That's right. And so's the chocolate.

IOANA: *(who hasn't understood)* I didn't hear you very well.

ALEXANDRA: Nothing... I haven't had the time... to go and see a doctor.

IOANA: So, are you getting used to things?

ALEXANDRA: I miss you. I miss everything.

IOANA: Same here. We miss you. I've been getting your letters. All of them, I think. There've been twenty-three.

ALEXANDRA: There must be two more on their way. I've become a graphomaniac.

IOANA: Are you getting used to things?

ALEXANDRA: It's still too soon to tell. But I'm doing my best. I'm still the brave little soldier. *(She gives a brisk salute.)*

IOANA: Are things very different?

ALEXANDRA: I don't know yet.

IOANA: Is it true that you find everything... and with no waiting in line.

ALEXANDRA: It's true you find everything but also everything is so different.

IOANA: Like what?

ALEXANDRA: The people, especially.

IOANA: How are they?

ALEXANDRA: Dead... lifeless. Like teeth that are too well cared for.

IOANA: *(horrified)* Is that true?

ALEXANDRA: *(trying to laugh)* No, of course not. They're just a little sad. And tight-lipped. They're gray... like stuffed animals. Not unfinished artworks, like us.

IOANA: I read that there's a terrible crisis over there...

ALEXANDRA: Terrible! Everyone wants to get into the Iron Curtain countries, like ours, and become an economic refugee.

IOANA: This must be costing you a fortune. Where are you phoning from?

ALEXANDRA: From a public phone. At the train station. The others are all closed at night.

IOANA: Mama's not home. She'll be sorry you missed each other.

ALEXANDRA: She hasn't missed with me, she's had a big hit. *(She laughs nervously.)*

IOANA: I don't like it when you laugh like that. It's a sign that all's not well with you.

ALEXANDRA: Kiss Mama for me. Grandmother, too. Kiss everybody.

IOANA: We're thinking about you. All of us.

ALEXANDRA: I'll call again. As soon as I've got a little money.

IOANA: I love you.

ALEXANDRA: I love you, too.

IOANA: Is it cold over there?

ALEXANDRA: Yes.

IOANA: Here, the springtime is still so far off.

ALEXANDRA: Here, too.

IOANA: Don't forget: together!

ALEXANDRA: Always.

Each in her own space, they hang up at the same time.

7

LETTERS

ALEXANDRA: My dearest, this evening we spoke over the phone. For the first time since I left. Five minutes, a short time. They were the shortest five minutes of my life. We have so much to say to each other. But we've got to be reasonable: we'll only talk for five minutes each time, otherwise all my money will go for phone calls. Your voice was soft, yet strong... and I drawled along. I'm slowly wasting away; I may not even live to see twenty. Every gardener knows you can't change a plant from one pot to another when it's too old.

IOANA: *(alone in her room, rehearsing the role of Puck)*

> "I am that merry wanderer of the night.
> I jest to Oberon and make him smile
> When I a fat and bean-fed horse beguile,
> Neighing in likeness of a filly foal;
> He smiles... I jest to Titania in lurking 'twixt
> A gossip's thighs in likeness of a crab.
> She laughs... Then slip I' neath her bum,
> Down topples she, old legs upraised, and falls
> Into a cough...
> At that the quire, the whole world which behold
> The impish Puck

(At this she weeps.)

> Do hold their hips and laugh,
> And waxen in their mirth, and neeze, and swear
> A merrier hour was never wasted there..."

(Without transition) Examination Day: I'm playing Puck.

ALEXANDRA: Oh, the exams! How I wish I were there instead of you. *(Wearily)* Instead of sitting in this room of mine growing moldy while I write up my résumé and fill out job applications... for department stores. *(Returning to the subject)* It's too early for you to know the results, but I'm sure you passed.

IOANA: I've finally figured out what the play is all about, in your adaptation! Puck is only a jester in a horrible masquerade in which the tyrannical king and queen of the Gods enjoy clouding the minds of mortals. In the joyful section at the end, I started to cry. And, in fact, you had written in the notes, "his tears come from joy or his laughter from woe." I didn't see it before. It came to me during my exam performance, because I was playing the part for you. I didn't give a damn for the judges at that moment. The teachers were just flabbergasted, absolutely amazed, applauding just like the students... What will I do next year when you're not around to help me? Your teacher, Gina, said to me, "If you write to Alexandra, tell her that I heard her voice today, in Puck."

ALEXANDRA: My dear little sister, I'm so proud of your success. Rest assured that only Shakespeare and yourself deserve congratulations. And as I hadn't the pleasure of meeting the author (at whose feet I'd have thrown myself, unabashedly), it's on you that I rain down my bravos. *(Suddenly somber)* You advise me in your letters to "get myself moving." I'm trying. I've taken my manuscripts to every theater in town. Afterwards I've phoned each one of them at least four times. And you know how uncomfortable I am with wheeling and dealing. No one seems to want to read my plays. They say I should be recommended by a stage director. I took it all as a joke. So I wrote a letter as Alexandra-Popesco-stage-director concerning Alexandra-Popesco-promising-young-author whom I greatly admired and whom I warmly recommended and whose work I said I would be ready to stage in under a week. That didn't amuse them, either. Now I have no more manuscripts. That's what's so funny: in our country everybody reads and the problem is finding a Xerox machine that's not under surveillance. Here the Xerox machines abound, like mushrooms after a rainstorm. You even find them on the street corners but I have no more money to make copies. Here everything comes down to money. The only person who took the trouble to read my plays is the director of a tiny avant-garde theater. He called me to say that if I could find the money for a production, my play would suit him to a "t." I asked him what I would need him for if I had the money for a production, considering I wrote the play and can stage it myself. You'd never guess what he said to me then. It's an expression that we use all the time. For a moment I thought I was home again. He said, "That's the way the system works." Of course, I responded just the way we always do to that remark, "That's the way the system sucks." The only difference was, unlike in our country, he was able to answer me back with, "You're right. The system sucks."

IOANA: My little darling, you've been away nine months and already you've forgotten so many things. About your last letter: "The system sucks." Well, Aunt Prudence didn't much care for it. I was called in so that they could tell me that something like that might be tolerated once, because it did contain a severe critique of the capitalist system but that in future it would have to stop. They're already doing us a big favor in allowing us to write to each other. One of Aunt Prudence's employees happened to be, in his younger days, the student of our uncle Ioan Popesco, the painter, and he worshipped him. That's why Aunt Prudence is letting us send our notes back and forth, but we'd better not press our luck, if you know what I mean... Poor Aunt Prudence, she's getting on in years, and as you're well aware, old people want to have the final say in everything, they're very suspicious, especially where young people are concerned...

ALEXANDRA: *(typing furiously)* The weather is fine, the sky is blue, the clouds are white and billowy! The temperature is 23 degrees in Lausanne and 14 degrees in Saint-Cierges...

> *She stops, goes and gets out the wedding dress, puts it on, then crosses down stage right, as if she were in the wings, waiting to make an entrance. We hear music:* The Wedding March *from Mendelssohn's* A Midsummer Night's Dream. *She enters, looking contrite, looks around the room, and opens her suitcase. Then she drops her wedding bouquet into it and piles two manuscripts on top of the bouquet. Closing the suitcase, she makes a*

laughable little attempt at a waltz to this triumphal music, holding the suitcase in her arms like a dancing partner. Suddenly, the music goes sour, becoming an indescribable noise, out of which finally emerges Beethoven's Ode to Joy. *She opens the suitcase, letting manuscripts and bouquet fall to the floor. She tips the suitcase upside down over her head and a shower of white confetti rains down on her as she exits from the room, leaving the door open.*

IOANA: *(crying as she writes)* It's snowing at our house.

*

*   *

IOANA: *(delightedly)* A personal triumph: Puck is being revived as a curtain raiser at the Bulandra Theater. I'm performing there every night. Last evening, as usual, it was "standing room only." The sound of applause was intoxicating to me. But, as my older and unassuming sister, you're only entitled to my hangover, and to my eternal "I love you," as well. *(Very excitedly)* What are this year's fashions like, where you are? I need something to wear for the end-of-the-year party at the theater. You must have such beautiful dresses!

ALEXANDRA: *(snickering)* Yes, indeed. My closet is a wonder! *(She opens wide the doors to her wardrobe closet: it's completely empty.)* Over here you find marvelous dresses and inspired lunatics, considered the top fashion designers. They create magnificent dresses, so off-the-wall that nobody can wear them. It all goes to furnish the dailies with lovely photos. You should see their magazines... nothing but gossip. World-famous widows, and singers with no voices, starlets who want to be writers and writers who warble like songbirds. Boxers and princesses: they get married, they get divorced, they come down with a cold, among myriad other metaphysical upheavals. It's a fact. A world headed for cultural underdevelopment, as I heard it put to some poor native who was trying to hold out against progress. I don't even want to get into the political situation. In that area, they see about as clearly as a mole. Among other pearls of wisdom, they call Alfred a great political figure, a defender of human rights. They say those of us who have escaped his influence are paranoids, out to make excuses for ourselves, at best, or, at worst, just out to make more money.

IOANA: Really, thinking Alfred a defender of human rights... Are they all crazy?

ALEXANDRA: No. What they are is blind. I've gone to work as a sales clerk in a department store. Selling accessories and little knick-knacks. You see, I am well on my way to being both hopeless and helpless. For eight hours each day, I sell umbrellas and belts and handkerchiefs. Today an old lady explained to me in detail how you fold up an umbrella, bearing in mind that the shortest distance between two points is a straight line, hence the metal rod. This private lesson lasted for half an hour, punctuated with many a "Do you understand what I mean?" which she shouted at me as though I were deaf. Finally I said to her, "Just 'cause I talk with an accent doesn't mean I've gone deaf." She replied, "Speak louder. I can't hear a thing."

IOANA: Mama was called in and told that it was out of the question for her to make even a short trip out of the country. The guy even said, "If I had a daughter like yours, I'd shoot her dead." Mama was sick about it. Watch out for our fellow countrymen who you run into over there. As you yourself used to say, you can't be too careful.

ALEXANDRA: I sold an umbrella to a pregnant woman. I got choked up about it. Because I was jealous. When I make a mistake on the cash register, instead of making a void slip, which is difficult to do and for which you have to call the head of the department over from the other end of the store, I deduct the excess amount from the next purchase or, if I haven't counted enough, I add on the difference to the next charge I ring up. I do this without thinking; you know I've always had a head for figures. I thought they'd be pleased with me because I didn't have to disturb my boss and I didn't have to bother the accounting department with a lot of void slips. Well, little did I know! I was told, and I quote, "You foreigners, you've always got an angle, haven't you?"

IOANA: It's a good thing you left. They're talking more and more about getting rid of the directing class at the Institute. They say it's become a hotbed of troublemakers.

ALEXANDRA: *(She enters carrying a large wrapped package in her arms.)* Whew! In honor of your theatrical successes, I took the first of my paychecks as a sales girl and used it to buy you a real evening gown. I ought to mention, whenever I have a customer who wants a belt shortened, I head for cover. I've already ruined three belts this month. The price was deducted from my paycheck each time. I've never been very good with my hands. The matching shoes to go with your dress will have to wait until the next pay period. *(She takes a plate from a cupboard, cuts a hard-boiled egg in two and eats one of the pieces during Ioana's next letter.)*

IOANA: The dress is marvelous. Everyone was astonished at the sight of it, myself most of all. I'm going to wear it to celebrate the publication of your first book. Something strange is going on, there's talk about mandatory gynecological exams in the work place. It must be just a rumor... Do you have enough to eat?

ALEXANDRA: Of course I do. How can you ask such a question? *(As if "caught in the act," she takes the plate with the uneaten half of the hard-boiled egg and hides it in the cupboard.)* I share my room with another girl. The trouble is, she can't stand having the light on when she's asleep. So, since I do my writing at night, I find my inspiration in what the English call "the water closet," which is right down the hall. Somewhere it must be inscribed in stone that, no matter what I do, I'll always end up a closet dramatist. Whenever I've had it up to here, I go for a walk to see the swans at the edge of the lake. Wear that evening gown as often as you can. Don't save it for the publication of my first book in French. That won't be anytime soon. I make mistakes in grammar, my vocabulary is pitiful, and don't get me started on those damned rules about "agreement of tenses." *(Cutting another egg in two, she eats half and puts the rest on a plate in a safe place.)* But it's not like I'm not trying hard. I don't read a thing in our language, except for your letters and my plays. Maybe no one wants them but I patiently translate them every night, at the breathtaking speed of two pages a day, I mean, a night...

IOANA: Mama has a cough and she refuses to do anything about it. Ask her to go and see a doctor. She always listens to you. But whatever you do don't say anything about this in the letters you send me. I have her read them all and she doesn't like me telling you about her health problems for fear of worrying you.

ALEXANDRA: It will no doubt come as a shock to learn that I am tremendously upset by a fact that everyone's aware of, but this is a very serious matter: Switzerland has no seacoast. You're going to say that someone as supposedly up in her geography as I am shouldn't be quite so taken aback by this "revelation." And yet... Knowing it may be nothing. But realizing it... In the eyes of everyone on the street, I can see it, I can sense it: this is a country that has no sea. Their eyes are beautiful, quite often bright, melancholy or wistful, but there's a color missing: the color of the sea. At home, I guess I didn't realize it, it was so obvious. Even when everything was going wrong, we could always fantasize about our people setting out to sea on little makeshift boats, ranging from foot basins to wine barrels, setting sail from our beloved shores to seek refuge where the sky meets the sea. But Switzerland has no sea. *Oh, les choses que l'on ne peut pas acheter!* Today I treated myself to a long walk beside the lake, in the woods at Vidy. I was almost feeling happy when all at once I happened on the silver cube which is the Vidy Theater. It was like a reproach: What have I done with myself? What have I accomplished? I'm so far from the theater now... It was my twentieth birthday.

IOANA: Happy birthday, big sister. Your life is spread out before you, and so is the world. Gabriela has gotten married to a foreigner. She'll be leaving as soon as she gets her passport. The boys have all gone off to the army, carrying their wooden cases, it was a sad sight. Radu has been sent to a village in the mountains. Every week I send him a care package... like a good little prisoner's wife. I'm working on the role of Ismene for the new season. Ana died as a result of you-know-what: blood poisoning... she was in the third month.

ALEXANDRA: I'm working at a center for children. It's in a marvelous mountain setting. I take the train from Lausanne to Vevey, then another quaint little commuter train to Blonay. I who love children, I'm really getting my fill of them now: autistic, severely retarded, little human vegetables. They have to be watched constantly. Especially outdoors. They eat grass. They have to be stopped from jerking off, too. I asked the director why. She gave me a dirty look and said that she thought I was a well brought up young lady, and how disappointed she was in me. Which, as far as I'm concerned, still doesn't explain why the poor kids aren't allowed to jerk off. At the very least. I got my advanced diploma in French at the Alliance Française. My progress was rated "highly honorable." Well brought up, honorable... you see, I'll never escape my past. My application for asylum has finally been accepted. I can travel as a Swiss resident and I now qualify for a scholarship. If I take the exams for a high school diploma again. And since my diploma isn't recognized over here, I have to start all over again. I'm sick and tired of having to do everything twice. These things only happen to me...

IOANA: Something awful happened to Cristina. You know that she was crazy about that architect. And he seemed very nice, of course. But he never paid any attention to her. At least not until this last summer when, after three years of indifference, he suddenly began to show some signs of real interest. Dates, gifts, the whole shebang. Well, our Cristina was on cloud nine. Especially since she had just passed the qualifying exam to get into med school. After ten blissful days, the guy wanted to marry her right away and wouldn't take no for an answer. Cristina, delirious with joy, didn't want to seem in too much of a hurry, so she gently pointed out that they had never really gotten to know each other intimately, and she could certainly understand how such a healthy, normal guy would have the desire, and the right, even before their marriage... Well that threw the guy into a tailspin. He's the romantic type, see, not just somebody out to get laid, so don't lump him in with the others, get the picture? Cristina got scared of losing him, that's how mad he was. Well, she agreed to marry him. So one night, he makes her get all the necessary documents together, and wouldn't leave her except to get some sleep.

Wanted to keep himself pure until the wedding. Then at eight a.m. he shows up to take her to the People's Council where they go through all the formalities before they can publish the banns. After that, she doesn't see him again for two months. He says his work site is three hundred miles from the capital. Cristina offered to come along and he turned her down flat saying he was afraid of spoiling the chastity of their union, if he let his desires get the better of him. He came back for their civil wedding ceremony. I was one of the guests. Cristina was radiant, so beautiful. Truly. Well, the ceremony goes off without a hitch, and we all leave to change clothes for the evening. At nine o'clock we get to Cristina's place, only to find her alone. So we wait, one hour, two hours. Around midnight, feeling embarrassed for her, we all go home. The guy never did show up. Radu made some inquiries, only to learn that he had left the country as soon as he got his hands on his passport. As you know, the only men who get passports are ones with a family that stays behind. And this guy was an orphan. So what's he say to himself? "Gotta get myself a family right away, if that's what it takes." Cristina found out. After two months of electroshock treatments, they put her away in a home, for good. She wanders up and down the corridors, carrying a picture of her virtuous husband, asking people if by any chance they've seen him, showing them her wedding ring, and the marriage license...

ALEXANDRA: Happy, happy, happy! I got my Swiss high school diploma. No big deal. It was a special exam, just for foreigners. And their level was, all in all, abysmal! The president of the examining committee said to me, "Mademoiselle Popesco, I speak for the entire committee, as well as myself, when I say how pleased we are to have been present at your exam." I strongly suspect the majority of the candidates couldn't even speak French. Among the group was the daughter of our ambassador in Berne. She was being chaperoned by a classmate who was her own mother. You should have seen how they avoided talking to or even looking at me from the moment we found ourselves in the same waiting room. You'd have gotten such a laugh. I actually felt sorry for them. Of course, she failed her exams. But I wouldn't worry about her. No doubt there's a nice little scholarship set aside for her at Lomonosov University... and a diplomatic post after that. One of the teachers who'd quizzed me for my finals asked me out for dinner after the results were in. I feared for my virtue, but he acted like a gentleman. He spent the evening going into ecstasy over my intelligence. Fortunately, he also slipped in a comment about my beauty, or I'd have been extremely put out. You see, I've already some admirers to wine me and dine me. Don't send me any more food packages. It's silly. You have almost nothing to eat, and here we're in the lap of luxury. If you really want to send me something, send me some comedies by Caratchek. If I can't write, I should at least be able to translate. You know, you start out thinking you're a general in your own little war and you wind up discovering you're just a buck private. Autumn's here.

IOANA: I wanted to send you the plays of your dear Caratchek but, and this will surprise you, I couldn't find any. His works aren't being published any more. This despite the fact that he's one of our classic writers and you can find excerpts from his writings in our textbooks. You see, Alfred is even going after the classics. I'm sending you these few pages of Caratchek which I tore out of my high school textbook. More and more, I find myself thinking that you made the right decision.

ALEXANDRA: I have found myself a niche, at least for the next four years. Because I did so well on my exams, I qualified for a scholarship. But only if I study law. Well, why not? For three square meals a day I can put up with a little judicial mumbo-jumbo. Now it can be told! I went hungry for a whole year. I lived off lettuce and, for the protein, a half an egg a day. To think I was born in a third world country but had to come to Switzerland to find out what hunger is. Why do I always have to be different? Well, let's say no more about it, that's all behind us now. Still, even with my food provided, survival is sometimes difficult. I've met a few of my future classmates at law school. By chance, the conversation happened to come around to Alfred. I told them he's insane. They said, "Why are you so hostile?" I said, "I'm not hostile, I'm impassioned." Meaning I'm alive. They said, "We don't shout here; this is a democracy." After the first law class, one of my fellow students, very well-meaning, no doubt, asked me if in our country we have shops like in Switzerland. I, of course, informed him that we all go around wearing animal hides and that our wedding ceremony goes something like this: a man clubs his future mate over the head, then drags her by her hair back to his cave where he lights a fire by rubbing two sticks together. Since he still didn't catch on, I resorted to a parable. I told him, "where you come from, there's a sign on the shop marked 'John, the Butcher's', and inside you find meat. Where I come from the sign says 'Meat' and inside you find John, the butcher." No response. Today was our first course in Constitutional Law. What was the horrendous outcome of the violent Swiss Revolution? Four people dead. A real blood bath! And to think that with a past like that I expected them to understand my parables. That almost amounts to mental cruelty.

IOANA: When are you going to start writing again?

ALEXANDRA: Today in the lunchroom, I heard another student say that the sausage she was eating was magnificent. That's right, you read that correctly, "mag-nif-i-cent." A sausage! It wasn't all that good, incidentally. If a sausage is magnificent, what word do you use for Beethoven? As for me, I give up: I'm at a loss for words. And being at a loss for words is something of a handicap for a writer. I also went to a gathering of theater-types. One of the actors said to a playwright, "Give me the key to your universe so that I can find my way inside." That jerk! Our Caracheck would have answered back immediately, saying, "Read, you animal, read! It's there on the page!" But we don't shout here.

IOANA: *(attempting to do her yoga exercises)* Calm down. Find your peace and your inner strength. Ignore their lack of understanding. It will take just as long as it takes, but you will succeed. *(Suddenly very upset, she abandons the yoga position and stands with arms akimbo, like a fishwife.)* It's getting so the men here have the most awful mind-set. They're only looking out for themselves now, so a girl had better have a college degree, a house and, if possible, a car, if she has any hopes of getting married. Needless to say, she's got to be pretty, too, and sweet and even at that... it's expected she'll settle for any man at all. And even after she gets married, her troubles aren't over. He'll divorce her at once if she can't have kids. And some of the big mouths hanging around the cafés will tell you, with a big satisfied grin, that what matters isn't how a woman looks, it's what she's got in the oven.

ALEXANDRA: I've forbidden myself to read or to write in our language. It's either sink or swim. Only with you, do I allow myself that pleasure. Otherwise, it's too painful. Oh, Inaccessible, Beloved Mother Tongue... Will you remain forever ensconced in the depths of my heart, preventing me from giving myself to other loves? Dear little sister, I had the most awful dream. I dreamed we were allowed a five minute meeting in some no man's land. I wanted to shout something to you but I couldn't speak. After a desperate attempt, I was finally able to shout out to you, "Always together." I knew that these were my last words, that the effort had cost me so much that I would never again be able to speak. So I shouted with all my might, "Always together!" And that's when I realized you had gone deaf.

IOANA: It's seems incredible to me that there are people there who love Alfred. Are you sure that you're hanging out with the right crowd?

ALEXANDRA: *(laughing)* Yesterday, I went to see a doctor. When he found out what country I was from, he said, "So, don't they need young people like you, over there?" He was so smug. At school, I'm always getting into fights. With three young demonstrators who call themselves Marxists. I'm sure you'll say, "Why bother with them?" Well, strangely enough, it's because they're the ones who seem the most alive, out of all the students. Doesn't matter, though, there's no way we can get along. The difference between them and me is that I've read Marx and, even if I had to be forced to read him, that didn't keep me from understanding... and from loving certain passages. Whereas they haven't even gotten a quarter of the way through the first volume. This Thursday, the First of May, 1975, marked the fall of Saigon. We saw on TV the pictures of people scrambling on board trucks, families torn apart, the first settling of old scores. The students in theology were so ecstatic that they gleefully bought us all a round of drinks... What's become of Oberon? You never mention him to me, any more...

IOANA: I'm working on Medea. Radu has left me. He's getting married next month. Of course, as usual, I was the only one who didn't know about his other liaison. But the revival of Puck as a curtain raiser has been a great success. As a matter of fact, Oberon was in the audience last night. Right now he's writing odes to Alfred and organizing shows with thousands of extras. He's very famous and very powerful. It really made a big impression, having him show up.

ALEXANDRA: *(looking over her sister's letter)* A big impression? Puck between the two thieves... *(Very quietly, she exits the stage by the upstage door.)*

IOANA: He came backstage to my dressing room to congratulate me and, obviously, to ask me for any news of you. It's odd but he didn't realize that the text had been changed or even suspect that it was you who changed it. I thought he knew you better. Don't be sad for me. I don't give a damn about Radu. I can do better.

> *Alexandra enters by a side door in the house, comes down the left side aisle as far as the apron, then climbs to the stage, down stage right.*

ALEXANDRA: I've finally had the classic refugee's dream. All the others have had it over here, and I was starting to worry because I hadn't. Now what worries me is that I might have it again. It was awful. I was back in our country again, without really knowing why. I was horrified. I knew perfectly well that I wasn't allowed back. I would hide my face whenever someone passed me on the street, for fear of being recognized. I kept saying to myself over and over, "What was I thinking, coming back like this? Why did I do it? They'll arrest me any moment." I was on the outskirts of the city and my one hope was to be able to see you before I got arrested. All at once, this crowd of people took to the streets, I couldn't possible hide. I was carried along by the

crowd, half frightened and half delighted. It was so good to
see so many familiar faces, and to hear everyone speaking our
native language. I relished every syllable, every inflection. I knew
the language but I couldn't understand a single word. It may
be that I'd been recognized and they were talking about me.
Without knowing how, I had come back. Only one thing ran
through my mind, how to get back out of the country...

IOANA: For my summer vacation, I went to the beach. Alone. I
mean, without Mama. I'll tell you more later.

*Alexandra sits facing her mirror, clumsily putting rollers in her
hair. She's never been good with her hands.*

ALEXANDRA: So, who is he? That handsome stranger you were
with at the beach, the one who rushed to your side, ready to mend
the heart that Radu broke? As for me, I was in Provence with some
of my classmates. It's the first time I've been outside of Switzerland.
Now that I've got a travel permit, one with a big, beautiful Helvetian
Cross on the cover, why deprive myself of the pleasure? The world
is my oyster. We started off by visiting Orange. They had a terrific
rock concert. I heard a band there that was so great; I'm sending
you one of their cassettes. They performed outdoors in a Roman
amphitheater. Until dawn. All the kids were stretched out on the
seats, smoking grass. I wouldn't touch it. Maybe I should have. But
since everybody made fun of me, I went right on saying no.

IOANA: *(rock music in the background, she's dancing at a party.)* I
don't understand why people were smoking the grass in Orange.
Didn't you have any cigarettes? Was it to save money? Or is it
the newest thing? Thanks for the cassette. You're right, it's really
great. I can just imagine how wonderful it was to listen to that
music in a Roman theater under a ceiling of stars. Your cassette
has made the rounds of all our friends and they've all copied
it. You know how Aunt Prudence feels about rock music. So
of course everybody couldn't wait to hear that music, which
supposedly doesn't exist over here.

ALEXANDRA: We also went to the theater festival in Avignon. It was crazy: so many productions at so many locations with so many theater people. Performing whatever they want, and not needing prior approval. Do people lucky enough to have their plays put on, or who put on plays themselves there, ever realize they're in heaven? And when will I have a play put on in Avignon? When pears grow on poplar trees and primroses grow on willows...

IOANA: The new theater season is starting. Get busy with your scripts. You're going to have a big hit... Just get one staged, that's all it takes.

ALEXANDRA: *(bursts out laughing)* That's all it takes... *(She laughs uproariously.)*

IOANA: Then leave the rest up to the audience. They've always followed your lead.

ALEXANDRA: *(pretending to be nervous)* You think so? I don't see anyone behind me.

IOANA: *(putting on a chic black outfit, very 60's looking)* Keep your fingers crossed for your little sister. If all goes well, before I even graduate from the Institute, they might be offering me a contract at the National Theater! Mama's having some health problems. She coughs almost constantly. A bout of flu followed by a bad case of bronchitis. And springtime is still so far away... *(She begins to put on her makeup.)*

ALEXANDRA: Here, half the time and energy of people in the theater goes into trying to finance a production. It's a continuous quest requiring other talents than those of a playwright. It's an altogether different profession: that of an institutionalized beggar or a professional money grubber, and I have no gift for it. I'm just now starting to realize how lucky we were over there. At least money was never a problem. All you had to do was ask the government for it. On the other hand, we had to write tame little plays or plays that at least seemed tame. Like the artists-slash-servants of some slightly dimwitted prince. It was so easy. Aside from that, I always show up late for my classes when

I'm not out-and-out playing hookey. With a marked preference for Constitutional Law which I skip systematically. And delightedly. On the other hand, I haven't missed a single one of my Civil Rights classes. It must be their novelty that appeals to me.

Alexandra crosses to the public phone, down stage right and dials a number. Ioana's phone rings and she stops putting on her makeup to answer it.

ALEXANDRA: It's me.

IOANA: *(very embarrassed)* Oh, it's you?

ALEXANDRA: Am I bothering you?

IOANA: No, I'm expecting someone but it doesn't matter.

ALEXANDRA: You're in a dither, Puck. It must be a man.

IOANA: Uh-hunh.

ALEXANDRA: So your old flame, the incorrigible Radu, has come back, hey?

IOANA: No.

ALEXANDRA: Well, so it's a newcomer...

IOANA: You might say that.

ALEXANDRA: Tell me all about him!

IOANA: Not right now.

ALEXANDRA: *(hurt)* I understand, he might come by at any moment. *(Ironically)* Whereas, I telephone you each and every day...

IOANA: Don't over-react, darling. You're so kind, so considerate and I'm so... swamped. *(Looking at her ring)* It was sheer madness, sending me the ring that Andrei gave you. Are you sure you've gotten over him? Wouldn't you be just a little upset if you found out he was seeing some other girl?

ALEXANDRA: Why? Has he found someone new?

IOANA: *(a bit too quickly)* Oh no, he hasn't. Well, I really don't know. But if he had... would that bother you at all?

ALEXANDRA: Two years have gone by. Besides, I can't wear his ring now anyway. My joints are all swollen. None of my rings will fit me. Lausanne is right beside a lake and rheumatism runs rampant.

IOANA: You should see a doctor.

ALEXANDRA: Sure, sure... How's Mama doing?

IOANA: Not so well. I sent you a letter listing all the medicines she needs. No need to add they can't be found here.

ALEXANDRA: I'll send them off just as soon as I get the list... Well, since you're eagerly awaiting your visitor, I'll say good-bye.

IOANA: *(on a note of false gaiety)* Very well then. I'll let you go. Talk to you soon! *(She hangs up. Alexandra, looking stricken, stands with the receiver in her hand. At the sound of the door buzzer, Ioana rushes to the door and opens it, exclaiming as she does so.)* Andrei! Come in. *(But first she goes out onto the landing, disappearing from the audience's sight.)*

ALEXANDRA: *(She hangs up the receiver, gently. She collects the unused coins which gush from the pay phone into her hand, a stunned look on her face.)* Thirty... *(Pensively)* Thirty pieces of silver? *(She crosses to her room, opens a book, begins searching feverishly.)* A Midsummer Night's Dream... Ah-ha! Here it is. *(She pinches the pages of the book between her fingers, lets go of them, and the book opens at random. She searches the page which chance has put in front of her.)* Oberon... Oberon... not here... etc., etc., etc. Wait, here it is, at last. Puck! *(Reading aloud)*

"Then fate o'rrules, that, one man holding troth,
A million fail, confounding oath on oath."

(She remains pensive, thumbs through the book some more, and reads.)

"Shall we their fond pagent see?
Lord, what fools these mortals be!"

(She stares off into space, with a sad smile on her lips.) Shakespeare, you really shouldn't tell on us. *(She tosses the book aside, rushes to the door, bumping into Ioana who is just entering. Ioana looks very different than in the previous scene. She is somber, still dressed in black but with a head scarf covering her hair, signifying mourning. The two sisters glance at each other in passing, as if surprised by the incongruity of this chance encounter. Alexandra stands aside to let Ioana pass.)* Excuse me, Ma'am.

IOANA: *(crossing to her room, as if she hadn't recognized Alexandra)* Excuse me, Miss. *(She drifts over to her bed, and sits down, looking defeated.)* Be strong, my sweet, beautiful sister. Thank you for the various medicines. They arrived yesterday. And today Mama died. We are her survivors.

ALEXANDRA: I'm going out of my mind. I'm caught in a trap. If I go back home, I'll lose my exile status here in Switzerland. And over there, I'll be picked up before I even get to the cemetery. After I got your telegram, I took the next train to Bern. I did everything in my power. The Federal Office of Refugees, the Foreigners' Police Service. Everyone understands that I want to bury my mother. And everywhere the answer is NO! They say, in no uncertain terms, "If you go back to your country, even for one hour, you can never return to Switzerland. You ask us for exile because you're persecuted over there, and the first chance you get, you go back there." "But the first chance I get is my mother's funeral!" "Well, these things just naturally happen." All I could do was take the train back, and get off in Geneva to go and light a candle in the Orthodox Church. I prayed and prayed... for a miracle. But the Lord must know I've been a long-standing atheist. I hate myself for leaving two years too soon. All I had to do was wait for a while, stay with Mama while she was still alive and breathing. Maybe she wouldn't be dead now, if I had stayed...

IOANA: *(writing her letter)* It's hard for me as well! I'm all alone now with Grandmother who says anything that pops into her head. She's prophesying the revolution, she's insulting the people in power. Today, at the funeral, she started in again predicting the fall of the dictator. *(Aghast, she hastily crosses out the previous word, and rewrites.)* The fall of Alfred! It was just lucky that there was virtually no one around to hear her. Mama is buried in Bellu Cemetery, next to Uncle Ioan, since our father, as you know, has no grave. Except for a reed, somewhere between the Danube and the Black Sea...

ALEXANDRA: *(contemplating her manuscripts)* I dreamed that I would be dedicating my first book in French to Mama. Once again, I'm too late. And I'll never make up for it.

IOANA: Getting cast in a role here in the city is proving to be a herculean task. You have to pull just the right strings. There are all these middlemen who have to be wooed with presents. And after making your first visit, just to show respect, you have to follow up by paying them lots of courtesy calls. And you don't even know if this'll do you any good.

ALEXANDRA: Getting even a short article published in a newspaper here is proving to be a herculean task. You have to pull just the right strings. There are all these middlemen who have to be wooed with presents. And after making your first visit, just to show respect, you have to follow up by paying them lots of courtesy calls. And you don't even know if this'll do you any good.

IOANA: It's getting harder and harder to find enough to eat, the lines you wait in are endless, I don't know how I'm going to get by. Just to keep them from assigning a new tenant to live in Mama's old room, I had to have Grandmother come and live here. She didn't want to, I had to keep begging her. What she really would have liked was to go and live with Aunt Lucia. I've never seen a mother-in-law who's so stuck on her dead son's wife! Of course, by going to our uncle's widow, like that, she'd get to live in a huge apartment decorated with her son's paintings. But Lucia doesn't have the same problems I have. They leave her alone in her seven-room place out of respect for that museum she looks after so well. Whereas, in my case, if they stick me with one of Aunt Prudence's chums, right there in Mama's room, it's good-bye friends, good-bye phone calls, good-bye letter writing! I asked Grandmother to come and live here as a favor to me. She finally said yes but she never stops telling me that she's sick of doing favors. She gives me dirty looks. I think she hates me and would have much preferred to live with you. You remind her so much of Papa. She's like a child, so capricious. She's positive that Alfred's days are numbered and she's stocking up on food, even though we don't have enough to eat, just for your return. She's sure she's going to see you again. Yesterday, we had one orange, three hours in line to get it, I won't even talk about that, and Grandmother insisted that we put three pieces of it in the fridge and save it. "If Alexandra comes back, we've got to have something nice to give her." She opens the door to the fridge every fifteen minutes just to check that I haven't eaten *your* dessert. "Ever since you were a little girl, you've always swiped your sister's desserts." *(She laughs between her tears.)* Do you want me to send it to you, express mail? And if all that weren't enough, I'm in love and I'm afraid. Mostly of getting pregnant.

ALEXANDRA: Dear ungrateful little sister, you have a suitor and you haven't said a thing, not even to me whose desserts you were always swiping, during the best years of my life? Don't worry, I'm only teasing. You know I don't have a sweet tooth... So who is he? Tell me everything, this is really great! Who is this mysterious Don Juan? Have you, shall we say, crossed the Rubicon with him yet? Is it true that it's painful the first time you do it? Try to be understanding of Grandmother. She's gifted with second sight. Papa and Uncle Ioan, her own sons, always said so. And I've always believed it. Even when what she predicted seemed ridiculous to us, it always came true in the end, if you recall.

True, this time she seems to have gone a little too far...

IOANA: You're much too excited about all this. You're making far too much of this boyfriend of mine. All this is not as important as you think. It's clear that you're still a... girl. If it's finally dawned on you that I'm not a virgin any more, I suppose I should mention that this transformation dates back to the time of Radu.

ALEXANDRA: Was it Radu who was your first lover? But you broke up with him a year ago. And you've been hiding this from me all this time? Don't you tell me anything any more? What's gotten into you? You used to tell me everything.

IOANA: Maybe I'm feeling overly guilty. I don't know how this all happened. Everybody has a right to their own little "secret garden." Reading your letters, I get the feeling you wanted to march me down the aisle in all my virginal purity. *(In a hurry to finish her letter)* Success for Puck beyond all imagining. Thinking of you.

ALEXANDRA: Oh now, don't give me that... We made a solemn vow that whichever one of us was the first to lose her virginity would tell the other about it. Sometimes I don't know you any more. Your letter about finding someone for Mama's old room, it put me into a cold sweat. Why didn't you let Grandmother go and live with Aunt Lucia if that that's what she wanted. You ignored her wishes, just to hold onto that room? The wishes of a woman who deserves our love and respect and who raised our own father and Uncle Ioan? What's gotten into you? How can you have changed so much? And so suddenly? Unless it was just that I didn't want to see it...? I can't stop thinking of Mama. I'm so ashamed. I ought never to have left while she was still alive.

IOANA: *(to herself)* That's right. With me, Mama was bound to croak. With you, of course, she would have gone on living indefinitely.

ALEXANDRA: Did Mama know your boyfriend?

IOANA: It's too late for regrets and it doesn't matter.

ALEXANDRA: It doesn't matter that I'm dying of impatience? You change so fast... And why not just tell me all about it? I'm sure it would make you feel better and there wouldn't be such a hostile tone to your letters. You know, I might just understand this. If it's you who explain it to me.

IOANA: I haven't changed. It's the life around me that's changing. If you don't toughen up, you don't survive. And our age is changing too. You're over there, well protected. You can afford to dream and to make up crises to test your conscience with. But I've got Grandmother to deal with every single day, and long lines to stand in, and performances to give. We're not dreamy little schoolgirls any more. Well, not me, anyway. I've gone out into the world, working as well as being the head of a household. And it's hard! Oh, it's not so much a jungle, it's more like a salt mine. You want me to share some of my secrets? Well, I haven't got either the time or the energy to keep my private little diaries, full of metaphysical speculations. Okay, you want to know a secret? Here's a hot one: you almost became an auntie. But you're not going to be, and I'm not going to be a mother. I can't have children any more. I thought I was getting rid of just one; it turns out I'll be rid of them all. For good.

ALEXANDRA: And what did the father have to say about this? What did he do?

IOANA: Nothing... Didn't I tell you there was plenty to be ashamed about?

ALEXANDRA: Leave him!

IOANA: And how are your legal courses going? *(She continues, shifting into the role of Puck.)*

> "My mistress with a monster is in love.
> Near to her close and consecrated bower,
> while she was in her dull and sleeping hour,
> A crew of patches, rude mechanicals,
> That work for bread within the city walls

> Were met together to rehearse a play,
> Intended for the tyrant's wedding day."

ALEXANDRA: *(also assuming the role of Puck)*

> "The cunning sly fox of that barren sort,
> A lover's role enacting in their sport,
> Forsook his scene and entered in a brake.
> When I did him at this advantage take,
> An ass's nole I fixèd on his head....
> When they him spy,
> As wild geese that creeping fowler eye,...
> Sever themselves and madly sweep the sky,
> So at his sight away his fellows fly,...
> When at that moment (so it came to pass)
> Titania waked, and straightway loved an ass."

IOANA:

> "Thou art as wise as thou art beautiful. Fairies,
> Tie up my lover's tongue, bring him silently."

ALEXANDRA: *(in a state of exultation)* Sometimes I wonder, my dearest, if any husband could ever put up with us. With me, especially. You know so much better than I do how to handle matters, how to keep important things to yourself, how to do exactly as you please while seeming to give in to someone else's wishes. The people I love are all characters right out of books, and that's the only thing on my mind these days: writing, reading, making images with words. *(As if sex-crazed)* That's the only thing on my mind these days. I can't imagine anyone other than a book worm ever wanting me. Who knows, I may just go and rape a dictionary... *(Dropping the pose)* My new friends here at the University are so different from the boys we used to know... They stand so stiffly but have such languid looks. Their faces are smooth and handsome but their gestures... like an old man's. They'll tell you, "I'm not for it or against it, quite the contrary." And they're actually proud of that. When called upon to perform, I do my little "basic-freedoms-trampled-in-the-dust" routine, and I'm hailed as a martyr. I'm sick to death of it all.

Why don't they just go and see for themselves. I'm broken down. The knell of good conscience has ceased to toll in me. A broken down martyr. A martyr... say, that reminds me of something you said to me the day I left, about how you didn't have a calling for martyrdom. That frightened me so at the time, and I didn't even know why. Just writing about it now makes me feel that same fear, fear mixed with a shameful, uncomfortable feeling, as if all of a sudden, your face had changed. *"The while he slept, an ass's nole I fixèd on his head."* Sorry, I'm getting off the track. Still, that was the day when you started to change. Don't change too much, little sister, you were so nice when you were little. Sorry, it's just that I'm so happy everything makes me want to laugh. I've got some people to pal around with, like I had before, if not exactly to be friends with. We sneak into the movies together. Oh, I saw Fellini's *Roma* recently, and, right on the spot, we decided to go to Italy.

IOANA: We still take after each other. I'm traveling, too. *(In a very low voice)* As part of our mandatory volunteer work, we're putting on cultural programs at some center for manual laborers out in the suburbs. The audience is wiped out from their day's work. Row after row, they're falling asleep in their seats. And all they want is to send us to hell, and themselves to bed, the sooner the better!

ALEXANDRA: *(not listening)* Someone has been putting flowers on my doorstep; quite a few of the boys (and not among the least seductive, either) have claimed responsibility for these attacks. That comes as a relief after being a hungry, cultural misfit for so long, stuck behind the accessories counter at La Placette Department Store. Yesterday, a venerable parliamentary journalist was talking to me at a party given for a group of judges. When he mentioned how worried all the media have become about the future of Europe, I told him that the media were being a little slow. They still haven't picked up on the fact that, since the war, half of Europe has already been lost. *(Suddenly worried)* Why don't you write me anything any more? I strike myself as being a word factory even though I have nothing particularly metaphysical to say and I'm still waiting for some news from you. You must be happy with your handsome stranger. When will

I have the great honor of knowing his name? I'll never forgive him for the mystery in which you two have so long enveloped... me...

Alexandra suddenly stops, not moving a muscle. Ioana puts on a record: Beethoven's Ode to Joy, *which she listens to for a moment before it seems to become unbearable to her. She stops the music.*

ALEXANDRA: *(still not moving:)* No need to tell me who it is. A friend stopped by. With a recent copy of our great national newspaper. There was a photo in it with the caption, "Andrei Vornicou and his companion." You were the companion. A photo taken at a show honoring Alfred. I really don't know which of your two betrayals pisses me off more.

IOANA: Forgive me. I wanted to write you about it at least a hundred times, but I was always so afraid of how you'd judge me. You who are so pure, so unyielding. I'm not looking for an excuse, but I really don't know how it happened. I can't even explain it to myself. As for that show... I've got to survive somehow. You don't for a moment think they'd let me play Puck if I didn't toe the line, do you? The ground is shifting under my feet. You're angry with me and Grandmother, after pounding Andrei with insults, has fled from me to be with Lucia. I understand you but who in the world wants to understand me?

ALEXANDRA: *(with a vacant look)* I've chosen the dumbest student at the law school, a real dimwit, even for a future judge. And he's the one I've chosen to lose my virginity to. *"My mistress with a monster is in love."* That way we'll continue to be together, to take after each other. You were the one who made the decision... for both of us. I don't know what's got into me. Today... *(She pins the tag with her school ID number to her dress.)* I went walking around like this all day. Right in the middle of a store, someone called out to me. He thought this was a sales clerk's name tag. I'm sure that stranger saved my life. *(She tears up the letter she has just written.)*

IOANA: I'm getting married to Andrei in May. I won't lie to you ever again. I won't hide anything from you any more but write to me!

ALEXANDRA: Do you remember that white fox fur toque? The one I used to wear every day? I was hoping I'd never have to tell you this. The year I left, I went for the umpteenth time to Veritas. For some strange reason they kept putting off the publication of my book. As soon as I went in, the literary editor's secretary told me how splendid it looked, and where did I ever get it? What? In Poland? Oh really? They certainly do make some lovely things in Poland. She would love to have one of her own, I should remember that, you know: that sort of thing. I could see a dotted line running straight from her eyes and ending at my fur toque. A diagonal of desire, so to speak. Finally, I get around to talking to her about my book, she tries to change the subject, I end up begging for her pity: she might as well tell me the truth, I'll never tell any one who told me and I'll find some way to pay her back for letting me in on the secret, well, you get the picture. I tell her, "Don't have me come back every week for nothing, I bother you, I bother your boss... and I wear myself out. I live at the other end of town. Tell me the truth. That's what the name Veritas means, dammit! You'll be rid of me once and for all. Only fools bear a grudge against the bearer of bad news, etc., etc., and so on. In fact, I'll remember you the next time I'm on a trip to Poland. Give me your hat size... No, even better, try on my toque. Oh, that's marvelous, it looks like it was just made for you..." Groveling, I was simply groveling... and it worked! She finally admitted that she'd heard from her boss that the book would never be published! All the while she spoke to me, she was admiring her reflection in the mirror in front of her. She must have found herself very pretty in that toque, it made her quite chatty. So, it seems her boss was already afraid of getting rapped on the knuckles by the higher-ups if the book sold too many copies. "With all those references to the regime, a success could hardly go unnoticed." But, what's worse, the loyal comrades over at the Ministry of Culture had expressed certain fears. *(Imitating these comrades)* "Say, this author's name is Popesco, the same as Alexander, that francophile deviationist found guilty of self-centered cosmopolitanism. Could she be from the same family? Oh, his daughter." So, to quote her, the well-intentioned comrades at the Ministry advised, in the unlikely event that the book ever did get published, that I change my name. I suggested Ionesco. That's as far as we got when a mad kind of recklessness suddenly came over me. So I say to her, "Listen, that toque looks so good on you... I really haven't the heart to take it back. Oh, you must, no, I can't! You must, I can't, you must, you must, you must let me do something for you, in that case." And then I heard myself saying, as if in a dream: "Let me have the readers' reports." "The readers' reports," she says, "You must be joking!" And then, suddenly backtracking, "In fact, what readers' reports are you referring to? There simply aren't any. The editor is the only reader." And I, with tears in my eyes, go on to add (with supreme hypocrisy), "That toque looks so good on you." *(Looking crushed)* "That toque looks so good on you." Three reports... *(She can barely get it out, her sobs constricting her throat.)* Three reports in all. Two of them signed by some old fogies who write poems in praise of the party and Mr. Big. Nothing above and beyond, nothing unusual, either. Just the same old farts producing the same old farts, about self-centered cosmopolitanism, avoiding reality, seditious comments, perverted images of today's youth, and the absence of our beloved leader, the Danube of profound thought, the Volcano of the Carpathians... the usual stuff. But the third note, the subtlest and the most vicious, was infinitely more cunning. *(Imitating)* "Publishing her book would surely be doing this talented young writer a disservice. She needs ample time to become seasoned, and, once she's gained experience, any future publication should depend upon her assimilation of our national values and her willingness to support the victorious regime, attributes which, due to her family values, she sadly lacks." That third report was signed by Andrei... my beloved. The same man who, every day, would assure me that he was doing all he could to see that my book got published. I politely thanked the comrade sitting at her desk, and handed her back the reports which she immediately returned to my file. Then I left. Bareheaded... perfect, I thought, it's snowing.

IOANA: Why don't you write to me? It's been two weeks already without a letter from you. Before, you used to write me every day... several times a day, at first. *(She takes a new sheet of paper.)* This is the second letter I'm sending you today. Some people pay on the way in and some pay on the way out. Now it's my turn... *(Taking another sheet)* I'm begging you, write to me! I'm going to go on, stubbornly writing to you in spite of your silence, my whole life long, if necessary... Andrei got mad at me a week before we were to be married. We've made up again but now he doesn't want to set another date... I should focus more on the parts I'm playing but I just can't... At last, I have a note from you, for New Year's Day, 1977! *(She opens the envelope, takes out a greeting card and reads it, pensively.)* Just two words, no date, no signature: "Always together"... a reminder of a New Year's Eve when we spoke those words to each other. Exactly five years ago. It's a reproach... which I deserve. Andrei is fine. He never stops working, which means he's always away. Marriage now is out of the question. But he has me acting in his shows. Which isn't exactly doing Shakespeare. Unless it's like playing the king's fool. And you, what about you? *(She takes another sheet of paper.)* I'm sending you the first snowdrop I picked this spring. Let me explain. You may suspect that I advised you to leave so I could take your place in Andrei's life. I swear to you that's not what happened. It was just after the start of Mama's illness that he came to see me. After she died, I was so frightened of everything, of my responsibilities, of Grandmother's hostility. I got involved with him at a time when it was either that or suicide. Don't be so cruel, give me a sign, at least let me know you read my letters and that you don't just throw them away without even opening them.

ALEXANDRA: *(She grabs some wadded-up letters and starts tossing them into the audience, with a wide, swinging motion as if she were sowing seeds. Then she begins singing at the top of her lungs.)*

> "Mother wants to see me wed
> Little stars upon my head,
> Incense in my linen chest
> And a dagger in my breast."

IOANA: *(She wanders through the audience, looking haggard, as she picks up the wads of paper.)* To find out any news about you, I've had to ask people who know you and who can travel to other countries. Radu, someone I haven't wanted to speak to for years, was one I stooped to contacting. I knew he was supposed to visit

Switzerland. Yesterday, he finally came back. I know he didn't tell you that he went to see you because of me. I was afraid you'd refuse to see him. He told me that you look very beautiful and very sad, that you've stopped writing, that people call you The Fair Alexandra, and that you passed your doctoral exams magna cum laude. He also said that you live in a marvelous little house at the edge of the woods.

The stage lights go down suddenly, to be replaced by the light from a TV cathode tube.

OFF-STAGE VOICE OF A TV ANNOUNCER: Catastrophic earthquake in Bucharest. Eight on the Richter Scale. Rescue workers are still struggling to pull survivors out of the rubble. The list of casualties, already long, has increased steadily in the last few hours. A team of Swiss rescue workers with St. Bernard dogs left the airport in Geneva last night...

Alexandra rushes to the public phone, down stage, and stuffs it with coins. Then she dials a number and listens.

IOANA: Hello. Hello. It's me...

Alexandra hangs up the receiver, gently.

IOANA: Dear Alexandra, I have this idea in my head that it was you that called me after the earthquake, just to find out if I was still alive. Maybe it's just a mistake on my part... The person who phoned me didn't say a word, but it comforts me to imagine it was you. I'm deluding myself; no doubt you're going to think I'm insane. The only good news to come out of the quake is that the literary editor who turned down your manuscript was found crushed to death in the rubble of what used to be Veritas. Aside from that, we're all stupidly fearful of the earth starting to shake again. The housing shortage is going to be impossible to manage. Out of your high school class, two people have already been found dead: Cristian, found in the Casata Candy Shop, and Doru, who was at home... *(Nearly in tears)* Let's make peace, while there's still time...

The light from the cathode tube gives way to the regular stage lighting. Alexandra using a spray can, paints the words "Always together" in large letters. Ioana feverishly opens a letter.

IOANA: For the 1st of January, '83, I received my usual greeting card. "Always Together." It's the seventh. I was wrong, I realize that now, and I'm paying for it every day. I think that Andrei has always been in love with you but you wouldn't have been happy with him. He only thinks of himself. If I could, I'd take the first plane out of here and see you, hear you, talk to you... I'm on TV now in those huge productions you know about. They make you memorize the script right down to the last comma. If you don't, you could easily be accused of sabotage. And me with my memory like a sieve.

ALEXANDRA: *(She places a small white hat on her head as she does her make-up, from time to time she puts pen to paper, writing a portion of a letter.)* The big day is here... and everything is so different from what I dreamed it would be like. *(Imitating the Coué method of self-improvement)* Always bright, always gay, on the happy wedding day! Strange, it seems like a rehearsal, one that's going badly. My scene at the Institute, where I wore the wedding gown, that was my real wedding. This one seems more of a masquerade. It must be genetic, the way we do these things. Do you remember the day Alfred got an honorary degree? We played our parts so well. And made our lines sound so convincing. Especially this one: "Always together." Especially when you said it. *(With no transition)* My engagement ring is a two-carat emerald surrounded by ten pure white Wesselton diamonds, all in a platinum setting. *(She tears the letter up into tiny pieces, and drops them like confetti; they fall straight to the floor.)* The weight of the paper?... or of time? *(She exits by the upstage door, carefully slamming it behind her.)*

IOANA: I found out you've been writing to Grandmother. And that you've been phoning her. Some people have all the luck! Me, I got my annual "Always together" card. I found out you're married. I haven't even seen a picture of your husband. What does he look like? I hear he's very rich. I found out you had a book published. In French, of course. Bravo! Andrei is never around. My health is getting worse... I'll never be able to have a child. You've become a Swiss citizen. You could come back here. Don't do it! You're still considered a national here. Andrei told me so, he who never worries about anything except himself. He told me more than once. He seemed genuinely troubled. He even spoke to Grandmother to try and get her to stop you from coming. The articles that you write over there about Alfred have made them very angry... Andrei really loved you. I'm sure he still does, but he's so bad at loving... I was wrong when I said he hadn't recognized your revisions to the Shakespeare play. Yesterday, right in the middle of an argument, and we argue all the time, I asked him why he came to see me play Puck, the very first time. He told me it was to hurt you, to make you jealous and... to make you come back... and after three words of the text he heard your voice, while I was "reciting." He's never stopped being with you. And he'll go on making my life hell. He finds me repulsive because I'm not you... *(She turns around and around in her room, unable to stand still, then resumes her letter writing.)* January 1st, 1984. I still haven't had my New Year's card. Andrei cheats on me, whenever and wherever. He humiliates me every chance he gets. I don't really care, but I'm scared of him. He's becoming so powerful. He's on close terms with Alfred. He goes on hunting trips with him and on trips to foreign countries and he's lost in his own delusions of grandeur. He thinks he's the power behind the throne. And that's what he's becoming. If I leave him now, no one will offer me a part, no matter how small. Among other things, he's head of the theater section at the Ministry. Nobody wants to cross him. I saw a picture of you in a Swiss newspaper. You were dancing with your husband at a ball. You're so beautiful, so elegant and you've stayed so young...

ALEXANDRA: *(starting a letter)* Ioana... *(crossing this out)* Dear... *(crossing this out)* Perfidious Puck *(crossing this out)* "At last I've found that magic flower which, placed on mortals' eyelids, opens up their hearts and lets their souls blossom within their bodies." *(After reflecting a moment, she tears this letter up.)*

IOANA: I just heard you speaking on the radio. I'm all choked up. We listen to all the programs in Romanian on Radio France...

It's part of our routine and suddenly... your voice. You're going to laugh at this: You speak Romanian with a slight accent. Andrei was with me. He listened right to the end. Then he was quiet for a while, Andrei, who's always shouting. Finally he said, "She's done it again. She's found a way to be right." And he went out. Everybody heard you, they can't stop talking about it. People I haven't seen for years keep calling me. They're happy. They thought you were dead. They congratulate me. As if I had something to do with it. Your program was wonderful. Even here, we learned something from it about the plans to "systemize" Bucharest. Usually, all we can do is notice what's being torn down in our own neighborhoods, without knowing what's going on in other parts of the capital... and we listen to radio programs from the West. I heard that you're getting a divorce. That must be rough on you... You see, we're still alike. I also got my Christmas present: I left Andrei on December 23rd and on the 24th I got fired from the theater. The head of organization for the Party is a close friend of Andrei's. I'm almost thirty, I can't have any children, and I'm out of work. I'm a woman who's all washed up. Last night, I went over your scene with the wedding gown. I hear you have a child. I'd really like to see his picture...

ALEXANDRA: *(taking a baby picture and writing on the back)* He's an only child. At least no one will be able to fool him with their "Always together." *(After a long hesitation, she adds these words.)* "Chin up!"

IOANA: What a lovely baby! He looks like you did at that age. Naturally, I've never known you as anything other than my big sister, but it's often seemed to me that I used to know you as an infant. That must have been in another life when I was strong enough not to lose you... At last you've written me! I am so happy. Seven years of silence built up between us. Do you remember the swan brothers in that fairy tale by Andersen? Their ditsy little sister had to weave tunics out of nettles for years and years to earn forgiveness. We've finally finished weaving our nettle tunics, both of us... and spring is still so far away... Alexandra... I knew that you were going to forgive me, even if it was in the next world. As for Andrei, I was wrong. It wasn't love... You would have forgiven me that. Maybe jealousy toward you, but without being aware of it. I was so mixed up... You've always been the stronger one. Even stronger for not even realizing it. Forgive me, oh please forgive me. I found a little maid's room, with a toilet down the hall. I've gotten fat and ugly, but I'm happy because we're back in touch. When I smile, I don't open my mouth too wide. I'm missing a tooth. I'm embarrassed but have no money to see a dentist. As soon as I get a few coins together I run to the phone and call you.

ALEXANDRA: Forgiveness is the most magical and therefore the most mysterious thing in the world. We're thirty now, we're not madcap schoolgirls any more and yet... You are almost another person; so am I, no doubt. And for that other person you are today, this other that I've become has wiped the slate clean.

IOANA: I'm so happy! Everything's lousy, I'm out of work, I'm getting fat, but at least I'm in touch with you now... If it'd been me, I would have forgiven you right away. I already forgive you from now on for every bad thing you could do to me over the next thousand years.

ALEXANDRA: One who can sin with ease can forgive with ease. As for me, I could only bring myself to forgive you after I'd forgotten... a little. And I still don't understand how I managed to do it. (*She goes back to her typing.*)

IOANA: I'm performing in Galatzi now, in cold, unheated theaters. Our audiences are so tired after working all day, standing in various lines and squeezing into their trains and buses that they fall asleep as soon as they get in their seats. And their snoring is so loud that sometimes I can't hear my cues on stage. I was afraid the other actors would turn against me because I lived with Andrei. But that didn't happen, thank God. The company has welcomed me with open arms. Here in the provinces the shortages are far worse than in Bucharest. We knit our own underwear, and you can't even get cotton in a drugstore, so you can imagine how we have to improvise to get by every month.

ALEXANDRA: We all have our cross to bear. Mine is writing fluff,

and writing it badly. I make up stupid gags for the so-called enter-
tainment programs on TV. Even so, I'm glad I can provide for my
son through my writing. Your cross is Galatzi. See Galatzi and die.
Remember how we dreamed of being the greatest playwright and
the greatest actress of our generation? We're not exactly leaving
our mark on the twentieth century. I don't know if I already told
you this in a letter, but since a year ago I've had to wear glasses.

IOANA: In my case, it's been two years. Or it should have been.
I've been walking around all that time with the prescription still
in my pocket. The opticians here demand to be paid under
the counter and no one has the cash unless they're in good with
Aunt Prudence. What about your new husband? Tell me about
him, I'm longing to know more.

ALEXANDRA: You know what Chekhov said, *(laughing)* it was in
The Three Sisters, by the way, "A wife is a wife." Therefore, a husband is a husband. Mine is even more so. Maybe the only husbands we're cut out for are our own homegrown macho-men.
The men over here are a different breed: civilized, responsible,
willing to do household chores, clean, delicate... in a word, limp.
But don't take it all to heart; who *doesn't* have the feeling their
life's a failure, after age thirty?

IOANA: Our Gideon now has a police file, just like a criminal. I
had to take him to Aunt Prudence's where they took a sample
of his writing, his "fingerprints." Instead of a sample, I was
tempted to give them your rejected manuscript. Poor Gideon,
since you went away, all he's written are answers to some want
ads, and that was just so he wouldn't get rusty. His only real function is as a holy relic. Rationing has gotten terrible here. We all
have our tickets. A pound of meat per month. Don't send us
anything; hoarding is punishable by six months in prison. There's
even a program of scientific food consumption. A manual laborer
must eat twice as much as an office worker. *(Waving her fist in
the air and chanting the following slogan)* We demand the right to
be manual laborers!... Our gas and electricity is cut off at
night. The city is dark as of nine o'clock. It never gets warmer
than around fifty-five indoors.

ALEXANDRA: I don't know how to put this in a letter. I can now "buy you." There is someone in London... who can do wonders. Fairly quickly. He's gotten hundreds of people out. And with no risks.

IOANA: I have to stay. It's to pay up... I don't really know why but I know how. I've got to go on acting in unheated theaters. If you could see the people there! They sit through the show wearing their coats and hats. At the end they applaud for the longest while, their hands encased in gloves. There's even a real experimental theater going on. Plays by "New Writers" are being put on. One of your scripts was revived this way, performed in an apartment.

ALEXANDRA: Whose apartment?

IOANA: My darling, you've forgotten everything. "Whose apartment?" If I could put that in a letter... I wouldn't be acting in apartments, but at the National Theater... You asked me in your letter if it was some kind of a joke, these reports of unscheduled gynecological exams in the workplace, to keep tabs on pregnant women and stop them from having abortions. Yes, it is a joke... one that's been going on since 1984...

ALEXANDRA: Be careful what you put in your letters. Aunt Prudence is a light sleeper.

IOANA: I don't give a damn, nobody gives a damn, we're way past being afraid. At the present time, our city is living through the historic days of complete systemization. Churches are being torn down, whole neighborhoods are being razed. The first of these to go was the Uranus. Our Aunt Lucia received two eviction notices. Her building was being condemned. She came to see me for advice. I told her to leave, that they weren't kidding. She shook her head without saying a word, a strange little smile on her face. She put Grandmother in an old folk's home. When the bulldozers got to the entrance of her building, Lucia threw herself out the window. Ninth floor. They hardly took time to pull her body out of the rubble and throw it on a nearby embankment before going back to tearing down the building. The whole house collapsed. With all Uncle Ioan's paintings inside. Seven rooms, a museum filled with paintings, all destroyed.

ALEXANDRA: Find Grandmother and get her out. Now!

IOANA: Don't worry, I did. She wanted to come here. Now, she's much nicer to me. The two of us live in my tiny room. But it's brilliantly lighted, just like the rest of the city. With 15 Watt bulbs. That's all they're allowed to sell. There was an accident in the building next to ours. A defective water heater. Six people dead. But that could happen to any of us. We do whatever we have to get hot water, to cook. In theory, we're only allowed to cook at night, during the two hours when they turn the gas on. But you know that Romanians aren't good with theories, we're a nation of poets. And defiant. What with the frigid temperatures in these unheated apartments, some people have put up signs on their doors saying, "Please don't leave your windows open in winter. You might cause people on the street to die of pneumonia." How long was it that it took an act of courage to leave? And when did it become an act of courage just to stay here? Ten years after you left? Twelve? I hear you're getting famous over there and that you've gone back to writing for the stage. They're putting on your plays in Avignon. Do you remember how you used to dream of that happening, ten years ago? When you thought it would never happen to you...

ALEXANDRA: I lost ten years of my life but it was worth it. I'm back at the starting point. As far as my duty to report what I went through, forget it! A fiasco. Nobody wanted my works on the situation over there. Too gloomy. Exaggerated, no doubt. They implied that I was a bit paranoid or that I'd made these atrocities up to justify my leaving... So, I sold them comedies, light and witty. Racy stories or scenarios. Cut to measure for the highest bidder. *(Imitating a newsboy)* "Get your ready-to-act plays from the exiled author!" Some reporter I made! And every day I run into these armchair radicals who say, "If I'da been in your shoes, I'da knocked the block off that Ceau..." *(crossing out what she was about to write)* "Alfred of yours, long time ago. Say, whatsa matter with you people, anyway? Over here, we'd never put up with that shit."

IOANA: I'm performing in unheated cultural centers. I tried playing Puck again but I'm too old for the part. Andrei has gotten to be so influential... that everybody hates him. His hymns of praise to Alfred take up almost all two hours of the daily TV programming. Grandmother was very sick. For ages now they haven't been sending ambulances for sick people over the age of sixty-five. We called them and, naturally, they didn't come. And even if they had... in the hospitals now, you have to supply your own surgical thread, your own alcohol, your own cotton. Where can you get such things? Our neighbor is a doctor and, according to him, Grandmother was dead at eight o'clock that evening. She was asleep for two whole days. I kept listening to her breathing to make sure she didn't slip into a coma. On the third day, she got up. She demanded to have chicken breast with vinaigrette sauce, as if you could get any, and then she declared she wasn't going to die and miss out on a revolution she'd been waiting forty years to see... For her, it's just a question of a few days, as always. Only this time she added, "Too bad Alexandra isn't here to see this." Grandmother, in a strange frenzy, even for someone naturally excitable like her, began shouting that the First-Among-Us would be toppled from power before Christmas. She's very convincing, but crazy as a loon. Here it is, mid-December, and we all know this is the year that, whether from hunger, illness or cold, we're all going to croak...

> *A TV comes on. The stage is plunged into the light emitted by the cathode tube. Alexandra fascinated, watches the program on an imaginary screen.*

VOICE OF THE TV ANNOUNCER: And now a brief round-up of the events which suddenly occurred over the last two days. On December 21st, the demonstration in front of the presidential palace, which had been organized in celebration of the dictator, suddenly turned into a protest demonstration. While the tyrant was booed to his face, he stood there transfixed, his mouth open and the national television service ceased all broadcasting.

ALEXANDRA: *(writing a letter which is balanced on her knees)* You won't believe it. Yesterday, I went out and bought a TV set, just so I wouldn't miss anything that's going on. I've never actually had a TV before, even though I've written TV movie scripts for the last several years. I spend my time channel surfing so as not to miss a thing...

VOICE OF THE TV ANNOUNCER: The dictator and his wife are said to have fled the city yesterday. A helicopter is believed to have taken off from the roof of the Palace of the Republic, carrying the couple to an unknown destination.

IOANA: *(She is seated down stage, in the "no man's land" between the two rooms. Unable to see each other, the two sisters are sitting side by side.)* Darling little sister, it's so incredible. Everything has happened so fast in the last three days. Faster than since we were born. I'm writing you a brief note from the street in front of the Intercontinental Hotel. You can't hear anything. There's non-stop shooting. Cannons, rifles, pistols. Grandmother is impossible. I had to practically call out the army yesterday to keep her from going out into the streets. She started weeping and told me I was spoiling her rendez-vous with History. The moment my back was turned, she got away. That was yesterday afternoon. She came back this morning, her face flushed with excitement, telling me how she went to the big demonstration in front of the Palace. That's where most of the sniping was going on, naturally. She stayed home just long enough to ask me for some bread to give to the men in the tanks. I let her go. She looked twenty years younger.

ALEXANDRA: *(in her room, on the phone as she watches TV)* What do you mean, there aren't any flights?

VOICE OF THE TV ANNOUNCER: Members of the secret police are said to be hiding out in basements around the capital. Like desperados, they emerge in unexpected places, spreading terror as they fire at random into the crowds.

ALEXANDRA: *(into the phone)* You say some people have been

waiting three days for a flight? Well, listen Miss, I've waited eighteen years. *(She disappears from the room.)*

IOANA: *(She is wearing a tricolored armband, blue, yellow and red, and holds a newspaper.)* I'm a member of the Civil Guard protecting the Museum. There's danger of looting and especially of a possible raid by the followers of our Aunt Prudence... *(She crosses out the last words, vigorously.)* How dumb of me! Now we can actually put it in writing. We're protecting the building from the secret police and their goon squads. I hold in my hands the first newspaper published in complete freedom...

8

DECEMBER, 1989

Alexandra presses the buzzer, then opens the door. Silhouetted in the doorway, she continues to buzz; she carries in her hand the same suitcase that she had when she left.

ALEXANDRA: Hello!

IOANA: You...

ALEXANDRA: You see, there's no getting rid of me. Together again! *(They embrace, with great emotion.)*

IOANA: *(trying not to cry)* That's the same suitcase?

ALEXANDRA: *(nodding)* And that's all the luggage I brought.

IOANA: You've come back... Of course, it's taken you eighteen years.

ALEXANDRA: When you love someone, the years don't count.

IOANA: You haven't changed.

ALEXANDRA: You've changed, too. I brought you a bottle of *Martini Bianco.* For New Year's Eve.

IOANA: We two seem to see each other mostly between Christmas and New Year's...

OFF-STAGE VOICE OF A CHILD: Mommy, are you coming?

IOANA: *(leaning out the window)* Is that Alexander?

ALEXANDRA: Alexandru Popesco, in all his glory! I have the honor of introducing you to the next generation.

IOANA: He's beautiful... Does he speak our language?

ALEXANDRA: He'll learn.

IOANA: You mean you're coming back... forever.

ALEXANDRA: Always together, didn't we say?

IOANA: *(observing her)* After all this time, it's going to be hard for you.

ALEXANDRA: I'll just have to learn our language all over again, that's all. Haven't you heard? They say it's a lot like French.

IOANA: *(laughing through her tears)* What'll become of us?

> *They exit laughing, each with her arm around the other's waist. Only the lighted TV set remains on stage.*

VOICE OF THE TV ANNOUNCER: This is the... *(Static covers some of the words)* Television Network. And here's our News at Noon. This morning, Mister Andrei Vornicou, who holds an honorary degree from the University of... *(More static)* was named our nation's ambassador to... *(More static)*

> *A song is heard, overlapping the broadcast. It is one of the songs that will be sung a few months later, in University Square, when the newly-installed government uses its tanks to brutally crush the intellectuals and students peacefully assembled there to demand more freedom.*

~

LOLEH BELLON

BONDS OF AFFECTION

Translated from the French by

BARBARA BRAY

UBU REPERTORY THEATER PUBLICATIONS
NEW YORK

Loleh Bellon was an actress for thirty years. Performing many roles in plays by Jules Romain and Armand Salacrou, Chekhov and Claudel, Giraudoux and Genet, Garcia Lorca and Pirandello, Marlowe and Henry James. She made her breakthough as a dramatist with *Thursday Ladies (Les Dames du jeudi)* in 1976. An immediate hit, the play won the Prix Ibsen and the Prix Tristan Bernard, was translated into several languages and performed throughout the world. It had its American premiere at Los Angeles in Barbara Bray's translation in 1990. Since then, she has written seven other plays, all produced in Paris: *Changement à vue,* in 1978; *Le Coeur sur la main,* in 1980; *De si tendres liens (Bonds of Affection),* in 1984; *L'Eloignement,* in 1987 — for which she was awarded the "Molière" prize—; *Une Absence,* in 1988; *L'une et l'autre* in 1992; and *La Chambre d'amis,* in 1995. She was awarded numerous prizes, such as the prestigious Prix de l'Académie Française, the Prix du Théâtre de la Ville de Paris, and the Prix du Théâtre de la SACD (Société des Auteurs et Compositeurs Dramatiques) in 1995. *Bonds of Affection* had successful runs in several countries, including Italy, Belgium, Switzerland, Turkey, Scandinavia, Hungary and Brazil. Ubu is pleased to present its American premiere.

Barbara Bray was born in London, England and graduated with honors in English at Cambridge University. After lecturing in Egypt, she became BBC Radio Drama Script Editor. Since the 1960s she has lived and worked in Paris as a free-lance writer, critic and translator. She is well known for her translations of works by Marguerite Duras (published here by Pantheon Books and Grove Press), including the award-winning translation of *The Lover.* Barbara Bray has collaborated with Harold Pinter and Joseph Losey on the film adaptation of Proust's *A la recherche du temps perdu* (published but not yet produced). She is the president and metteur-en-scène of "Dear Conjunction," a bilingual professional theater company based in Paris.

Bonds of Affection, in Barbara Bray's translation, had its American premiere at Ubu Repertory Theater, 15 West 28th Street, New York, NY 10001, on March 12, 1996.

Director. . . . . **Shirley Kaplan**
Set Designer. . . . . **Watoku Ueno**
Lighting Designer. . . . .**Greg MacPherson**
Costume Designer . . . .**Carol Ann Pelletier**
Sound Designer . . . . **Robert Gould**

CAST

Charlotte . . . . **Kathryn Rossetter**
Jeanne. . . . . **Kristin Griffith**
Pierre. . . . . **Paul Hoover**
Jacques . . . .**George Hosmer**

Produced by **Ubu Repertory Theater**
Françoise Kourilsky, *Artistic Director*

"Restless memory stirs accurately and uneasily in *Bonds of Affection,* an admirable play by Loleh Bellon. [...] This sharply observed examination of the relationship of a mother and daughter sifts through decades of yearning, disappointment, growth and decline. As it does, *Bonds of Affection* lays bare the reversal of roles that accompanies the maturing of the daughter, [...] and the descent of her mother toward loneliness, infirmity and the darkness of death."
—Lawrence Van Gelder, *The New York Times,* March 20, 1996

INTRODUCTION

Roles are exchanged; laughter, tears are now on one side, now on the other. Time passes and yet stands still. The same words are repeated, the same scenes re-enacted with the situations reversed. Different periods of history merge together. Wounds do not heal. Resentments always lurk near the surface; so do affection, hope and exasperation. Memory, though infinite, is never quite the same for both Charlotte and Jeanne: each of them shadows the other, tries to break away, then returns. They wear the same coat: you can't tell them apart, yet they do their utmost not to be like one another. The little girl is afraid of the darkness that goes by the name of death; the old lady fears the death that goes by the name of darkness. There are no more frontiers. Men appear, and disappear even when they remain: they don't really understand this story without a beginning or an end; they think they've left it behind them, or never even entered it. So they keep it at a distance, preferring to live their own lives. Yet it's for the men the women make themselves attractive and charming; to them they direct their love; in them they find pleasure.

But what if passion lay elsewhere? What if it were to be found in the nameless, ageless bond that can never be broken, the bond that grows stronger and stronger all the time because it is forged by loss?

Through many little things, Loleh Bellon's play speaks one of the greatest things in life.

J.-B. PONTALIS

CHARACTERS

CHARLOTTE, *The mother*
JEANNE, *The daughter*
PIERRE, *Charlotte's lover*
JACQUES, *Jeanne's husband*

SETTING

Minimal décor. The mother's bedroom. The set arranged to allow easy movement. Everything that will be used in the play, including furniture and props, is there somewhere from the start, and can be used for various purposes. Except for the two identical, brightly colored coats, everything is old and much used. Styles and periods intermingle.

The characters move around as though the acting area were the landscape of their memory. Charlotte and Jeanne, the mother and the daughter, are played by actresses of the same age, between 45 and 50, in the middle of their lives. The play is not in any way realistic: it is the "inner history" of their relationship.

Between the first and last scenes—they are really one—time and memory are unfolding in Jeanne's mind. But time may be arrested momentarily by some word, gesture or feeling that was especially significant for her.

The costumes too are reduced to essentials, with each actress wearing the same dress throughout. Only the details change, with the addition of a coat, a scarf, a low cut top, etc.

There is only one act. It should flow without interruption from beginning to end, with changes of scene indicated by blackouts and other lighting effects. No intermission.

As the play opens the stage is in shadow. We hear the sound of an older woman's voice, a kind of moan.

CHARLOTTE: No! Mother! Mother! *(Jeanne enters.)* Who's that?

JEANNE: Me. Jeanne.

CHARLOTTE: Oh.

JEANNE: Did you call?

CHARLOTTE: When?

JEANNE: Just now. I heard you cry out. *(She goes nearer.)* What were you saying? I couldn't make out the words. Do you need something?

CHARLOTTE: No.

JEANNE: Have you been asleep?

CHARLOTTE: Yes. I think so.

JEANNE: You know the doctor said you should have at least an hour's sleep every afternoon. *(Pause.)* Did he come this morning?

CHARLOTTE: Yes. On his way to the hospital.

JEANNE: Did you tell him about that giddy spell you had yesterday?

CHARLOTTE: No. I forgot. It's nothing. I stood up too quickly, that's all.

JEANNE: How do you know?

CHARLOTTE: He's always in such a hurry. It would be a shame to hold him up.

JEANNE: Even to help you get better?

CHARLOTTE: Am I really getting...

JEANNE: *(interrupting)* Now, now! *(Pause.)* Have you taken your drops?

CHARLOTTE: Yes.

JEANNE: Stay there and rest a bit longer.

CHARLOTTE: I dropped off and had a horrible nightmare. I was just going into a cinema. But when I looked through the swing doors, all I could see was flames. And the noise! Like the inside of a furnace. A sort of roar. The exits were blocked. The people were screaming. Their shrieks woke me up.

JEANNE: Would you like a glass of water?

CHARLOTTE: Mmm...

JEANNE: You would or you wouldn't?

CHARLOTTE: I wouldn't. *(Pause.)* It seems like a miracle just to be lying here. To have escaped from that fear. That dread. *(Pause.)* Would you mind switching the light off, please? It's shining right in my eyes.

Jeanne switches off the ceiling light.

JEANNE: Is that better?

CHARLOTTE: Yes. Don't shut the door. *(Pause.)* It's nearly dark, isn't it?

JEANNE: It's five o'clock.

CHARLOTTE: When I opened my eyes I couldn't remember where I was. I felt as if I were shut up in the dark. I couldn't breathe. It was awful!

JEANNE: Are you all right now?

CHARLOTTE: Yes. *(Pause.)* Have you been here long?

JEANNE: A little while.

CHARLOTTE: Why didn't you wake me?

JEANNE: I only stopped by to see how you were. The phone was busy all morning.

CHARLOTTE: What time?

JEANNE: Before lunch.

CHARLOTTE: That's funny.

JEANNE: Not really. When I got here I found the receiver hadn't been replaced properly.

CHARLOTTE: Really?

JEANNE: I might have gone on calling forever!

CHARLOTTE: Madeleine came to lunch. She talked about coming to stay for a few nights. What do you think?

JEANNE: Good idea. You can start quarreling again. Very good for the health.

CHARLOTTE: Why don't you sit down? Stay for a little while?

JEANNE: *(looking at her watch)* I haven't much time.

CHARLOTTE: Just for a moment. Haven't you got anything to tell?

JEANNE: Marie's coming at seven. She's on duty at the hospital this weekend and I said I'd take the baby till Monday.

CHARLOTTE: Five minutes, stay with me for five minutes.

Jeanne, who has gone over to the door, freezes. The light fades so that all we see is Jeanne in profile.

JEANNE: Don't leave me. Stay with me. Kiss me goodnight. Again. Do you love me? Say it. Am I your own dear little girl? Why not? I have to say I love you first? All right, I love you. But I am your own dear little girl too, aren't I?

A faint ray of light shows Jeanne wandering around the room.

No, don't switch the light off. Why must you? When it's dark I feel all alone. You're not there any more. You've gone.

Complete fade-out. Then a faint light shows Jeanne lying on the bed. Charlotte has gone.

Don't shut the door, I can't see you any more. I can't see anything. I can't remember where the walls are. I can't remember where I am. Everything's dark. When I breathe it's dark, when I swallow it's dark. Mother, why have you shut the door? *(Pause.)* You've left me all alone. You've gone. Mother! *(Silence.)* Mother! *(Silence.)* Mother!

Pause. A figure appears, outlined against the light from the door.

CHARLOTTE: Aren't you asleep? Do you know what time it is? Almost ten o'clock. Come along, you must go to sleep.

JEANNE: I can't.

CHARLOTTE: What do you mean, you can't? Who won't hear the alarm in the morning? Who'll be asking me to write her a note for the teacher?

JEANNE: I'm not doing it on purpose! It's not my fault! I just can't!

CHARLOTTE: Try. You're not really trying. *(The figure goes over to the bed, switches on the bedside lamp. Charlotte sits on the bed.)* What's bothering you? Didn't you finish your homework?

JEANNE: Yes, I did all my homework. It's not that.

CHARLOTTE: Have you had bad grades ? Are you afraid I'll be angry when I have to sign your book? *(Pause.)* Come on, tell me the worst!

JEANNE: It's not that.

CHARLOTTE: What is it then? Why can't you sleep?

    Pause.

JEANNE: I'm frightened.

CHARLOTTE: Now what on earth have you got to be frightened of? Here you are in your own bed, in your own room, with your own mother just next door. I don't understand.

    Pause.

JEANNE: *(in a small voice)* I'm afraid of dying.

CHARLOTTE: *(putting her arms around Jeanne)* Jeanne! What's the matter with you, you silly girl? What in the world makes you think about things like that?

JEANNE: I'm not "thinking," I've got a lump! Here! I can't breathe!

CHARLOTTE: *(rocking her)* There, there. There, there, my little girl.

JEANNE: I can't breathe. Really!

CHARLOTTE: I know, dear, I know. Calm down, now. You're not alone any more. I'm here, we're together, nothing can happen to you. *(Pause.)* Don't cry, sweetie. You mustn't get upset like this. You must learn to be calm, relax. Lie down straight now. And breathe.

Breathe deep. *(She massages Jeanne's stomach.)* Fill your lungs right up. That's right. Now empty them out. That's right. Better?

JEANNE: *(small voice)* Yes.

CHARLOTTE: *(kissing her)* All right again now, my darling? Not frightened any more?

JEANNE: When I open my eyes in the dark, it's not black. And it's not black when I shut them, either.

CHARLOTTE: What do you mean, it's not black?

JEANNE: There are lots of little shiny dots.

CHARLOTTE: Does your head hurt?

JEANNE: No. *(Pause.)* Am I going to... stop being able to see... Am I?

CHARLOTTE: What on earth are you talking about! Your sight's perfectly normal. I see little dots myself sometimes. It's nothing serious. It can happen to anyone when they're tired. I'll make an appointment with the doctor tomorrow.

JEANNE: Oh no!

CHARLOTTE: Why not? When something goes wrong it should be seen to right away. *(Pause.)* Well? Feeling okay now?

JEANNE: Yes.

CHARLOTTE: Would you like a glass of water?

JEANNE: Yes, please. *(Charlotte goes out.)* Why didn't you answer?

CHARLOTTE: *(off)* When?

JEANNE: Just now. When I called.

Charlotte comes back with a glass of water. Jeanne drinks.

CHARLOTTE: Because I didn't hear. Why do you think?

Pause.

JEANNE: Are you alone?

CHARLOTTE: Yes.

JEANNE: Really?

CHARLOTTE: Yes ! Someone dropped in to lend me a catalog I needed. That's all. Why?

Silence.

JEANNE: Who was it that phoned?

CHARLOTTE: When?

JEANNE: Just now. I heard you talking.

CHARLOTTE: Oh, that. That was Lucien. Your father. He's going away again sooner than he thought, so he can't have you on Thursday. He sends his love.

JEANNE: But I am going to stay with him on my vacation, aren't I?

CHARLOTTE: Of course.

JEANNE: I was supposed to last year and I didn't.

CHARLOTTE: Patrick had whooping cough. You didn't want to catch whooping cough, did you? *(Silence.)* Jeanne?

Pause.

JEANNE: Will you be going out?

CHARLOTTE: No, of course not!

JEANNE: Promise?

CHARLOTTE: I don't have to promise. Kindly remember that when I say something I mean it.

Short pause.

JEANNE: The other day you said you were going to bed, and when I went to the bathroom you weren't in your room.

CHARLOTTE: Well, I'm very sorry, but I do sometimes like to see my friends. I'm not a little girl, you can't expect me to go to bed every night right after dinner. Try to understand... You do understand, don't you?

JEANNE: Yes. *(Pause.)* Will you be here tomorrow when I get home from school?

CHARLOTTE: I don't know yet. I'll try. If I can't manage it, you can go next door as usual. Madame Vergère will give you a snack. Goodnight, darling.

Charlotte kisses Jeanne goodnight.

JEANNE: Do you love me?

CHARLOTTE: *(smiling)* What do you think?

JEANNE: How much?

CHARLOTTE: *(opening her arms wide)* As much as that!

JEANNE: *(opening her arms wider)* I love you as much as that!

CHARLOTTE: *(her arms wider still)* And I love you as much as that! Look!

JEANNE: I love you as high as the Eiffel Tower.

CHARLOTTE: The Himalayas!

JEANNE: The moon!

CHARLOTTE: The sun!

They embrace.

JEANNE: Stay with me just a little longer.

CHARLOTTE: Five minutes. No more. After that you must go to sleep.

JEANNE: Won't you just lie down a minute?

CHARLOTTE: All right. But not for long.

Charlotte lies down beside Jeanne.

JEANNE: Let's talk.

CHARLOTTE: All right.

Long pause.

JEANNE: What shall we talk about?

CHARLOTTE: You choose. *(Pause.)* Hurry up or I'm going to turn the light off.

JEANNE: You didn't finish yesterday.

CHARLOTTE: Didn't finish what?

JEANNE: The story. She was in her castle. She was sick.

CHARLOTTE: Oh yes... She'd stopped eating. She never got out of bed. Just lay there with her eyes shut. The king sent for the best doctors in the kingdom, but they didn't know what was the matter with her. They couldn't cure her. Everybody was in despair. Then one evening there came a knock at the castle gate. It was a messenger. Tristan had been wounded, and sent his sweetheart a ring as a token of his eternal love. Isolde listened to the messenger. "Where is Tristan?", she whispered. "I want to see him." The messenger said, "He's sailing home to you, but he's badly hurt. The captain of the ship has two sails ready, one white and one black, so that you may know as soon as possible whether Tristan is alive or... " *(Pause.)* Days went by. Weeks. Isolde turned her face to the wall. *(Charlotte speaks more and more softly.)* Then one morning, at sunrise, the ship appeared on the horizon. Isolde opened her eyes. Her lips moved. "The sail," she whispered. "What color is the sail?"

JEANNE: *(pleadingly, though she is almost asleep)* White! White!

CHARLOTTE: Yes, my love. The sail is white. *(She gets up gently, bends over Jeanne kisses her.)* Sleep, my little treasure.

> *Charlotte switches the light off and goes out.*
> *Blackout.*
> *In the dream, the sound of rigging, wind, sails.*
> *The light gradually fades back.*
> *Charlotte and Jeanne cross the stage, Charlotte carrying Jeanne's*
> *suitcase and a bag.*

CHARLOTTE: Don't touch the doors when you're on the train. Be careful when you go to the toilet. Keep clear of any open doors when you're on the platform. Don't get off at any stops on the way. In short, behave like a grown-up young lady.

JEANNE: Will Father meet me at the station?

CHARLOTTE: Of course. And Patrick. If they're late, just wait quietly at the ticket window.

JEANNE: What's the name of the station?

CHARLOTTE: Quimperlé. That's the third time you've asked.

JEANNE: I keep forgetting.

CHARLOTTE: You mean you don't listen. Anyhow, I've written it down on a piece of paper so that you can be ready ahead of time. Here... *(She rummages in her purse.)* And here's ten francs. You don't have to spend it. The comics are in your bag. With something to eat on the journey.

> *Charlotte gives Jeanne the bag. Jeanne looks to see what's inside.*

JEANNE: Where's "La Semaine de Suzette"?

CHARLOTTE: It doesn't come out till tomorrow. Your father will buy it for you.

JEANNE: Who's going to give me my pocket money?

CHARLOTTE: Lucien.

JEANNE: Did you tell him to?

CHARLOTTE: *You* ask him. He *is* your father.

JEANNE: I get extra on my vacation!

CHARLOTTE: Sort it out with him!

JEANNE: What is there to eat?

CHARLOTTE: A couple of hard-boiled eggs, a slice of fruit tart...

JEANNE: Yum yum!

CHARLOTTE: Some orange juice and a chocolate bar. But don't eat it all at once or you'll get sick. And don't speak to anyone. Especially not to men. And write every other day. Promise?

JEANNE: Yes.

CHARLOTTE: You don't have to write much. Just a line to let me know you're all right.

JEANNE: Will you come and see us?

CHARLOTTE: I don't expect so. I'm all behind with my work.

JEANNE: Oh, try! You never come...

> *They go off, talking, Charlotte carrying the suitcase, Jeanne following with the bag. Then they reappear, with Jeanne carrying packages and Charlotte following. They are going home to Charlotte's place.*

CHARLOTTE: Let me carry something. You're loaded down like a mule...

JEANNE: *(interrupting)* Jacques will take you to the station. He'll call for you at nine o'clock, so don't be late. Pack your suitcase tonight to be on the safe side. And don't take your whole wardrobe!

CHARLOTTE: Do you think I ought to pack my beige suit?

JEANNE: No! Whoever heard of anyone wearing a suit at the seaside!

CHARLOTTE: But what if I'm asked out?

JEANNE: Wear your black pants with a dressy blouse! That'll be just right. And be sure to take some sweaters. You never take enough warm things, and then you complain that you've been cold. And what about shoes? Which ones are you taking?

CHARLOTTE: Casuals?

JEANNE: That's right. And you'll need some espadrilles. Have you got a pair?

CHARLOTTE: I'll buy some there.

JEANNE: If you can. It's safest to get them beforehand.

CHARLOTTE: Is the hotel far from the station?

JEANNE: There are taxis. I phoned to ask.

CHARLOTTE: Does the train stop there long?

JEANNE: Long enough for the passengers to get off, I imagine! Ask some gentleman to help you with your suitcase. Be ready ahead of time. And whatever happens, don't panic.

CHARLOTTE: I hope there'll be someone.

JEANNE: Of course there will. I'll call you tomorrow evening to see how it went. *(She puts down some papers and magazines.)* I got you "Le Monde" and "L'Observateur".

CHARLOTTE: Thank you.

JEANNE: What is it? What's bothering you?

CHARLOTTE: Do you think there'll be a restaurant car?

JEANNE: How should I know? Look at your ticket, that'll say.

CHARLOTTE: Right. Just a minute. *(She opens her purse and takes out her ticket and her glasses.)* No. No little forks.

JEANNE: What time do you arrive?

CHARLOTTE: Two o'clock.

JEANNE: Splendid. You can have lunch when you get there. Have a good breakfast to help you last out.

CHARLOTTE: Do you think the hotel restaurant will still serve me?

JEANNE: Oh yes. Sure.

Charlotte has put her ticket away in her purse and taken out a telegram. She holds it out to Jeanne.

CHARLOTTE: Look what came this morning!

JEANNE: *(reading)* "Love this year as always to my dear sister... Madeleine." You're on speaking terms again, then?

Jeanne hands the telegram back to Charlotte.

CHARLOTTE: Do you know what day it is today?

JEANNE: No.

CHARLOTTE: The fourteenth of April.

JEANNE: Oh?

Jeanne undoes a package of things from the pharmacy: cotton swabs, Q-tips, rubbing alcohol, etc.

CHARLOTTE: Doesn't it ring a bell? The fourteenth of April?

JEANNE: No. I don't think so.

CHARLOTTE: It's my birthday.

JEANNE: So it is!

CHARLOTTE: Sixty-eight! *(She gives a little laugh.)* No, not me, it's not possible! There must be some mistake. *(Pause.)* But you get used to it. Get into the habit. Answer quite naturally. "Me? I'm sixty-eight." You forget. You feel quite well. The time goes by, and so does the year, and before you know it, it's the fourteenth of April again. And this time you're sixty-nine. And it starts all over again. *(Pause.)* When I was a little girl we always had a big family party on my mother's birthday. After dinner everyone gave her a present. Even the little ones. A drawing or a poem. It was so nice.

JEANNE: And she used to stand up when dinner was over and say it was bad enough getting older, without having to celebrate the fact every year.

Jeanne has gone again. Pause.

CHARLOTTE: Why do you say that?

Blackout.
In the darkness, a little voice from outside the door.

JEANNE: Mother! *(Pause.)* Mother! *(Charlotte gives an inarticulate groan. Jeanne is in the room by now.)* Are you asleep?

CHARLOTTE: Yes.

Pause.

JEANNE: Did I wake you up?

CHARLOTTE: Yes.

JEANNE: Oh, sorry! *(Pause.)* Shall I draw the curtains?

CHARLOTTE: No!... Well, just a little, then. *(The light comes up. Charlotte is lying in bed.)* That's enough. Thanks.

JEANNE: *(kissing her)* Hello, Mother.

CHARLOTTE: Hello, darling.

JEANNE: Did you sleep well?

CHARLOTTE: *(yawning)* Not too badly.

JEANNE: I heard you come in. You ran the bath.

CHARLOTTE: Mmm. *(She yawns.)* What time is it?

JEANNE: Nine o'clock.

CHARLOTTE: Nine o'clock! Why are you still here then? Why aren't you at school?

JEANNE: Mademoiselle Forge is sick. She tripped over a hole in the stair-carpet. I don't have a class till ten.

CHARLOTTE: So why did you wake me up so early?

JEANNE: To give you a surprise.

CHARLOTTE: *(yawning)* Oh?

JEANNE: I've got you your breakfast.

CHARLOTTE: That's nice.

JEANNE: Can I turn the radio on?

CHARLOTTE: Not too loud.

> *Jeanne switches on a radio. Appropriate music, singing and publicity.*

JEANNE: Shall I bring it in now?

CHARLOTTE: Yes, please. *(Jeanne goes out. Charlotte settles herself comfortably. Jeanne returns carrying a tray with a little bunch of flowers on it.)* Oh, how pretty! And it smells good too... Mmmm...

JEANNE: I took them from the vase in the leaving room. The ones that weren't too faded.

CHARLOTTE: Thank you.

JEANNE: I was waiting for you to wake up...

CHARLOTTE: And then you thought you'd give me a little hand, eh? *(She pours herself some coffee.)* Toast! My word, what luxury!

JEANNE: I buttered it, too.

CHARLOTTE: You're an angel.

Charlotte eats, Jeanne watches.

JEANNE: Is it good?

CHARLOTTE: Delicious.

Pause.

JEANNE: Don't you notice anything?

CHARLOTTE: Where?

JEANNE: There. *(She points to a little package on the tray.)*

CHARLOTTE: What is it?

JEANNE: Look and see.

Charlotte opens the package and finds a pair of earrings.

CHARLOTTE: Ooooh... ! Are they for me?

JEANNE: Yes.

CHARLOTTE: But why?

Jeanne flings her arms around Charlotte and kisses her.

JEANNE: Happy birthday!

CHARLOTTE: What?

JEANNE: Happy birthday! It's your birthday!

CHARLOTTE: Today?

JEANNE: Yes. Father told me. You were born on April 14th, 19...

CHARLOTTE: Please, please! It's sweet of you to have thought of it, but it's bad enough getting older...

JEANNE: You're not old.

CHARLOTTE: Without having to celebrate the fact every year! Three more wrinkles, one year less left to live, not a particularly cheerful occasion, is it? *(She turns to Jeanne, but she has disappeared.)* Jeanne, where are you? Your earrings are beautiful! *(Charlotte sits for a moment holding an earring in each hand, then gets out of bed and goes out calling.)* Jeanne!

> *Quick lighting change. Upstage brightly lit. Jeanne is talking on the telephone. The light gradually comes up to include her.*

JEANNE: No, Mother, really... she's only seven. If you're not careful you'll turn her into one of those horrible little brats who polish their toenails and wear bras before they've got any breasts... All her friends have their ears pierced? Too bad... You should ask me before you promise her things... Fashion! I suppose if it was fashionable to wear a hearth brush sticking out of your behind you'd buy her one with sequins on... I'm not getting worked up, you get on my nerves! It's easy for you. I kill myself trying to bring her up decently, then you come along playing the doting grandma and undermine all I... No. She's inclined to show off anyway... After all, I see more of her than you do... I don't want her to be a tomboy, but neither do I want her to spend all her time preening herself in front of the mirror... Yes, if I let you have your way... I may be her mother, but that doesn't stop me facing facts...

> *She stops, as if the words reminded her of something. The light fades on her and comes up on Charlotte, sitting by the telephone.*

CHARLOTTE: Do you think so?... Oh no, yours is much prettier... No comparison... No, Jeanne's very sweet, but that's a different matter. *(Jeanne has entered, carrying her little suitcase and wearing a sweater that is too big for her. She stands upstage, motionless.)* Really beautiful... Her eyes... I'd have loved to have a daughter with blue eyes... Why? I may be her mother, but that doesn't stop me facing facts... Yes, she's very sweet, very easy to manage. A good little girl... Next Thursday? Of course she'd love to come... Good-bye then... See you soon... Good-bye. *(She turns around.)* Oh, it's you. I'd forgotten what we decided. Whether you were to stay there tonight or...

JEANNE: I'd rather sleep here. I need to collect my books for school in the morning.

CHARLOTTE: As you wish. You know your father and I like you to decide things for yourself. But what's all this you're wearing? Sweater, coat, and scarf as well, you're smothered! You'll catch a chill.

JEANNE: It's cold out.

CHARLOTTE: Well, did you have a good weekend? Enjoy yourself?

JEANNE: Yes.

    Pause.

CHARLOTTE: What's their new apartment like? Big?

JEANNE: Yes! Patrick's got a room to himself. He needs it with all those toys.

CHARLOTTE: What about you? Where did you sleep?

JEANNE: In the dining room. They've got a convertible couch. *(Pause.)* Who were you talking to?

CHARLOTTE: When?

JEANNE: *(pointing to the phone)* Just now.

CHARLOTTE: Paulette's mother. *(Pause.)* I went to the Paramount yesterday to see your idol.

JEANNE: Greta Garbo?

CHARLOTTE: That's right.

JEANNE: "Camille"?

CHARLOTTE: Yes. It was marvelous. I cried my eyes out!

JEANNE: Why didn't you wait and take me?

CHARLOTTE: You can go with Paulette. My treat.

JEANNE: When?

CHARLOTTE: What about Thursday? Her mother's invited you to lunch. If you've finished your homework!

JEANNE: *(kissing her)* Oh, you are sweet!

CHARLOTTE: Here, look at me... You've got a speck on your nose. *(She takes a handkerchief out of her pocket, moistens it with saliva, and rubs at the tip of Jeanne's nose.)*

JEANNE: *(struggling)* Ow, you're making me all wet!

CHARLOTTE: I'm making you presentable... There!

JEANNE: Father asked me to give you this. *(She hands Charlotte a note.)*

CHARLOTTE: *(reading)* He's sorry he's late with the alimony. *(Putting the note away in her pocket)* Since it barely pays for my cigarettes...

JEANNE: Have you ever tried to ride a tandem?

CHARLOTTE: No, why?

JEANNE: Father and Denise said they had and it wasn't at all difficult. They took Patrick along behind them in a basket.

CHARLOTTE: And who am I supposed to ride a tandem with?

JEANNE: Me, of course!

CHARLOTTE: *(smiling)* And has he found a job?

JEANNE: He didn't say anything about that. We took Patrick for a walk in the Bois de Boulogne.

CHARLOTTE: Did you?

JEANNE: And we bought some ham and some bananas and rented a boat and had a picnic on the lake.

CHARLOTTE: How nice.

JEANNE: Did you know bees had a queen?

CHARLOTTE: Vaguely.

JEANNE: She just lays eggs and the others do all the work. Yes, really! The workers clean the hive and get food from the flowers and look after all the little bees...

CHARLOTTE: Do they really?

JEANNE: Yes. Father said so.

CHARLOTTE: *(smiling)* Father knows everything, doesn't he? *(She is unpacking Jeanne's suitcase. She takes out a blouse.)* Why is this collar all stiff? It looks as if it's been starched.

JEANNE: Denise washed it yesterday evening.

CHARLOTTE: *(brandishing the blouse)* Washed it! But it was perfectly clean!

JEANNE: I don't know. She said it wouldn't do it any harm.

CHARLOTTE: She must be out of her mind! I sent you there in clean clothes from head to foot—socks, underwear, everything... You even had a bath. *(Pause. Resentfully)* Anyone would think I let you go out looking like a hobo.

JEANNE: She didn't say that.

CHARLOTTE: And what have you got on under your sweater? Don't say you're wearing it next to the skin?

JEANNE: Oh, no! Denise gave me one of her old blouses that had shrunk in the wash. It's very pretty. Look, smocking!

CHARLOTTE: Yes. *(She looks again at the blouse that was in the suitcase.)* I hate starched collars. They hurt your neck. *(Pause.)* I think I'll rinse it through. Soften it up a bit. It won't do it any harm!

> She exits. Blackout.
> Jeanne's voice can be heard as Charlotte goes to and fro getting ready to go out. Jeanne is sitting on the floor reading out her essay.

JEANNE: "Am I, like Pierre Loti, afraid of growing old? I have reflected long upon the difficulty of the question before us. Which do I prefer, Time Future or Time Past?" *(She looks up.)* Do you like it?

CHARLOTTE: *(She hasn't been listening properly.)* Yes, sweetie, it's very good.

JEANNE: *(reading)* "At first I thought Loti's fear of aging paralleled my own feelings. True, I dread the problems and uncertainties of the future, and would like to prolong my childhood happiness. The past is but a hastily scribbled chapter in the book that is our life. But the present is elusive: it is already the past."

(To Charlotte) Can you understand it?

CHARLOTTE: Can I understand what?

JEANNE: Madame Binet says I muddle things up.

CHARLOTTE: Read me the last few lines again. I didn't quite follow.

JEANNE: "True, I dread the problems and uncertainties of the future, and would like to prolong my childhood happiness. The past is but a hastily scribbled chapter in the book that is our life. But the present... "

> *She stops. Charlotte is putting on her stockings. Real stockings, with garters or a girdle. Jeanne watches, fascinated, forgetting her homework. Pause.*

CHARLOTTE: *(noticing the silence)* What's the matter?

JEANNE: Nothing. *(Pause.)* Where are you going?

CHARLOTTE: To see some friends. You don't know them.

> *Pause.*

JEANNE: You've been to the hairdresser's.

CHARLOTTE: How did you guess?

> *She puts on the earrings Jeanne gave her.*

JEANNE: They suit you.

CHARLOTTE: A perfect choice.

JEANNE: Paulette's mother let her have her ears pierced. She says you don't feel a thing. *(Pause.)* Paulette's mother is an usherette in a cinema.

CHARLOTTE: Yes, I know.

JEANNE: So Paulette can get in at the movies without having to pay. *(Pause.)* She's seen "The Bengal Lancers" three times. Have you seen it? She wants to be a movie star when she grows up. I'd rather be a history teacher. In a girls' school. *(Pause.)* Which do you like best—the Greeks or the Romans?

CHARLOTTE: *(putting on her make-up)* Will you pass me my purse, please? *(Jeanne goes to fetch the purse, drops it.)* God, honey! You are clumsy sometimes.

JEANNE: I didn't do it on purpose.

CHARLOTTE: I should hope not.

JEANNE: What was it you wanted?

CHARLOTTE: My lipstick. *(Jeanne rummages in the purse.)* No, give it to me.

Charlotte looks in the purse, finds lipstick, starts to apply it.

JEANNE: Madame Binet says we have to have new notebooks for recitation. Can I have some money? *(Groan from Charlotte, still putting on lipstick.)* I can, can't I?

CHARLOTTE: Just wait a minute, sweetie, or I'll smudge it.

Pause while she finishes. As soon as she has, Jeanne starts again.

JEANNE: I'd like the money tonight, please. We have to copy down some poems in the morning.

CHARLOTTE: Cross my heart and hope to die.

Charlotte goes out.

JEANNE: *(watching her as she dresses)* When did you buy that dress?

I haven't seen it before.

CHARLOTTE: *(off)* It isn't mine! Solange lent it to me. I had to look elegant this evening.

JEANNE: What's it made of?

CHARLOTTE: Satin.

JEANNE: I love the way it shines. *(Charlotte enters wearing a low-cut top.)* It shows your bosom.

CHARLOTTE: So what? What's wrong with my bosom?

JEANNE: I don't like low necklines. It doesn't look nice.

CHARLOTTE: Too bad. *(She looks at herself in the mirror.)* I think it looks great. *(Pause. She looks at Jeanne.)* But I'll take a scarf.

JEANNE: *(rushing to look for one)* Which one? The white one? I'll get it.

CHARLOTTE: No, the beige silk. It's softer.

> *Charlotte picks up a necklace and starts to put it on. Jeanne comes back with the scarf, arranges it over Charlotte's shoulders and takes the necklace from her.*

JEANNE: I'll do it up for you.

CHARLOTTE: Thank you. *(She looks at herself in the mirror.)* Do you approve?

JEANNE: Oh yes. Will you come in and kiss me goodnight when you get back?

CHARLOTTE: I always do, don't I? But promise you won't stay awake reading till all hours?

JEANNE: I promise. *(Charlotte starts brushing her hair.)* What time will you get back?

CHARLOTTE: How should I know? Early if I'm bored, late if I enjoy myself.

JEANNE: Six in the morning?

CHARLOTTE: What *is* all this? Just because for once in my life I stay out all night... Anyone'd think I'm always out on the town! *(A ring at the doorbell. Jeanne gets up.)* No. I'll go. *(Charlotte takes a last look at herself in the mirror and goes out. Off)* Good evening, Pierre.

PIERRE: *(off)* Good evening, Charlotte.

CHARLOTTE: *(entering)* It wasn't a bother coming to pick me up?

PIERRE: On the contrary!

CHARLOTTE: Really?

PIERRE: A pleasure.

CHARLOTTE: I don't think you've met my daughter. Jeanne, this is Pierre.

PIERRE: How do you do?

JEANNE: How do you do?

Jeanne and Pierre shake hands. Charlotte laughs.

CHARLOTTE: Aren't we formal? *(She kisses Jeanne.)* Goodnight, darling. Don't read too late.

JEANNE: You haven't given me the money.

CHARLOTTE: Oh hell. I'll leave it in your satchel.

PIERRE: Goodnight, Jeanne.

Charlotte and Pierre leave the lighted area but are still visible in the shadow upstage. The light goes slowly down on Jeanne, lying curled up mid-stage.

PIERRE: *(more intimately than before)* Are you cold?

CHARLOTTE: No. Why?

PIERRE: The scarf.

CHARLOTTE: Jeanne doesn't like me in low necklines.

PIERRE: What about me?

CHARLOTTE: *(starting to take off the scarf)* Do you prefer me like this? *(Pierre kisses her shoulder. Pause.)* No, we must go, we'll be late.

PIERRE: No, we won't. They said any time after nine. The taxi's waiting just down the street.

He takes her hand and they go out. Complete blackout for a few moments. Then Jeanne's voice.

JEANNE: Mother! Mother!

The light comes up again. Jeanne hasn't moved.

CHARLOTTE: *(off)* What's wrong?

JEANNE: *(to herself)* Nothing.

CHARLOTTE: *(on stage now)* What a face! What is it?

JEANNE: ... Blood.

CHARLOTTE: *(guessing)* It's nothing to be frightened of, sweetie. It's normal. I told you about it. Don't you remember?

JEANNE: Perhaps. I forget. It's disgusting.

CHARLOTTE: Of course it's not disgusting! It's natural. It happens to every girl.

JEANNE: Does it happen to you?

CHARLOTTE: Of course.

Pause.

JEANNE: How long does it go on?

CHARLOTTE: As long as you can have children.

Pause.

JEANNE: I was supposed to be going swimming with Paulette.

CHARLOTTE: I'll call and tell her you're not coming.

JEANNE: *(running off)* No, I'd rather tell her myself.

> *Sudden change of lighting. Charlotte sits outlined against brightly lit backstage. After a moment, Jeanne enters, talking to someone unseen.*

JEANNE: Thank you, doctor.

> *Light comes up from front to cover the whole stage.*

CHARLOTTE: *(standing up)* Well?

JEANNE: The test was positive.

CHARLOTTE: *(kissing her)* Darling, how wonderful!

JEANNE: Wait a bit before you...

CHARLOTTE: *(interrupting)* But you are going to keep it?

JEANNE: I don't know. I'll have to talk to Jacques.

CHARLOTTE: Oh, keep it!

JEANNE: Why?

CHARLOTTE: What do you mean, why? Because it's the most beautiful thing in the world!

JEANNE: I suppose so.

CHARLOTTE: You don't sound very sure.

JEANNE: It depends. Beautiful for whom?

CHARLOTTE: For you, of course!

JEANNE: And what about him?

CHARLOTTE: Jacques?

JEANNE: The child.

CHARLOTTE: That depends on you.

JEANNE: Exactly.

CHARLOTTE: You don't intend to make him unhappy, I suppose?

JEANNE: No. But shall I be able to make him happy?

CHARLOTTE: You're both young. And in love.

JEANNE: For the moment.

CHARLOTTE: You're in good health, Jacques has a job. You could still take your own exams, you wouldn't be the first... It's the ideal moment. Couldn't be better, if you ask me.

JEANNE: Calm down, *please!* There's no point in getting excited. It's a decision that could change our whole lives, and I don't mean to make it lightly.

CHARLOTTE: *(unstoppable)* I'll do all I can to help. Only too glad! I'll make such a fuss of it!

JEANNE: Listen, Mother, I'm not going to have this baby just for you.

CHARLOTTE: Sure, sure.

JEANNE: If we keep it we must be able to look after it ourselves. On our own. It'll be our responsibility.

CHARLOTTE: Yes, but I'll be there. *(Smiling)* For whenever I'm needed.

Jeanne bends forward, strokes her stomach lightly and talks to it.

JEANNE: And what do you think, eh? Do you want to come into this awful world? You won't regret it? You won't hold it against me? Will you? *(Pause. She stands with her hand still on her stomach, exhausted.)* Will you ever feel deserted? Will I always be there when you want me? Will I always put you first, before everything else? Before every*one* else? My little one. My little life. *(Pause.)* If I do keep you, I'll make you happy. I promise.

CHARLOTTE: *(going)* Amen.

The light goes down slowly on Jeanne, who comes and lies down on some cushions near the front of the stage. When she hears her mother, she picks up a book and pretends to be absorbed in it. The light fades up.

CHARLOTTE: *(off)* Jeanne! Jeanne! Are you there? *(Jeanne doesn't answer.)* Jeanne! *(Charlotte enters with a towel in her hand.)* You might answer when I call you.

JEANNE: *(pretending to be concentrating on her work)* I didn't hear.

CHARLOTTE: "Didn't hear!" Do you take me for an imbecile? Do you think I haven't noticed your airs? Her ladyship is up in her ivory tower, thinking great thoughts. "Ordinary mortals, keep out!" *(No reaction from Jeanne.)* I'm sorry to interrupt such lofty meditations with merely material trivialities, but I'd like to know what the hell you do with the towels in the bathroom! I change them three times a week, and there's never one that's decent. Look at this! I found it under the bath, all scrunched up and sopping wet. Pools of water everywhere. You'd think a herd of elephants had been taking a shower. How on earth...

JEANNE: I don't know.

CHARLOTTE: It's more like a pond than a bathroom. All it needs is the ducks. If you really can't wash without splashing water everywhere, at least get a cloth and mop it up. It's not so difficult to keep things reasonably clean and tidy, is it?

JEANNE: It's just the same as usual.

CHARLOTTE: You mean it's always a horrible mess! *(Pause.)* You're a young woman now. You can't leave your things strewn all over the place. You ought to be neat and tidy and well-groomed.

JEANNE: You keep saying that. I've had it up to here.

CHARLOTTE: Well, whose fault is that?

    Pause.

JEANNE: I'm not the only one who uses the bathroom.

CHARLOTTE: If you're referring to Pierre, you know very well he's tidiness itself. If he doesn't complain to you about the bathroom it's only to avoid unpleasantness. *(Silence.)* What?

JEANNE: I didn't say anything.

CHARLOTTE: I know what you're thinking. If he didn't live here I wouldn't keep on about all this. Well, so what? What am I supposed to do? Throw him out? *(Silence.)* I don't know what you've got to complain about. Isn't he nice to you? Doesn't he take you with us every time we go out, and spend hours helping you with your homework? Though heaven knows he's got too much work of his own. He treats you as if you were his own daughter.

JEANNE: I never asked him for anything.

CHARLOTTE: Anyway, all that's got nothing to do with the towels in the bathroom.

PIERRE: *(off)* Anybody home? Charlotte? Are you there?

Pierre enters.

CHARLOTTE: Hello, Pierre!

She joins him upstage. They kiss. Jeanne seems to be working.

PIERRE: *(taking Charlotte in his arms)* I thought I'd be home earlier, but...

CHARLOTTE: *(girlishly)* I didn't say anything.

PIERRE: No. I feel only warmth coming from you. *(He kisses her.)* How are you, my darling?

CHARLOTTE: And how are you, my love?

PIERRE: On top of the world.

They move down stage, talking.

CHARLOTTE: Someone called Feinstein phoned.

PIERRE: Oh?

CHARLOTTE: I could barely make out what he was saying.

PIERRE: He's only been in France a few years. And he's not young.

CHARLOTTE: Apparently he's lost his job... in a hotel. What was he doing in a hotel?

PIERRE: Working as a night porter. In Berlin he was a political journalist.

CHARLOTTE: And that went up in smoke with the Reichstag.

PIERRE: He's got a wife and two children. When they left Germany their train was held up for a while in a station. It was night-time, and there were some other cars standing there on another track. And they could hear groans and cries coming from them. As if instead of being ordinary passengers, the people inside were...

CHARLOTTE: Prisoners?

PIERRE: Who knows? *(Pause.)* The Feinsteins' train went on. Nobody said anything. There was an SS man in the compartment. *(Pause. Then Pierre turns to Jeanne and bows ceremoniously.)* Good evening, mademoiselle.

JEANNE: *(mumbling)* Hello.

CHARLOTTE: *(whispering)* Leave her alone! She's impossible today.

PIERRE: *(to Charlotte)* I can always try. *(To Jeanne)* May I inquire whom I have the honor of addressing? Is it Miss Anthropy of Gloomville, or her charming cousin, Sunny Side Up?

   Silence. Jeanne makes a great show of getting on with her work.

CHARLOTTE: Have you lost your tongue?

JEANNE: I'm working.

PIERRE: Excellent! And might I ask what problem your augustness's mind is addressing? *(Silence.)* Should my humble powers be able to assist you in your endeavors, I should esteem myself highly honored. *(Pierre and Charlotte exchange looks.)* But of course I must respect the secrecy with which you choose to surround your distinguished labors. *(Silence. Jeanne doesn't look up.)* What's the matter, Jeanne?

JEANNE: Nothing.

PIERRE: *(going over to her)* Look at me. *(He tilts her chin up.)* Say "cheese." *(He gives an exaggerated grin.)*

JEANNE: *(expressionless)* Cheese. *And she looks straight down again at her books.*

PIERRE: Very well. I was going to take you to the movies, but as the meteorological conditions are so threatening we'd better wait until they improve.

> *He goes out. Charlotte follows him, but stops at the door.*

CHARLOTTE: Thank you.

JEANNE: What for?

CHARLOTTE: For the atmosphere you create in this house.

> *Charlotte goes out. Blackout.*
> *The sound of "Alexander's Ragtime Band" played on the gramophone. Jeanne is practicing dance steps in front of the mirror with an invisible partner. The light comes up on the whole stage. Charlotte crosses, carrying a tray with plates on it, and exits. Jeanne goes on dancing. Charlotte passes again with the tray. Pierre is seen from behind, sitting in an armchair reading the paper.*

CHARLOTTE: Will you give me a hand, please?

> *Jeanne goes on dancing. Charlotte exits, but returns a few moments later, goes over and stops the gramophone. Jeanne stops dancing.*

JEANNE: What's the matter?

CHARLOTTE: I asked you to help.

JEANNE: In a minute.

CHARLOTTE: Not "in a minute." Now! After lunch it's usual to clear the table and wash the dishes. Come on, now. You can't let Pierre's mother do everything.

Charlotte exits. Jeanne goes on looking at herself in the mirror. Charlotte comes back with some glasses. Jeanne makes a half-hearted effort to help her.

JEANNE: Can I have a pleated skirt?

CHARLOTTE: We'll see.

JEANNE: There are pictures of them in "Marie-Claire". And one of a straw hat with a ribbon hanging down behind. Like Deanna Durbin. Do I really look like her?

CHARLOTTE: Like who?

JEANNE: Deanna Durbin. Everyone at the beach says I do.

CHARLOTTE: Why ask me, then?

Pause.

JEANNE: Do you think I've got a nice voice?

CHARLOTTE: *(going)* Yes... yes...

Jeanne starts to sing "Some day my prince will come."

PIERRE: *(folding up his paper)* Mercy, mercy! We're only here for two days. Don't go and blot out the sunshine! *(He gets up. Jeanne has stopped singing.)* Sing after we've gone. *(As he goes)* They say rain is good for the complexion.

JEANNE: *(through clenched teeth)* Very funny!

> *She puts a Jean Sablon record on the gramophone, listens to it with her head in her hands. When she hears Charlotte's voice she stops the record and goes and sits down.*

CHARLOTTE: *(off)* Jeanne! Jeanne! *(Jeanne reads, or pretends to. Charlotte enters.)* Are you coming? We're going for a walk. Come on!

JEANNE: I don't feel like it.

CHARLOTTE: You can't waste this lovely afternoon indoors reading. You're supposed to be on holiday! *(Jeanne gets up and goes and looks out of the window. Charlotte speaks to her back.)* What do you do here all on your own? What do you think about? I hate to see my little girl worried. *(She kisses Jeanne.)* What do you say to a lovely pistachio ice-cream with whipped cream on top? Ah... I see a flicker of interest...

JEANNE: I'd rather stay here.

> *Pause.*

CHARLOTTE: As you like. *(Pause.)* It's not very nice for Pierre. He might have to leave at any moment. We came all this way in the heat just to spend a few days with you, and you go and shut yourself up in your room. What's wrong?

JEANNE: Nothing.

CHARLOTTE: Pierre's parents are so glad to have you. And you must admit it's very pleasant here. The sea's only a stone's throw away, and your friends are staying just opposite. So what's the problem? *(Silence.)* Have I done anything you don't like?

JEANNE: No.

CHARLOTTE: Did I offend you just now? *(Silence.)* I'm sorry. You're the image of Deanna Durbin. You sing like a lark.

JEANNE: It's not that.

CHARLOTTE: What is it then? *(Silence.)* You can tell me anything, darling. I'll understand. But I can't bear to see you with that stony expression. Smile!... No? All right. Some other time... Sure you don't want to come? You won't be sorry afterwards? *(Silence.)* All right. I'll go, then. *(She goes, and turns at the door.)* We'll be back for dinner. If you decide to join us, come on your bike. We'll be bathing off the point. And then having a drink at the two little old ladies' place on the square. All right? *(She kisses Jeanne.)* My own little girl.

PIERRE: *(off)* Charlotte! Jeanne! Are you coming? It's four o'clock!

CHARLOTTE: *(calling)* Coming! *(She joins Pierre upstage. To Pierre)* She'd rather stay in her room. I tried to find out why but she shut up tight as a clam.

PIERRE: She'll get over it.

CHARLOTTE: What can I do to make her loosen up? She's so touchy... She can't take the slightest joke.

PIERRE: Yet we're supposed to put up with her prancing about in front of the mirror all day long.

CHARLOTTE: And those headaches she's been complaining of lately... Do you think they could have anything to do with it? Her hands are very hot.

PIERRE: Nonsense! It's ninety in the shade and she's got a terrible temper, that's all.

> *Their voices have faded in the distance. Jeanne comes and lies on the floor down stage.*

JEANNE: I'm fed up. Fed up. *(Pause.)* I have got a headache. I'm going to be ill. That'll show them. It'll serve them right. They ought to have been nice to me before. Now it's too late. *(Pause.)* They'll be sorry when I'm dead. *(She is starting to fall asleep.)* It must be sad, dying, but at least it'll teach them a lesson.

> *She is asleep. We hear Deanna Durbin singing, Charlotte calling "Jeanne! Jeanne!", then sirens wailing in the distance. This is Jeanne's dream.*

CHARLOTTE: *(pulling violently away from Pierre)* No, don't touch me! Don't come near me! It's all your fault. You were always against her. You hated her! My poor little girl... *(To Pierre)* You wouldn't believe she was really ill, you said it was just affectation! Jeanne, my angel! You died all alone, without your mother... *(To Pierre)* I don't want to see you again, ever. It's all over between us. I shall stay with my darling, my love, my little one!... Jeanne! Jeanne!

> *Pierre has vanished. Charlotte shakes Jeanne to wake her.*

JEANNE: *(waking)* What is it? *(She sees Charlotte.)* What's the matter? *(She hears the sirens.)* What is it?

CHARLOTTE: War.

> *Blackout. Sirens continue throughout the blackout, ending, just as the next scene begins, with the "All Clear." Suddenly the lights come on. Charlotte is in bed. Jeanne is caught standing with her shoes in her hands.*

CHARLOTTE: And where have you been?

JEANNE: You nearly frightened me out of my wits!

CHARLOTTE: I asked you where you've been. The curfew's been over for two hours. I phoned Françoise and she couldn't tell me anything, she hadn't seen you for three days. Why do you tell me fibs? I let you go out alone at night when you're only fifteen, and you take advantage of my kindness and lie to me. Why. Eh?

JEANNE: Because otherwise you wouldn't have let me go.

CHARLOTTE: Bravo!... And where were you?... Answer!

JEANNE: At a friend's place. You don't know her.

CHARLOTTE: And where does she live, this friend?

JEANNE: Near the Etoile.

CHARLOTTE: And what did you do all the evening?

JEANNE: Played records... Danced...

CHARLOTTE: Very interesting. Just the pair of you, all on your own?

JEANNE: There were some boys.

CHARLOTTE: Perfect. And do you know what time it is? You promised you'd be home by midnight.

JEANNE: I had to walk. I missed the last metro.

CHARLOTTE: What do you take me for? An idiot? It isn't more than twenty minutes' walk from the Etoile to here. Where were you?

JEANNE: That's the third time you've asked that.

Charlotte slaps her.

CHARLOTTE: I'm your mother, kindly show a bit of respect. *(Jeanne starts to go.)* Stay where you are. *(Jeanne does so.)* Sit down. *(Jeanne obeys. Pause.)* You ought to be ashamed of yourself. There you are with your dizzy pals, and all you think about is flirting and jazz. Don't you know there's a war on? And that if you get picked up by a patrol they'll find out your mother's Jewish? *(Pause. She looks at Jeanne more closely.)* Look at me. What's that you've got on your eyelids?

JEANNE: Just a bit of blue.

CHARLOTTE: Horrible! And you think it looks nice?... Kindly go and wash it all off. And the lipstick. It's all smudged. *(Jeanne starts to go.)* Didn't you hear the sirens?

JEANNE: Yes, that's why I came. We thought it'd be easier to get through during the alert.

CHARLOTTE: Meanwhile I was worrying myself silly! What if there'd been some bombs? What if you'd been injured?

JEANNE: There weren't any bombs tonight.

CHARLOTTE: There might have been. *(Pause.)* You weren't on your own, I suppose?

JEANNE: No.

Pause.

CHARLOTTE: Would it scald your tongue to tell me who you were with?

JEANNE: Bernard.

CHARLOTTE: Who's he?

JEANNE: A friend.

Pause.

CHARLOTTE: Fine. I had plenty of time to think about our problems while I was waiting for you. It's crazy to stay on in Paris. I'm not legally supposed to be here. I'm not registered with the authorities, I can't work, I haven't got any money. And all you can do is run stupid risks. *(Pause.)* Pierre's parents are in unoccupied France. I've decided we'll leave next week and go and stay with them.

Pause.

JEANNE: What about school?

CHARLOTTE: Good heavens! Are you anxious about your studies now? That's a new one! By the way... *(She opens a school report.)* I just glanced at your report. Can you explain this? "More often absent than present. Can be relied on only for incompetence."

JEANNE: That doesn't count. It's only gym.

CHARLOTTE: And what about this? Does this count? "Geography, utterly lacking in application. Latin, main efforts directed toward disturbing the rest of the class. French, three and a half marks out of twenty. Position in class, twenty-first." Why twenty-first?

JEANNE: Jeanine Soulié's twenty-second.

CHARLOTTE: I didn't ask why you weren't twenty-second, I want to know why you didn't get better grades.

JEANNE: I tried to revise on my own, but...

CHARLOTTE: Oh, it was easier when Pierre was here, is that it? I'm delighted to hear it. *(Pause.)* Well, we'll let Jeanine Soulié be twenty-first now. I'll try to help you study at home. It's not a tragedy, you'll only miss a couple of months. And who knows what may have happened by then?

Pause.

JEANNE: But I'll be all on my own.

CHARLOTTE: Oh, there are worse things than not being able to go to parties. So, off to bed now, and I advise you not to say you didn't hear the alarm in the morning. I'm not writing any notes to the teacher. The rest of the bread's in the cooler outside the kitchen window.

JEANNE: There isn't any sugar left.

CHARLOTTE: I collected my ration this afternoon.

JEANNE: That's for you.

CHARLOTTE: I don't need it so much at my age. Don't gobble it all up in three days, that's all I ask. Try to be sensible. *(Jeanne gets up to go, and Charlotte takes a closer look at the shoes she's holding.)* Who said you could borrow those shoes? You've got some nerve, I must say! Give then back at once! *(She snatches the shoes and examines them.)* You're not to touch my things, do you hear? They're mine, they're for me to use. You'll completely ruin them.

JEANNE: All my shoes have got flat heels.

CHARLOTTE: So what? They're leather, that's a luxury.

JEANNE: Heels are better for dancing.

CHARLOTTE: Well, in future we won't be here and the occasion won't arise. *(Jeanne goes. Charlotte calls out after her.)* And don't make a racket in the morning. You've made me lose enough sleep as it is.

> *Charlotte switches the light off. Blackout. Sound of footsteps, door-bell, keys. Light. Charlotte enters, wearing a coat and carrying a suitcase.*

CHARLOTTE: Jeanne! *(Silence.)* Jeanne! *(Silence.)* Are you there? Jeanne! *(After a moment Jeanne appears, barefoot.)* Did I wake you? Sorry. I'm still on New York time. *(She looks at her watch.)* Midnight. You're getting up and I'm going to bed.

JEANNE: I didn't know you were arriving today.

CHARLOTTE: Neither did I. There was a seat at the last minute and I grabbed it. *(They kiss.)* Sweetie. Let me look at you... You've changed!

JEANNE: Not in two months!

CHARLOTTE: Yes, you have, really! You look more feminine. *(She kisses her again.)* That's a compliment! You can't imagine how glad I am to be back.

JEANNE: *(going)* I'll just get my bathrobe, it's not very warm in here.

CHARLOTTE: *(to Jeanne, who is invisible)* I was so worried! You might have written a bit more often. In San Francisco I didn't have any news for two weeks, I nearly went crazy. I know it's silly. At your age you're perfectly capable of managing on your own, but... *(Jeanne returns wearing a sweater.)* You promised to drop me a line once a week. Oh well... Did you miss me? You look tired. You're not working too hard, are you? Help me unpack my suitcase, I've got a surprise for you. Right at the bottom. Darling... So come on, tell me, how've you been getting on?

JEANNE: Just as usual.

CHARLOTTE: You and Madeleine got on all right together? You weren't difficult? You know how touchy your aunt is. Takes offense at the slightest thing. Like the princess and the pea. You did give her a hand sometimes, didn't you? You didn't leave all the shopping and so forth to her?

JEANNE: I have my meals at the cafeteria.

CHARLOTTE: Even so. You ought to think of her a bit. Where is she? Still asleep?

JEANNE: No. She's in Lyons. She had to go last week. An order for some painting on silk.

CHARLOTTE: So you've been all on your own? It hasn't been too much for you?

JEANNE: Mother, really!

CHARLOTTE: What about at night? How did you manage about the spiders?

YOUNG MAN: *(off)* Jeanne! Jeanne! Who is it?

Pause.

CHARLOTTE: Oh.

JEANNE: *(impassively)* So how did you find our liberators?

CHARLOTTE: *(affecting to be natural)* The Americans? Oh, fascinating. Absolutely fascinating.

JEANNE: And they gave you a hero's welcome?

CHARLOTTE: Very friendly. Very... moving. *(Pause.)* I met men who'd come three thousand miles to fight over here. In a country whose language they didn't know, a country they'd hardly even heard of. When you say you're from Paris they say, "Paris, France?" Because they've got places of their own called Paris, Amsterdam, Moscow and so on... *(Pause.)* Who is he?

JEANNE: A friend.

CHARLOTTE: So I imagine... And... ?

JEANNE: We've got together.

CHARLOTTE: I see. And... er... is it working out?

JEANNE: Mother, please! I hate smut.

CHARLOTTE: Where's the smut? I'm just interested. You are my little girl...

JEANNE: *(interrupting)* That's just it. I'm not a little girl any more.

CHARLOTTE: *(pressing on)* And because I'm interested in you I'm interested in the people you spend your time with. And your nights.

JEANNE: And I ask you to forget me for a while. I don't need anyone to supervise my...

CHARLOTTE: *(interrupting)* I have no intention of meddling in your love affairs!

JEANNE: So what are we talking about?

> *Pause. Charlotte takes a coat out of her suitcase and holds it out to Jeanne.*

CHARLOTTE: Do you like it?

JEANNE: But... it's the same as yours!

CHARLOTTE: Yes. Do you mind?

JEANNE: *(laughing)* No.

CHARLOTTE: Feel the material, pure wool! And look at the colors... Why shouldn't we both wear the same coat if it's pretty? All we need to do is make sure we don't wear them together. Try it on. I hope it's not too small. *(Jeanne tries her coat on.)* No. A perfect fit.

JEANNE: Yours too. *(They stand still for a moment, looking at one another. Exactly alike.)* Thank you.

CHARLOTTE: Shall we have lunch together tomorrow?

JEANNE: Well...

YOUNG MAN: *(off)* Jeanne!

JEANNE: *(calling out, calm)* Yes?

YOUNG MAN: *(off)* Can you come here a second?

JEANNE: *(to Charlotte)* Excuse me.

> *She goes out. Charlotte stands alone for a moment, looking after Jeanne, then goes out, carrying her suitcase.*
> *Blackout.*
> *Charlotte and Jeanne enter. Charlotte collapses into a chair.*

CHARLOTTE: I thought it would never end. What an idea, to keep people hanging around all that time! Did he... ?

JEANNE: Yes. He arranged all the details himself. Even the music. Clara Haskill playing the Mozart concerto in E flat.

CHARLOTTE: Not that anyone could hear it.

> *Pause.*

JEANNE: You got all dolled up, anyhow!

CHARLOTTE: Of course! What would they have thought if I hadn't, all those people I haven't seen in twenty years? "Doesn't Charlotte look old?" *(Pause.)* That's the worst thing about funerals. One of the worst.

JEANNE: Do you think so?

CHARLOTTE: I don't mean for those directly involved. I mean for the others. *(Pause.)* Their faces! The younger ones looked anxious, "If he's dead, it could happen to me too!" The older ones looked pleased, "I'm still here, anyway!" *(Pause.)* Why didn't you stay on with Denise and Patrick?

JEANNE: She had her own relatives. He had his girl-friend.

CHARLOTTE: He's a man now...

JEANNE: Yes.

CHARLOTTE: He's got your father's mouth. That humorous

twist. *(Pause.)* Do you know what the lawyer said? I'm entitled to part of the pension. I never remarried.

JEANNE: Every cloud has a silver lining.

CHARLOTTE: I wonder what Denise will say...

JEANNE: Oh, she's not greedy!

CHARLOTTE: She might need it all herself.

JEANNE: She works.

Pause. Charlotte kisses Jeanne.

CHARLOTTE: And how are you feeling?

JEANNE: *(impassively)* All right.

Pause.

CHARLOTTE: You don't say anything. You don't show anything. You're strong.

JEANNE: What do you expect me to do? Burst into floods of tears? Roll on the floor and howl? *(Pause.)* Grief takes time. You have to wait for it to sink in. "You'll find out," they say. I'm trying to learn.

CHARLOTTE: He died in his sleep. He didn't know anything about it. He didn't suffer.

JEANNE: No. But I am. *(Pause.)* When I was about nine or ten he used to play tricks on me. Silly practical jokes. We'd be walking along the street and suddenly he would run away. I'd run after him, but he would have disappeared around a corner. And I had no idea where I was. I was lost. I just stood there in absolute despair. Then, just as I began to cry, he'd dart out of a doorway, delighted at the success of his joke. *(Pause.)* This time

I'll have to manage by myself.

CHARLOTTE: I hadn't seen him for years. Not since that time you broke your leg and were in that clinic in Boulogne. One day he drove me back into Paris. That must have been ten years ago. *(Pause.)* When you don't see someone any more, it doesn't make very much difference when they die. You've got used to their not being there.

> *Pause.*

JEANNE: Why did you split up?

CHARLOTTE: Now you're going back to prehistory.

JEANNE: I never knew.

CHARLOTTE: It's all so long ago.

JEANNE: But you can't have forgotten? You do still remember?

CHARLOTTE: It's almost as if it happened to someone else.

JEANNE: Well?

CHARLOTTE: We were too young. We mistook a passing fancy for a grand passion. The more obstacles our parents put in our way, the more determined we were to get married. Then, when the obstacles weren't there any more, we found ourselves all alone with scarcely anything in common.

JEANNE: There was me.

CHARLOTTE: You... *(She kisses her.)* And, just because of you, I've never regretted that pointless marriage. *(She laughs.)* At the civil ceremony, in the city hall, I wore a sack dress. With you inside it.

JEANNE: Did you hide it from them for long?

CHARLOTTE: As long as I could. *(Pause.)* One day we were all going along the street, and I was walking in front with your aunt Madeleine—she was fifteen at the time—and my father said to my mother: "Charlotte's hips are certainly well padded!" And my mother called out, "Charlotte, you walk just like an expectant mother!" And I said, "That's just what I am!" *(They laugh.)* You should have seen their faces! But it was a great relief to me.

JEANNE: What about them?

CHARLOTTE: Oh, they made a great fuss, there was a lot of argument, and then they arranged for us to get married. Your exact date of birth had to be kept from all the relatives, hence the sack dress. *(She smiles.)* But Madeleine has always been famous for saying the wrong thing, and if anyone asked her how I was, she told them I was expecting a little girl called Jeanne weighing seven and a half pounds!

> *They laugh. Pause.*

JEANNE: How old was I when you separated?

CHARLOTTE: Oh, very small. About five, I think. *(Pause.)* There was no great drama. Just a divorce by mutual consent.

JEANNE: Yes. *(Pause.)* I've always envied big happy families. With white-haired grannies and babies in the cradle, and big houses where everyone goes in the summer. Meals where you can't hear yourself speak, and you go round the table saying goodnight to everybody before you go to bed.

> *Pause.*

CHARLOTTE: It didn't take long to go round our table.

JEANNE: No. Some nights I could almost have kissed my own reflection in the mirror.

CHARLOTTE: What about me? I was there, wasn't I?

JEANNE: In my memory I'm always alone.

CHARLOTTE: That's not true. You exaggerate.

JEANNE: I didn't say it was true, I said that's how I remember it. *(Pause.)* Did you often go out in the evening?

CHARLOTTE: No... Well, not very often. Hardly at all, with your father, he didn't like late nights. Nor did Pierre, come to think of it. And for years I lived on my own... Anyway, there was always Adèle.

JEANNE: Was she always there?

CHARLOTTE: Until the war.

JEANNE: Oh. *(Pause.)* Where did she sleep?

CHARLOTTE: In a little room off the kitchen, by the service stairs. You wouldn't have her in your room.

JEANNE: Why do I always remember you going out with your friends and leaving me alone?

CHARLOTTE: Do you know how old I was when we got divorced? Twenty-five. The same age as you are now. I could have sent you to boarding school, I wouldn't have been the first. You'd have come home at the weekends and thought yourself lucky. And there were times when that sort of arrangement would have made my life a lot easier, believe you me.

JEANNE: So why didn't you?

CHARLOTTE: Because I could never bear to part with you.

Pause.

JEANNE: Why did you always side with Pierre and never with me?

CHARLOTTE: I didn't side with anyone! I just tried to keep the peace. You were often very unpleasant to him. As if you resented his being there.

JEANNE: Brilliant!

CHARLOTTE: What would you have liked me to do, then? Shut myself up in a nunnery? Renounce the world?

JEANNE: I don't know. *(Pause.)* Why did you go away and leave me all alone with his parents?

CHARLOTTE: During the war, you mean? I had to earn my living. I couldn't live off them indefinitely. *(Pause.)* I didn't go and join Pierre in England because I didn't want to leave you. And when the war ended, he'd found someone else.

JEANNE: In other words, if it wasn't for me you and he would still be together?

CHARLOTTE: I didn't say that!

JEANNE: Why didn't you ever listen to me?

CHARLOTTE: What do you mean?

JEANNE: Why didn't you listen when I talked to you?

CHARLOTTE: I did listen. Not as much as you'd have liked, perhaps, but I did listen. Do you want me to show you your letters, the essays you wrote at school? I've kept them all. Do you want me to tell you all the words you couldn't pronounce properly? You always said "lubarb" instead of "rhubarb"...

JEANNE: How amusing.

Pause.

CHARLOTTE: I came across one of your letters from before the war. Asking when I was coming to see you. You said it wasn't a real holiday until I was there.

JEANNE: But you never were there.

CHARLOTTE: What do you mean?

JEANNE: You never came away with me on vacation.

CHARLOTTE: You're talking nonsense.

JEANNE: When did you, then? I used to go to summer camp, I used to go and stay with Pierre's parents, with a whole lot of other kids...

CHARLOTTE: Friends of your own age!

JEANNE: But never with you!

CHARLOTTE: I used to come and see you when you were staying with Pierre's parents!

JEANNE: Just for the odd day, when you weren't off somewhere else.

CHARLOTTE: Wasn't I ever supposed to go anywhere by myself?

JEANNE: I didn't say that. I just said you never came on holiday with me, that's all.

   Pause.

CHARLOTTE: What about Brittany? Didn't we go to Brittany together? There, you see, you'd forgotten that!

JEANNE: I remember you and Pierre dropped in one afternoon while I was at camp. We were supposed to be resting. Parents weren't really allowed to come; the teachers were afraid it might unsettle us. They were right. I didn't stop crying for two days. *(Pause.)* No, when I talked about holidays I meant just you and me, alone together. *(Long pause.)* Why didn't I learn to play the piano?

CHARLOTTE: I did arrange for you to have lessons, but after a few times you gave it up. You said you didn't have time because of all your homework.

Pause.

JEANNE: Why didn't you think I was pretty?

Charlotte tries to give Jeanne a kiss, but Jeanne turns away.

CHARLOTTE: But my darling, to me you were the most beautiful little girl in the world!

JEANNE: That's not true! You told Paulette's mother she had lovely eyes and I was only sweet...

CHARLOTTE: I said *that* ?

JEANNE: Yes!

CHARLOTTE: Well, maybe you did go through an awkward phase. Most girls do. But you were always perfectly charming, I assure you.

JEANNE: What's the good of that, now?

CHARLOTTE: Poor Jeanne! A dead father and a wicked mother. Bad luck.

Pause.

JEANNE: Why haven't I got any happy memories?

Pause.

CHARLOTTE: Why must you hurt me? All right, I plead guilty, you're unhappy, you never had a real childhood, all your memories are sad ones, and it's all my fault. So be it.

She goes out. The light remains on Jeanne. Doorbell. Jeanne goes to open. Enter Charlotte.

JEANNE: It wasn't too much of a bother?

CHARLOTTE: Not at all! It doesn't make any difference to me whether I spend the evening here or at home.

JEANNE: I don't know how else I'd have managed.

CHARLOTTE: Come, come, it's the least I could do. Are they in bed?

JEANNE: Supposed to be. But you know what they're like. Up to all sorts of tricks. If they bully you, be quite firm. Send them back to bed at once, switch the light out and shut the door. Otherwise it'll be chaos.

CHARLOTTE: I can just tell them a story?

JEANNE: Just a short one, then. They take advantage of you, and afterwards I can't do anything with them. Do you remember the song you used to sing me? The one about the little man who went to buy bread?

CHARLOTTE: *(singing)*

> When the little old man goes to buy some bread
> He never goes without his little old head.
> With a skip and a hop-a,
> He's at the baker's shop-a. *(JEANNE joins in)*
> "If you please, some bread! A brown loaf, mother said!"
> Nowhere will you find, look wherever you can,
> Such a clever errand boy as the little old man.
>
> When the little old man goes to buy some milk
> He never goes without his purse of silk...

JEANNE : *(interrupting)* The children always ask me to tell them the words, and I can never remember them... Oh, I must fly!

CHARLOTTE: Where are you going?

JEANNE: To see some friends. You don't know them. What time is it?

CHARLOTTE: A quarter to eight.

JEANNE: Hell and damnation! Jacques is picking me up in ten minutes. I'd better step on it!

CHARLOTTE: Can I help?

JEANNE: You could get my beige dress out, if you will. The one with the low V-neck. And the openwork shoes that go with it. Thank you. *(She sits at her dressing-table and looks at herself in the mirror.)* I do look a mess!

CHARLOTTE: *(looking at Jeanne's reflection)* You look very nice.

JEANNE: Do you think so? *(She starts to apply her make-up.)*

CHARLOTTE: I like your hair. Have you had it cut?

JEANNE: Yes, it's easier to manage.

> *Charlotte looks at herself in the mirror and tests the elasticity of her skin.*

CHARLOTTE: I wonder if it would suit me. I'd like to try. What do you think?

JEANNE: *(applying make-up)* Why not?

CHARLOTTE: *(watching her)* Where did you learn to make your eyes up? You do it so well. I admire you, I can't put on a bit of mascara without making myself cry.

JEANNE: Try the new kind, it's easier.

CHARLOTTE: Really? Where do you get it?

JEANNE: At the butcher's shop! *(Smiling)* At any drugstore, of course.

CHARLOTTE: I'm sure there was something I wanted to ask you. *(She rummages in her purse.)* Just a minute. *(She fishes out a piece of paper.)* Oh yes, Mother's Day...

JEANNE: *(interrupting)* Oh, come on, we're not going to bother with that ridiculous custom!

CHARLOTTE: It's not ridiculous! It's charming.

JEANNE: Nonsense! It's been completely commercialized.

Pause.

CHARLOTTE: *(rummaging in her purse again)* As you like... I've had a letter about my apartment that I can't make head or tail of. I wonder if you'd explain it to me? It's about doing up the building. Listen to this gibberish: "To all shareholders. Low-interest proposal based on five per cent of rentable value of premises over twenty years, allowing for increase in maintenance coefficient resulting from the work in question. Reimbursement over five years in quarterly installments, starting... "

JEANNE: Shit! *(She has put her eye-liner on wrong.)*

CHARLOTTE: What's the matter? *(Silence.)* I'm distracting you with all my talk about coefficients.

JEANNE: If you wouldn't mind keeping quiet for a second. I can't do two things at once without doing both badly.

CHARLOTTE: Sorry.

She puts the letter back in her purse. Jeanne goes on applying her make-up. Charlotte creeps about on tiptoe.

JEANNE: There's a "Le Monde" over there.

CHARLOTTE: Thanks.

She picks up the paper, sits down and starts reading, casting furtive glances at Jeanne as she finishes her make-up.

JACQUES: *(off)* Jeanne! *(He enters.)* Ready?

JEANNE: In two minutes. As soon as I've put on my dress. *(As she goes out)* You can keep Mother company.

JACQUES: *(kissing Charlotte)* Hello, Charlotte. Are you our baby-sitter tonight? That's very kind of you.

CHARLOTTE: A pleasure.

JACQUES: *(calling to Jeanne)* Are they in bed?

JEANNE: *(off)* In bed, tucked up, read to, kissed goodnight, and with the light switched off.

JACQUES: But still awake, perhaps. Perhaps I could go in and...

JEANNE: *(entering)* Oh no, please, darling. They've been so difficult. Gérard wouldn't eat his supper, and Marie did everything she could to stop me switching off the light.

JACQUES: You did leave the door open?

JEANNE: Of course. *(She listens.)* Did you hear anything?

CHARLOTTE: Not a thing.

JACQUES: Want me to go?

JEANNE: No! *(To Charlotte)* Now's your chance to ask him about your letter.

Jeanne goes out.

CHARLOTTE: *(looking in her purse)* Oh yes. I don't want to bother you with my problems, but if you could explain... *(She produces the letter.)* What does all this mean?

Jacques scans the letter.

JACQUES: It's very simple. They're offering a loan to pay for your share of the work on the building. The terms are very favorable. You ought to accept it.

CHARLOTTE: Do you really think so?

JACQUES: You asked for my opinion, Charlotte, and I've given it. I've no ax to grind either way.

CHARLOTTE: Of course not.

JACQUES: So why do you look so suspicious?

CHARLOTTE: It's just that I don't understand this sort of thing.

JACQUES: Trust me then. Or else why ask?

JEANNE: *(off, to the children)* All right, I promise... No, I'm switching it off... *(She comes in.)* Gérard wanted to know if Annie was coming to dinner again on his fifth birthday.

CHARLOTTE: Annie?

JEANNE: Annie Versary. Don't you know her? Very sweet, but a bit of a bore. Insists on coming around every year.

CHARLOTTE: *(understanding)* Oh, I see!

They all laugh .

JEANNE: Come on, Jacques, or we'll be late.

JACQUES: *(looking at Jeanne's low-cut top)* You look smashing. A real cover girl!

JEANNE: *(laughing)* Thank you!

JACQUES: I hope you're proud of your daughter!

CHARLOTTE: I certainly am!

JEANNE: If you need anything to eat or drink you know where everything is. We'll be back around midnight. Jacques'll drive you home. All right?

CHARLOTTE: Perfect. Have a good evening.

JACQUES: You too. There's a good program on television about the mating habits of spider crabs.

CHARLOTTE: Ah... ?

JACQUES: The male pins the female down beforehand.

CHARLOTTE: What for?

JACQUES: Otherwise she'd eat him.

CHARLOTTE: How horrible!

JACQUES: But only *after* ...

CHARLOTTE: Even so!

JEANNE: Coming?

Jeanne and Jacques start to go off upstage. The light slowly fades until all that can be seen is Charlotte's face, and their figures, embracing.

JACQUES: You look really charming...

JEANNE: Thank you very much.

JACQUES: Suppose we just stayed at home and went to bed?

JEANNE: What about Mother?

JACQUES: She'll be watching TV.

JEANNE: Be serious, they're expecting us to dinner. Come on!

> *Jeanne takes Jacques's hand and they exit. Quick light change. Charlotte backlit in silhouette, then light comes up full from the front.*
> *Charlotte at home. She coughs.*

JEANNE: *(off)* Is that you coughing?

CHARLOTTE: Oh, it's nothing.

JEANNE: *(entering)* What do you mean, nothing? You've got a cough. Have you called the doctor?

CHARLOTTE: No.

JEANNE: Why not?

CHARLOTTE: It's not worth it.

JEANNE: It'll be worth it when you get pleurisy.

CHARLOTTE: Oh no, it's nothing serious.

JEANNE: Why won't you go and see him?

CHARLOTTE: I don't like to disturb him for every little thing.

JEANNE: It's his job. *(Pause.)* When something's wrong it ought to be seen to right away. *(Pause.)* Are you coming, then?

CHARLOTTE: *(standing up)* Coming, coming.

JEANNE: Sure you still feel like going for a walk?

CHARLOTTE: *(looking around)* Of course.

JEANNE: What are you looking for?

CHARLOTTE: My keys.

JEANNE: Why don't you always leave them in the same place? It would make life much easier. As it is, you spend half your time trying to find them.

CHARLOTTE: It's not my fault. As soon as I turn my back they start chasing around. *(She hunts for them.)* And where are my glasses? The ground they must cover in one day!

JEANNE: You ought to hang them around your neck on a ribbon.

CHARLOTTE: Oh no, I'd look like a salesclerk! Ah, here they are! How on earth they got under the cushions...

> She puts the keys away in her purse, taking out a lipstick and a mirror. Pause as she applies lipstick.

JEANNE: You know... I'm not sure it's a good idea for you to use eyebrow pencil.

CHARLOTTE: But my eyebrows are so thin now...

JEANNE: Perhaps a lighter color, then? And isn't—it's only my opinion—but isn't that lipstick a bit... dark, for you?

CHARLOTTE: *(poised with the lipstick in her hand)* Do you think so?

JEANNE: You're quite right to wear lipstick, of course, but...

CHARLOTTE: It makes one look so much healthier!

JEANNE: Maybe a paler shade?

Charlotte drops the mirror.

CHARLOTTE: Now how did that happen? It just slipped through my fingers!

JEANNE: *(picking up the mirror)* No harm done.

CHARLOTTE: But I was holding it quite tight. How could I have dropped it? It just fell...

JEANNE: It can happen to anyone.

CHARLOTTE: You gave me this mirror. Oh look, it's cracked!

JEANNE: I'll get you another one. Don't worry.

CHARLOTTE: I broke a plate in the kitchen yesterday. Exactly the same thing. One minute I was holding it in my hand and the next it was on the floor, in pieces. It was as if my mind had gone blank.

JEANNE: My cleaning lady's mind often goes blank. But if it'll reassure you, do make an appointment to see the doctor.

CHARLOTTE: Perhaps I will.

JEANNE: Would you like me to come with you?

CHARLOTTE: You must be joking.

JEANNE : Just a second! You can't go out with your coat undone, it's freezing outside. *(She buttons up Charlotte's coat.)* You'll catch a chill if you're not careful.

CHARLOTTE: Do you think so?

JEANNE: Yes. And take this scarf, too.

> *She takes off her own scarf and puts it around Charlotte's neck. They go out, then re-enter as if out on their walk.*

JEANNE: Watch the step.

CHARLOTTE: Thank you. *(They walk on. Pause.)* They ought to warn you.

JEANNE: What do you mean?

CHARLOTTE: When I used to help old ladies on to the bus I thought I was doing a good deed. If only I'd known it was myself... If you only wait long enough...

JEANNE: But between helping other people up steps and being helped up them yourself, there are quite a few years. You've had them, haven't you? Enjoyed them?

CHARLOTTE: Yes.

JEANNE: Well, then ?

> *Pause.*

CHARLOTTE: Sometimes, when I woke up in the morning, especially in the summer, I used to shout for joy, all by myself. Overflowing with happiness at being alive. But all that zest, all that vitality, is gone.

JEANNE: Don't think about what you used to have. Think about what you've got now.

CHARLOTTE: What I've got now is seventy years behind me and a weak heart. *(Pause.)* You were right, it *is* cold.

JEANNE: *(smiling)* You see, you ought to listen to what I say! You're not tired, are you?

CHARLOTTE: Oh no, not at all.

JEANNE: Tell me when you are. We could sit down on this bench if you like.

CHARLOTTE: All right. In the sun. *(They sit.)* There was a cat in that doorway over there the other day. A little black cat. Very thin. It followed me right up the street, mewing. But when I bent down to stroke it, it darted away as if it thought I was going to hit it. When I crossed over, it went back to its doorway.

JEANNE: So?

CHARLOTTE: The next day I bought it some chopped meat. But when I got here it had gone.

JEANNE: Probably found its way back to its owners.

CHARLOTTE: I hope so. *(Pause.)* Are you going away this year?

JEANNE: We always do, don't we? You wouldn't expect us to stay in Paris all summer?

CHARLOTTE: No, of course not.

JEANNE: We need to get away. The children look quite pale and wan. And Jacques is ready to drop; I'm quite worried about him. And he only wants to take a two weeks' vacation, it's ridiculous. *(Pause.)* Why, do you ask?

CHARLOTTE: No particular reason. *(Pause.)* Are you renting a place?

146

JEANNE: The same one as usual. What's the point in changing? The children have their friends there. Jacques has people to play tennis with. And I can cook for a dozen as easily there as here.

CHARLOTTE: Don't you have any help?

JEANNE: Oh yes! Jacques does the shopping, the children lay the table and my locally-engaged slave peels the vegetables and does the housework. No, that's not the problem. What's so tiresome is having to make all the decisions. What kind of meat to buy, which vegetables, when to eat them—being the boss, in short! *(Pause.)* I say that, but of course I love it. *(Pause.)* Did you make up your mind about that cruise?

CHARLOTTE: No. I'm still hesitating.

JEANNE: But why? It would be wonderful! The Greek Islands! Paradise!

CHARLOTTE: Not if you're all on your own...

JEANNE: But you wouldn't be. It's a tour group!

CHARLOTTE: But I wouldn't know anybody.

JEANNE: You'd get to know them. That's half the fun of a cruise. You set out on your own, and you come back with a host of friends.

CHARLOTTE: Or enemies.

JEANNE: You always look on the black side.

CHARLOTTE: So either I'm pleasantly surprised, or I have the satisfaction of being right. *(Pause.)* Am I still coming to see you for a few days at the end of September?

JEANNE: Of course. As usual. The children look forward to it. Does the 25th to the 30th suit you?

CHARLOTTE: Oh, any time suits me. It's up to you.

JEANNE: Until the 25th we'll be packed in like sardines, what with the children's friends and our own. Like the Marx Brothers in their cabin! *(Pause.)* I've kept the last week for you. The weather's usually fine, and the beach isn't so crowded.

CHARLOTTE: Oh, it'll be lovely. *(She kisses Jeanne.)* You are sweet.

JEANNE: Not at all. I'll enjoy it too.

CHARLOTTE: I don't see much of the children in Paris. They're always busy with the university or the hospital, judo or the guitar... It's difficult for me to find a slot, as they say. *(Pause.)* And like that we can all come back together.

JEANNE: To Paris?

CHARLOTTE: Yes.

JEANNE: Well... I'm afraid... What with sheets and blankets, and the suitcases, and the children. And Molotov... The room that dog takes up in a car you wouldn't believe! Seventy pounds of insatiable affection... *(Jeanne stands, helps Charlotte up.)* But don't worry. I'll put you on the train. A good night's sleep in a bunk and then you'll wake up in Paris. It's so tiring by car!

> *They walk off. Blackout. The telephone rings. Jeanne comes to answer it. The stage lights up from the front.*

JEANNE: Hello? Hello?... Oh, it's you! How are you? Did you sleep well?... No, not at all... No, I haven't got a sore throat, we didn't get to bed till late... No, tell me now, I have to go out... No, I'll be out all day... Who?... Yes, vaguely... Yes, you told me... Well, I don't see what it's got to do with me. I've never met them before, why should I start now?... Oh, family! People one likes, that makes sense, but just people with the same name! Might as well get them out of the telephone directory, there are three pages of Meyers... No, today I can't. *(She puts down the receiver in exasperation, then picks it up again.)* Sorry, I didn't quite catch?... Yes, sometimes the lines get overloaded... All right, Monday, then. And if I have a moment before, I'll ring and we'll meet for a few moments. All right?... Good-bye, then, take care of yourself. *(She hangs up, sighs, walks back and forth, looks at the phone, goes over and dials.)* Hello? Mother?... If you'd like to drop in at the end of the afternoon you'd see the children. Me too perhaps, if I finish early enough... They'll be delighted... Me too. Lots of love. Good-bye.

> *She hangs up and goes out. The light changes. We are now at Charlotte's. Jeanne enters with a vase of flowers, which she sets down.*

CHARLOTTE: I don't recognize that skirt.

JEANNE: I've had it for three years.

CHARLOTTE: It suits you. You look very elegant. *(Pause.)* Do you think it would make me look fat?

JEANNE: I don't know. Would you like to try it on?

CHARLOTTE: Some other time. Would you mind if I bought one like it?

JEANNE: No, why should I?

CHARLOTTE: We don't go out together all that often.

JEANNE: You haven't told me what the doctor said.

CHARLOTTE: Oh, you know what doctors are like...

JEANNE: What?

CHARLOTTE: They don't know much.

JEANNE: More than we do, anyhow. Why don't you ask Marie to go with you? She is a medical student. She should be able to understand.

CHARLOTTE: If you have to train as a doctor to be able to swallow a few tablets!

JEANNE: Well, what did he say?

CHARLOTTE: He thinks it's the gall-bladder. I have to have an X-ray.

Jeanne puts on her coat and picks up her purse.

JEANNE: Have you made an appointment?

CHARLOTTE: Not yet.

JEANNE: Why not?

CHARLOTTE: Because he's not quite sure. It might be something else. So he's prescribed some things for me to take for a month first. They cost a fortune. And the bother! It hardly leaves you time to do anything else. I'm not sure I've got the heart to begin... Are you going?

JEANNE: *(looking at her watch)* I must. I'm late.

CHARLOTTE: I thought you were staying for dinner.

JEANNE: This evening?

CHARLOTTE: It is Wednesday, isn't it?

JEANNE: Yes, the 28th.

CHARLOTTE: *(opening her diary)* I wrote it down so that I wouldn't forget. Look. "Wednesday: Jeanne to dinner."

JEANNE: But that's not possible. I *couldn't* have said I'd come today, we're spending the evening with friends. *(She gets out her own diary.)* Look, I wrote it down two weeks ago.

CHARLOTTE: I must have heard wrong. It doesn't matter.

JEANNE: It *does* matter. I'm so sorry. You must have misunderstood.

CHARLOTTE: But it's not important, I assure you. Don't worry.

JEANNE: Don't say that! You know I hate letting anyone down. And it's not even my fault! *(Pause.)* But I don't see what I can do now, I've got an appointment in half an hour on the other side of Paris. I was even going to ask you to give Jacques a message if he phoned, to remind him we're meeting at the theater. We'll eat after the show.

CHARLOTTE: I'll tell him. *(Pause.)* What are you going to see?

JEANNE: The ballet.

CHARLOTTE: How lovely! They were talking about it yesterday evening. A contemporary dance festival. It's ages since I saw any...

JEANNE: What about that wonderful program on Plissetskaya?

CHARLOTTE: It's not the same as going to the theater. Sitting among all the people. Having the dancers actually there in front of you...

JEANNE: Oh, you can see them much better on television.

CHARLOTTE: It's not the same.

JEANNE: Would you like to come with us?

CHARLOTTE: What do you mean ? I never asked... Anyway, all I want to do tonight is have a bath and go to bed. I'm exhausted. In a way I'm quite glad you can't stay.

JEANNE: Jacques has to discuss a project with this friend over supper. You'd be bored to tears. It's a business evening really...

CHARLOTTE: Of course.

JEANNE: But tell me if you ever want to see anything, and we'll get the tickets and take you. Nothing easier!

CHARLOTTE: Of course.

Short pause.

JEANNE: So I'll leave you.

CHARLOTTE: That's right.

JEANNE: Give me a call in the morning.

CHARLOTTE: All right. What time?

JEANNE: *(kissing her)* No, better if I call you. I've got to go out. Good-bye, then.

Jeanne moves upstage, freezes.
The light comes up on Charlotte.

CHARLOTTE: You're going. You'll tell me to have a good evening. You'll kiss me. Ask me if I need anything. I'll say no. Nothing at all. What could I need? I've got my television. Thank you. Thank you for coming to see me. You're so busy. You know what a pleasure, what an enormous pleasure it always is to me. You're all that matters to me. It's of no consequence whether I go or stay, get up or lie in bed, live or die. I scarcely exist. I don't count any more. Outside, in the street, everyone else is on the way somewhere. I'm there just for the sake of going out. *(She lies down on the bed.)* But you... You will come back, won't you? Say you will? You won't leave me all alone? I'll be good, I promise. I won't complain, everything will be perfect. You're going to shut the door and go. Wait, stay just a little while. Five minutes, stay with me for five minutes.

It's the same scene as at the beginning of the play. The same words, the same lighting, the same movements. Jeanne turns back.

JEANNE: All right. Five minutes. *(Pause. She bends over Charlotte.)* What's the matter? Are you crying? Mother... Oh, don't cry, I can't bear it when you cry. *(Charlotte turns her head away and puts her hands over her eyes.)* Mother, please, stop crying. What is it? Tell me.

CHARLOTTE: It's nothing. Really. It'll pass.

Jeanne takes Charlotte in her arms and rocks her to-and-fro.

JEANNE: Don't cry, my darling, my angel. If you don't stop, I'll cry too, without even knowing why. Then what a fool I'll look. There, you smiled! Just a glimmer of a smile, but still... I didn't dream it, did I?

CHARLOTTE: No.

JEANNE: *(kissing her)* I love to see you smile. You're beautiful when you smile. *(She kisses her again.)* Now let's have a serious talk. Is there anything worrying you? You must tell me if there is. I might be able to help. Have you got any money problems?

CHARLOTTE: Oh no! It's not that... I hardly spend anything.

JEANNE: You haven't quarreled with Madeleine?

CHARLOTTE: It's a long time since we quarreled. I almost miss it. The killing remarks, the unforgivable insults, we must have thought we were going to live for ever! Oh no, we treat each other like spun glass, nowadays.

JEANNE: Why were you crying, then?

CHARLOTTE: It's that nightmare I keep having. I was frightened.

JEANNE: Do you want me to stay?

CHARLOTTE: No. It's nothing. It's over now, I'm all right. *(Pause.)* What was I going to tell you? As soon as you start leaving I always feel there's something important I have to say. And then I can't remember what it is.

JEANNE: And if you could remember, you'd see that it wasn't important at all. That you might as well have just left it.

CHARLOTTE: Perhaps.

Pause.

JEANNE: What about those bits of paper where you write down what you want to ask me?

CHARLOTTE: Yes. *(Pause.)* But you'd need to write down your whole life. Every word in the dictionary. All the people you've loved. All the books you've read. *(Pause.)* Oh yes, I know... Switch the light on. Look on the table.

JEANNE: Where?

CHARLOTTE: Don't you see anything?

JEANNE: A photograph.

CHARLOTTE: I found it in a drawer. Don't you recognize it?

JEANNE: A young woman in a big straw hat holding a baby in a lace dress.

CHARLOTTE: On a terrace. By the sea.

JEANNE: The baby's turning its head, holding on to her blouse. She's looking at the camera. Smiling. *(Pause.)* It's you.

CHARLOTTE: And you. *(Pause.)* You were so sweet. You can't imagine. So... delicate. *(Pause.)* I sometimes think that after you were born I ought never to have done anything else... Anything else but revel in a wonder that will never come again. And that I yearn and yearn after, every second of it. *(Pause.)* All those days wasted away from you. *(Pause.)* I try to remember. What I did and what I didn't do. I feel guilty about it all.

JEANNE: You mustn't. I wanted you all to myself, but that was because I loved you. I could never have enough of you...

CHARLOTTE: You've reproached me so often...

JEANNE: I was wrong. I know that now. *(Pause.)* My poor darling, we only have one life, and I wanted to take the best years of yours away from you and have them all to myself.

She smiles at Charlotte, kisses her.

CHARLOTTE You're not angry with me any more?

JEANNE: What for? Because I loved you so much?

CHARLOTTE: Is there still some of that love left? You haven't used it all up?

JEANNE: *(on the defensive)* Why? Aren't I nice to you?

CHARLOTTE: Of course you are, my darling.

JEANNE: Don't I come and see you often enough? Don't I take enough care of you?

CHARLOTTE: Of course you do! I'm absolutely spoiled and pampered...

JEANNE: I do the best I can!

CHARLOTTE: What could I possibly complain of? No one was ever so well looked after as I am. You're a perfect daughter.

JEANNE: Well, you be a good obedient mother, then. Try to sleep now.

She gets up, kisses Charlotte on the forehead. Then she switches off the bedside lamp, so that the only light comes from the corridor. She goes.
Blackout.

∾

COLINE SERREAU

Translated from the French by

BARBARA WRIGHT

UBU REPERTORY THEATER PUBLICATIONS
NEW YORK

Coline Serreau is best known in the U.S. as the screenwriter and director of the highly successful comedy *Three Men and a Cradle* (1984). She has written and directed six other feature films: *Mais qu'est-ce qu'elles veulent* (1975), *Pourquoi pas* (1977), *Qu'est-ce qu'on attend pour être heureux* (1981), *Romuald et Juliette* (1987), *La Crise* (1992), and *La belle Verte* (1995). As an actress she has appeared on stage since 1970 in works by Shakespeare, Brecht and Pirandello, as well as in her own stage works and her first film, *On s'est trompé d'histoire d'amour* (1973). She played the part of the mother in *Lapin Lapin* when it was premiered in 1985 at the Théâtre de la Ville in Paris. The production directed by Benno Besson, moved to Geneva later the same year; it was recently given a revival in Orleans and Paris (January, 1995-February, 1996). During the 1993, 1994 and 1995 seasons she could be seen in Rennes, Geneva and Paris in her award-winning hit play *Quisaitou et Grobêta*, directed by Benno Besson. Coline Serreau's other plays are *Théâtre de Verdure* (produced in Geneva in 1987) and *Moi un Homme ancien marin* written in 1990.

Barbara Wright studied music in Paris and London and worked briefly as an accompanist. A contributor to the *Times Literary Supplement* since 1965, she also worked as a reporter for a local London newspaper and as a critic for the *Arts Review,* London, for twenty years. Her first translation was Alfred Jarry's *Ubu Roi,* and her second Raymond Queneau's *Exercices de style,* both for the Gaberbocchus Press in London. She has since translated ten other books by Queneau, as well as his short stories, is the translator of numerous other works by many twentieth-century French writers and playwrights, such as Robert Pinget, Nathalie Sarraute, Michel Tournier, Tristan Tzara, Alain Robbe-Grillet, Fernando Arrabal, Marguerite Duras, Jean Dubillard, Obaldia, Topor, Eugène Ionesco, Jean Genet. Her translation of *The Fetishist* by Michel Tournier was published by Ubu Repertory Theater in 1983. She has received the Scott-Moncrieff translation prize three times, and is Officier de l'Ordre des Arts et des Lettres.

Lapin Lapin, in Barbara Wright's translation, had its American premiere in Chicago, directed by Kim Rubenstein, on October 19, 1995, at the Bailiwick Repertory Theater, Cecilie Keenan, Artistic Director.

It had its first staged reading in New York, directed by Margaret Booker, on March 18th 1996, at Ubu Repertory Theater, Françoise Kourilsky, Artistic Director.

CHARACTERS

PAPA
MAMA
} *probably in their fifties*

Their children:
BÉBERT
JEANNOT
MARIE
LUCIE
} *probably in their twenties*

LAPIN   *twelve or thirteen years old*

Their neighbour:
MADAME DUPERRI   *probably getting on to sixty*

Madame Duperri's son:
HERVÉ   *probably in his twenties.*
                      He first appears as THE OFFICER
                      in charge of the "Forces of New Order"

Lucie's jilted fiancé:
GÉRARD   *in his twenties*

VARIOUS POLICEMEN AND SOLDIERS

ACT I

Scene 1

Lapin and Bébert are alone in the room. Bébert, at the table, is immersed in a chemistry book. Lapin, standing at the other side of the room, is miming a conversation with invisible people who seem to be somewhere up in the balcony. Enter the Father, exhausted.

THE FATHER: Evening. You okay?

BÉBERT *and* LAPIN: Yep.

THE FATHER: Mama not back yet?

BÉBERT *and* LAPIN: Nope.

THE FATHER: What's she doing?

BÉBERT: Shopping, I think...

LAPIN: She's shopping.

THE FATHER: *(going and sitting down in his armchair at the front of the stage)* You both okay? My God it's cold!

BÉBERT: Yep. *(Silence.)*

LAPIN: *(to the father)* You okay?

THE FATHER: Yep. *(Silence.)*

THE FATHER: Everything okay at school, Lapin?

LAPIN: Yep.

THE FATHER: Working hard, Bébert?

BÉBERT: Yep.

Silence. The Father looks at his watch and then at the front door. Bébert re-immerses himself in his book. Lapin daydreams.

THE FATHER: *(to himself)* It's freezing cold today... *(Silence.)*

BÉBERT: *(still immersed in his book)* Mmm, its cold all right.

The father stands up and goes and looks out of the window.

THE FATHER: You haven't got anything special to tell me, Lapin?

LAPIN: *(still daydreaming)* No... nothing special...

THE FATHER: Ah, that's her I think.

He goes over to the door. Bébert and Lapin prick up their ears. Enter Mama. She's a short, very fat woman. She's carrying two enormous, bulging string shopping bags. The moment she sets foot in the apartment, Bébert, Lapin and Papa go over to her and start talking to her very fast. They all help to put the shopping away in different cupboards, in the refrigerator, etc.

MAMA: Brrr, it's freezing cold! Filthy weather, evening Papa, everything okay at work?...

BÉBERT, LAPIN, PAPA: Evening Mama...

MAMA: I didn't buy any steaks the damn things cost more every day Bébert how're you doing? Lapin have you done your homework?

PAPA: Oh yes it's freezing cold plus there's no heating at work on account of it's supposed to be spring, bastards they'll freeze us all to death, if it's spring and it's snowing what can we do about it? Just because it says "Spring" on the calendar's no reason for us to have to catch our death.

LAPIN: Hey Mama my French teacher wants to see you she says I'm not doing well but actually I'm doing great, I got 99 out of

100 in math Bébert says I don't do a damn thing at school but it's not true I always get 99 in math because there's nothing they can teach me, Sémama the black boy kissed Charlotte on the mouth, Robert was jealous but Charlotte didn't mind.

BÉBERT: I'm doing fine thanks Mother but they've sent me to a different hospital I'm going to have to do night duty and I can't stand that but on the other hand it's a very interesting unit it's intensive care you know—guys with tubes all over them there's a couple of deaths a night.

PAPA: I'll have to wear my thick sweater tomorrow but I can't find it you don't know where on earth it is do you, and I've got something important to tell you...

LAPIN: I exchanged the book you bought me for my birthday for an advanced math book but don't worry if it bothers you I'll change it back Mama I'm hungry could you make me a sandwich?

BÉBERT: I'll be better paid in the new unit but I'll have to buy some books I'll need three hundred francs I'll pay you back I'll have saved enough by next month...

Mama has put all the food away, she sets the table and starts to get the meal. The three buzz around her like flies.

MAMA: Come on Lapin, bring the salt and pepper, but your sweater's put away with the winter things Papa, I'll get it out for you tomorrow, that's all we need, for you to catch your death, Bébert bring the bread, Lapin I know why your French teacher wants to see me, you don't learn any French you read math books during the class I know you do and I agree with her you shouldn't read anything else during her class. Papa are they finally going to change your pay check this month? No Bébert not that bread bring this morning's...

BÉBERT: I like it better fresh...

MAMA: Yes but we have to finish this morning's before we start on the fresh, what d'you want in your sandwich Lapin?

LAPIN: Cheese please.

MAMA: Get yourself a glass of milk.

BÉBERT: Why're you using the fresh bread for his sandwich? If we've got to put up with the stale...

MAMA: Bébert, he's your little brother... Lapin, bring me the butter damn it...

LAPIN: It's all the same to me, this morning's bread will do for my sandwich...

MAMA: Okay, bring it then, what's the important thing you've got to tell me Papa? Lapin a knife. But if you're on night duty how're you going to manage with your classes during the day? You'll be bushed again... Lapin, leave that chocolate alone it's for dessert!

PAPA: Well yes actually I've been wanting to tell you, we got a memo from the supervisor we couldn't make head or tail of it, I showed it to my pals in the union they're going to go over it this evening, it could be something to do with a transfer or even...

BÉBERT: Oh no I won't be bushed and anyway it isn't every evening that's not what's worrying me most, the other day I saw a guy wandering around with a hole in his windpipe, had tubes sticking out of it, people like that talk sign language, the nurses soon get used to it...

MAMA: Here, Lapin, let's have a look at your homework... What's all that about a memo from the supervisor? Not going to give us any more hassle are they? You too will get used to it, seeing people with tubes all over them, and anyway when you have your own nice little local practice you won't see any more of those guys with their tubes you'll earn a good living and that's all anyone asks of a doctor, to earn some good dough, we've been sweating for it for nine years we're nearly there a guy with tubes in his neck isn't going to get us down at this stage. Lapin, turn on the television...

Lapin goes and turns on the television. The newscaster is played by an actor in the TV set.

LAPIN: You'll have to go and see my French teacher pretty soon otherwise things might turn nasty the other day I had to read them my essay on Rousseau but it was a washout because although I'd prepared it very carefully every time I opened my mouth different words came out I told them about the last book I'd been reading about the Adamski case and I was all worked up and the teacher told me to go and sit down so I talked louder and louder and after that I don't remember what happened...

MAMA: What's the Adamski case? Right, come and eat, I haven't cooked much... it's all cold we'll have a better meal tomorrow evening but those damn steaks we can't afford them any more, they go up every day, what the hell do they put in them, gold nuggets or something? Bébert for the three hundred francs it's going to be difficult are you sure you need those books? Mind you, if your father gets a raise this month we might manage it but what's that you were on about Papa, what's that business of a memo from the supervisor? Did you a get a stupid raise or didn't you? Lapin, I don't like you changing the books I give you for any old stuff... Do me a favor and take it back... and your talk on Rousseau what exactly happened?

LAPIN: Well, I was talking...

MAMA: Wait a minute, shut up, that's the prime minister on the TV...

THE PRIME MINISTER: We are proud to inform you that everything is going well, everything is going well, we are rich, we are strong, we are intelligent, everything is going well, the Left and the Right have composed their differences, we are earning a great deal of money, we are very well placed everywhere, we love our country, the whole world loves us, we are helping the poor countries and we are very independent in relation to the ones that are richer than we are, we have a fine subway system, a splendid Ariane rocket, our trains run on time, we have a very strong central government, our children are happy at school, we are clean, our policemen never actually beat anyone to death and they protect our senior citizens, our camemberts sell well, so do our airbussy-wussies, everything is going well, we have a lot of wine and it's good wine, everything's going well, our young people are able to travel and our artists are famous, we are delighted to tell you that everything is going well here at home in spite of a few temporary problems, oh very temporary, everything is going well...

Bébert stands up, red with fury, and yells.

BÉBERT: Turn off that shitty, goddamn TV this minute or I'll smash everything. I'll make a scene, I'll smash everything, all they do is talk crap, crap, nothing but crap, turn that TV off this minute or I'll do something drastic...

MAMA: *(standing up, also yelling)* Ah Bébert don't you dare start again! Sit down and eat your supper. We're listening to the news.

BÉBERT: *(undaunted, still standing, shouts)* Turn off that shitty TV right now or I'll smash everything to smithereens in two minutes flat no one'll be able to stop me I'm going to smash that TV...

MAMA: *(still standing shouts)* Lapin, go and turn the TV off, your brother Bébert's having one of his fits. *(She glares at Bébert as she says this.)*

> *Lapin gets up and goes and turns the television off. Bébert sits down calmly and eats. Lapin sits down calmly and eats. Mama sits down calmly and eats.*
> *Silence. Suddenly Mama stands up and shouts.*

MAMA: Bébert, just for that you have to do the dishes today. *(She sits down again.)*

BÉBERT: *(shouting)* Yes Mama.

PAPA: *(bellowing)* Can't anyone say anything without shouting, huh?

MAMA: *(giving tit for tat, still shouting at father, reproachfully)* This is a frigging madhouse.

Everyone eats in silence.

BÉBERT: It's not a frigging madhouse at all. I blow my top because they talk crap on that TV.

MAMA: What d'you mean crap? Is it crap to say that we have some good things in this country? That we make things that sell well?

BÉBERT: Mama you know very well it's crap, you know very well that everything's going very badly.

MAMA: Okay, fine, everything's a mess but is that any reason to say so on TV?

BÉBERT: Mama I've told you before you're not logical.

MAMA: Oh Bébert, just because you're a student that's no reason to insult me.

BÉBERT: Oh great, fine, now I'm insulting her!

MAMA: Yes Bébert you're insulting your mother. I'm not logical okay, but I've had my nose stuck in shit all day long every blessed day since you, my first, were born, so in the evenings when I'm having my supper calmly with my little family I like to hear something cheerful on the television. That's all. And anyway we aren't stuck in that much shit. Your father's working, you're going to be a doctor, your brother Jeannot's got a good job abroad, he's engaged, your sister Marie's happily married, Lapin's in high school, he passes his exams, your sister Lucie's going to marry a decent boy and me I'm in good health, what more do you want? Think of the little Chinese kids, they don't even have any bread!

BÉBERT: But the Chinese don't eat bread, Mama, they eat rice.

MAMA: All the more reason.

BÉBERT: All the more reason for what?

MAMA: All the more reason, that's all. Eat up, Bébert, it's getting cold.

BÉBERT: What d'you mean it's getting cold, it's a cold meal.

MAMA: Bébert, you say that out of a pure spirit of contradiction.

Bébert abandons the struggle. He eats. Silence. The doorbell rings.

MAMA: Lapin, go and get it, ask who it is in case it's the bailiffs.

Lapin goes out in the direction of the front door and comes back a moment later.

LAPIN: Mama, it's the bailiffs.

MAMA: Come and finish your supper.

Mama stands up and disappears into the wings in the direction of the front door.

MAMA: *(from the wings, in a voice like thunder)* You dirty bastards, get the hell out of here aren't you ashamed of doing such a shameful job?... No, I won't open the door... That's right, come back with a locksmith, you'll see what I'll do to your locksmith, he won't leave with my furniture, he'll leave with his face smashed to pulp, so get the hell out of here. *(She comes and sits down again calmly, reading a sheet of paper.)*

PAPA: What's that paper?

MAMA: They're coming back in a week to seize the furniture. Another radish, Papa?

PAPA: No thanks.

Long silence, everyone eats. The doorbell rings.

LAPIN: Mama, there's the bell, should I get it?

MAMA: Ask who it is.

Lapin goes, and comes back a moment later.

LAPIN: Mama, it's Jeannot with some suitcases!

General stupefaction. Jeannot makes his entrance and throws two very battered suitcases down in the middle of the room. He is wearing a dirty, crumpled overcoat and looks exhausted.

JEANNOT: *(in a weak voice)* Hide the bags. Quick. The cops'll be here any minute.

MAMA: What? What bags?

Bébert pounces on the suitcases and hides them under the bed.

MAMA: Bébert, what're you doing?

BÉBERT: *(to Mama)* Get out all the dirty clothes, we'll bury him in the bath.

MAMA: What are you saying? What dirty clothes? Where've you been, Jeannot?

BÉBERT: Step on it Mama, shit! Didn't you hear, the cops'll be here any minute he said... We'll cover him with the dirty clothes and hide him in the bath.

He grabs hold of Jeannot and takes him into the next room, at the far end of which is a minute bathroom. He shoves Jeannot into the bathtub.

MAMA: *(following Bébert)* But what's he done for the cops to be after him?

BÉBERT: *(bawling)* How the fuck should I know Mama, they're after him, that's all. Get the clothes for Christ's sake!

Mama, impressed by Bébert's tone, quickly brings out the clothes and covers Jeannot with them.

MAMA: Lapin, come here.

Lapin goes over.

MAMA: Right, pull your pants down, sit on the seat, if the cops come in say you're doing a poo.

Lapin obeys. The doorbell rings. The father runs into the bathroom in a panic.

PAPA: *(to Mama in a low voice)* That was the bell!

MAMA: *(pressing one last pile of clothes down in the bathtub)* Quick, everyone back to the table.

Bébert and Papa rush back to the table and start eating with feigned enthusiasm. Mama goes to open the door.

MAMA: What is it?

VOICE: Police.

Two policemen enter and swiftly take in the whole room at a glance.

MAMA: Have you got a warrant? What d'you want?

FIRST POLICEMAN: Your son Jean is wanted.

MAMA: Why's my son Jean wanted?

FIRST POLICEMAN: Have you seen him recently?

MAMA: Why should I have seen him? He's in Belgium! He's an interpreter with the Common Market...

FIRST POLICEMAN: *(to Papa and Bébert)* Have you seen him?

Papa and Bébert shake their heads. The first Policeman signals to the other one to go and look in the other room. The second policeman goes into the small room.

MAMA: Where's he going? Do you have a warrant?

The second policeman goes into the bathroom.

LAPIN: *(very loudly)* I'm doing a poo.

SECOND POLICEMAN: Oh, sorry! *(He retreats very quickly, embarrassed, and comes back into the dining room.)*

SECOND POLICEMAN: There's a kid, that's all.

FIRST POLICEMAN: Listen, madame, your son is wanted he's neither in Belgium nor in the Common Market, he's trafficking in false papers for a terrorist organization. If you spot him I advise you to tell us.

MAMA: Tell you, tell you, I'm not married to you am I? I've nothing to tell you?

FIRST POLICEMAN: Right. Good evening.

The policeman start to leave calmly.

MAMA: *(following them)* What's all that about false papers? What are you, nuts? I tell you he's got a very good job in Belgium... and anyway what's the idea, coming and disturbing people without a warrant, if you think I'm going to let you...

The policemen slam the door in her face. Mama comes back into the room. Bébert and Papa look at her. She's deathly pale. She goes over to the sideboard slowly, takes out a plate, a glass and some cutlery and puts them on the table. She's trembling. Lapin appears at the door, rebuttoning his trousers. He observes the scene. Silence.

MAMA: *(to Lapin in a lifeless voice)* Go and get him, he must be hungry.

Blackout.

ACT I

Scene 2

Lapin makes his way to the front of the stage.

LAPIN: Good evening ladies and Gentlemen, I'm going to make you my monologue. I love my mother very much, I love my father very much, and my brothers and sisters too, I'm very glad I landed in this family, they're very nice to me, it's really as if I was one of them, they're even quite sure that I am. I arrived here in a spaceship and the ethers injected my fertilized egg into my mother's womb one day when she was fast asleep with her legs apart. Like a breath of air, an invisible puff of wind, I entered her and grew, feeding on her. I still don't know why they sent me here. But I see everything that happens with the eye of a stranger. I have powers, but I'm not using them for the moment. One power I have is that I see everything. This completely changes the way I feel for people. For example, I know the cure for every illness, for every misfortune. It's horrible, it's as if it was written in white chalk on a blackboard in front of my eyes. And I also see written on this blackboard that for the moment it wouldn't do any good if I were to tell these cures. So I observe their misfortunes in silence, I watch them grow and flourish like beautiful plants and I don't tell their cures. You, out there in front of me, I've learnt you. One day it may perhaps be written on my blackboard that it *will* do some good to tell these cures. And now I can see something written on my blackboard that is a bit useful for me to tell you. The cataclysms that are going to descend on this planet won't bother anybody. There's nothing interesting for the ethers here. They already possess your resources. They observe you, and they don't have any feeling for you. The big difference between them and you is that *they* know they aren't the center of anything. And now I can see it written on my blackboard that it won't do any good to say what I still could say, and nor will the last thing I said mean anything. Right, I'll go to bed. My love to you all.

Blackout.

ACT I

Scene 3

Jeannot is alone in the room with his back to the audience, he's looking out of the window. Enter Bébert.

JEANNOT: Well?

BÉBERT: Everything's under control. I gave them to your pals, I don't think I was followed.

JEANNOT: What did they say?

BÉBERT: That whatever happens you must stay put, you must stay holed up here, you aren't in any danger now that the suitcases are in a safe place. They've sent the cops off on a false lead, they're looking for you in Switzerland right now.

JEANNOT: What are the instructions if the cops come back?

BÉBERT: You can show yourself if you have to, here's your passport. They've no evidence against you, it was only the suitcases that might have got you into trouble. But you'll have to lie low until things settle down. How did you know the cops were on your tail?

JEANNOT: Just across the border I called my pals, they told me to watch out, they'd been searching everyone's homes the night before. No question of going back to my digs. I thought I'd be safer here, but as I came in under the porch I saw a van full of cops coming round the corner, no question of going out again or making a run for it...

BÉBERT: But you were completely crazy to come here!

JEANNOT: I'm sure they didn't see me come in...

BÉBERT: But you had the bags, you should have gone up and lain low on the sixth floor, anywhere but here!

JEANNOT: I know, it's idiotic, but on the stairs all I could think of was ringing the bell here... I was bushed, I hadn't eaten since...

BÉBERT: But don't you get what would have happened if they'd picked you up? Do you know what was in those suitcases?

JEANNOT: Passports and false residence permits.

BÉBERT: *(furious)* That's not all there was, pal!

JEANNOT: What else was there?

BÉBERT: There were enough explosives to blow up three apartment blocks at the very least...

JEANNOT: I didn't know.

BÉBERT: Enough to put you away for thirty years... and us too...

JEANNOT: I told you I didn't know.

BÉBERT: In any case, you and your pals work like amateurs and cretins. When you're carting junk like that around, at least you...

Enter Lapin, carrying his schoolbag.

LAPIN: Evening...

JEANNOT: Your pissy doctor's ethics—you can stick them...

Lapin takes off his coat and puts his schoolbag down.

LAPIN: Where can he stick them?

JEANNOT: Where I think!

BÉBERT: Not in his head, that's for sure!

JEANNOT: Chicken.

LAPIN: Why're you fighting?

Stubborn silence from Bébert and Jeannot.

LAPIN: Mama not in?

BÉBERT: Haven't a clue, look under the table...

LAPIN: *(turning his back on Bébert and starting to yell)* She isn't under the table, she isn't there that's for sure. And me, where am I? Where am I? What am I doing here with people like you? Who tell me "look under the table" and hurl insults at each other! *(Addressing the balcony)* Just tell me what the hell I'm doing here! Give me a sign, just one lousy little sign!

He runs into the bedroom, throws himself on his bed and hides his face in the pillow. Bébert buries himself in a book. Jeannot is lost in gloomy thought. Enter Papa, looking completely shattered.

PAPA: Evening...

BÉBERT AND JEANNOT: Evening...

Papa takes off his coat and goes and sits in his armchair, facing the audience. He picks up a newspaper and pretends to be reading it but actually he's staring into the distance with a haunted look. Mama comes rushing into the room with an enormous shopping bag.

MAMA: Oh! I only brought one bag up. Bébert, go and fetch the other for me will you, I left it downstairs, it's too heavy.

Exit Bébert, Mama puts things away.

MAMA: Lapin back?

JEANNOT: Yes.

MAMA: I've asked Madame Duperri to lend me a mattress, you'll have to go and get it, she's expecting you, we'll put you in here with us unless you'd rather be with Bébert and Lapin?

JEANNOT: Oh, it doesn't matter where... .

MAMA: She's had the bailiffs too, with her it's for her son's traffic violations, so every time they come she has to sneak down the fire escape and take her family silver to Madame Legrand, she's the one that sells the newspapers, she's taken her television too and her Louis XV armchairs, well she calls them Louis XV, to make a long story short, she's already carted them down three times and she's fed up with bringing them back up again so she leaves everything downstairs, all except the silver, that is. But Madame Legrand doesn't want the chairs, they clutter her place up, its very small, so they've come to an agreement, Madame Legrand is willing to keep the chairs on condition that she can watch madame Duperri's TV because hers is on the blink. Which means that Madame Duperri goes down every evening and watches her own TV at Madame Legrand's, sitting in her own Louis XV chairs. She's waiting until the elections to take them upstairs again, on account of the amnesty, personally I don't give a shit about the bailiffs, there's nothing for them to take here, to hell with them, I think we've got enough blankets, mind you, it isn't so cold this evening... Is it true that business of terrorists and false papers? *(She has now planted herself down in front of Jeannot.)*

JEANNOT: *(somewhat taken aback)* Completely false from A to Z, I swear.

MAMA: Why're the cops chasing you then?

JEANNOT: I've no idea Mama, haven't a clue, I swear.

MAMA: And those suitcases, what're those suitcases?

JEANNOT: Nothing, they're just my suitcases.

MAMA: Why'd you have to hide them then?

JEANNOT: It was a mistake Mama, I got scared that's all, I swear.

MAMA: What a filthy liar you are Jeannot.

Jeannot gives her an amiable look.

MAMA: *(between her teeth, glaring at him)* How did I get stuck with such a screwball! You got me good with your job in Belgium and all that malarkey! And your fiancée's just as phoney. You can tell me now...

JEANNOT: Oh no, that was true, I have got a fiancée, she couldn't come, she's working...

MAMA: I don't believe a word of all your nonsense.

JEANNOT: Mama, I swear...

MAMA: I don't know what's stopping me giving you such a licking...

JEANNOT: *(standing up)* Okay, I'll go and get the mattress.

MAMA: Yes, go and get the mattress.

Exit Jeannot. Enter Bébert carrying an enormous shopping bag. He begins to put things away.

MAMA: Bébert, you'll have to keep an eye on Jeannot for me, we've had enough crap, we won't let him out of our sight until he's got a job and somewhere to live, and...

Papa gets up from his chair, he's as white as a sheet.

MAMA: Ah, you're there Papa, I didn't see you, you okay?

Papa goes over to her, tense and trembling, and opens his mouth to speak.

MAMA: Lapin! Lapin!

LAPIN: *(from the bedroom)* Yes...

MAMA: Are you working?

LAPIN: Yes.

MAMA: Come and set the table... Bébert, why don't you go and help Jeannot bring Madame Duperri's mattress down...

> *Exit Bébert. Lapin enters and sets the table. Papa has sat down again, he can no longer find the courage to speak.*

MAMA: Papa, have you got any ideas for Jeannot? Couldn't you see your personnel manager, get him a job as a secretary or whatever, that way you could keep an eye on him... Don't you think?

> *Papa looks at her, and takes a long time to find his words.*

PAPA: Yes... The personnel manager... That's a good idea...

LAPIN: Mama, I feel sad...

MAMA: *(taking him in her arms)* What's the matter, my little Lapin? I'll go and see your French teacher tomorrow, I'll sort it all out... don't worry... You still haven't told me what your Adamski case is...

LAPIN: Adamski, he's a guy that got contacted by extraterrestrial beings, you should read the book...

MAMA: And you talked about that instead of reading your essay on Rousseau?

LAPIN: I didn't mean to, it wasn't me talking, I was talked...

MAMA: You shouldn't read all those stories...

> *Bébert and Jeannot come back with the mattress plus an enormous, hideous crystal vase.*

BÉBERT: Here, she wants to know if you can keep this for her on account of the bailiffs.

MAMA: *(taking the vase)* My God where'm I going to put that?...

Jeannot and Bébert put the mattress down in a corner.

MAMA: Can you imagine if it gets broken! And it will get broken, as sure as eggs... *(She puts the vase on the floor by the mattress.)*

MAMA: Good. Come and eat!

Everyone sits down at the table. Mama serves them.

LAPIN: In the metro they've put up some loudspeakers with music to chase out the people who're singing live. I smashed fourteen loudspeakers at the Bastille station.

MAMA: What?

LAPIN: The loudspeakers are a pain in the neck because we make money off the live singers.

MAMA: How come?

LAPIN: Me and my black pal Sémama, have got a scheme, he falls over in the subway, not far from the singer, he starts hollering, everyone turns and looks at him, and in the meantime I grab the singer's cash and bolt. We meet up at Châtelet and share the loot.

MAMA: You're crazy, Lapin, you mustn't do that!

LAPIN: The money's to buy science fiction books, I read them at the back of the class near the radiator, my math teacher confiscated four of them I don't care I'm better at math than he is, he's jealous. I'm even better at math than Bébert, aren't I Bébert?

BÉBERT: *(gloomily)* It's true.

MAMA: You're in trouble, Lapin, you haven't a clue what high school's all about. No one's asking you to be better than the math teacher, all they ask is for you to do your homework, be polite and get there on time, that's what high school's about. I'll go and see your French teacher tomorrow.

LAPIN: You'll see, she weighs about 300 pounds, she's a very sad sort of lady. She's always saying: "Life is just a tub of lard." I'm going to give her a loofah and my book on the Adamski case.

MAMA: Oh shut up about your Adamski case. If you go on I'll flush the book in the can.

LAPIN: It's there already, that's where I read it.

JEANNOT: What is the Adamski case?

MAMA: I forbid you to talk about it here.

LAPIN: It's about extraterrestrial beings.

JEANNOT: You'd be better off reading Marx, Lapin!

BÉBERT: You too, Jeannot, you should read Marx.

JEANNOT: *(cut to the quick)* Oh great, so you've heard of Marx? I can't believe that... It's not a good idea for a future doctor, you know, to spend his time on such things...

BÉBERT: *(between his teeth)* Asshole.

MAMA: Once and for all, I forbid you to talk politics at the table!

JEANNOT: Is "Asshole" politics?

MAMA: Jeannot, that's enough.

LAPIN: The Adamski case isn't politics.

MAMA: Papa, do something!

Papa stands up slowly, he speaks in a choked voice.

PAPA: I don't feel very well.

MAMA: Go and lie down for a moment...

Papa goes into the boys' room and remains standing in the middle of the room, looking distraught.

JEANNOT: What's the matter with him?

MAMA: He must be worrying about money. We've been waiting months for that goddamn raise. *(To Jeannot)* And with you on top of everything else! *(Shouting to Papa)* Papa, don't fret, we'll get by, as long as it comes in regularly we can still manage...

JEANNOT: I thought we weren't allowed to talk politics at the table!

MAMA: *(very angry)* Oh Jeannot, you get on my nerves!

JEANNOT: *(between his teeth)* How much longer is he going to put up with it.

BÉBERT: You can't decide for other people what they can put up with or not.

JEANNOT: What the fuck's it got to do with you? You've chosen your side, you've got it made!

BÉBERT: *(yelling)* People who shoot their mouths off get us nowhere!

JEANNOT: *(ironically)* How very true.

MAMA: *(exasperated)* Oh can it you two. Don't act like you did in the old days. All we need now is for your sisters to be here, and we'll be back where we were ten years ago!

The doorbell rings.

LAPIN: Mama, there's the bell...

Panic. Jeannot runs to hide in the bathroom, Bébert goes with him, getting ready to cover him with clothes.

MAMA: Ask who it is.

LAPIN: *(exits for a moment, then comes back)* Mama, it's Marie with some suitcases...

MAMA: Who?

LAPIN: Marie with some suitcases, shall I let her in?

MAMA: Yes...

BÉBERT: Who is it?

MAMA: It's Marie with some suitcases.

JEANNOT: *(cautiously getting out of the bath)* Who is it?

BÉBERT: It's Marie with some suitcases.

PAPA: *(emerging from his prostration)* What's that? With some suitcases?

Enter Marie. She drops two enormous suitcases down in the room, she's positively glowing.

MARIE: Hi Mama, hi everyone, I've come to live here for a few months, I'm getting a divorce.

She takes off her coat, very much at ease, very much at home. Mama sits down on a chair.

PAPA: You what?

MARIE: I'm getting a divorce. But there's no need to put your-selves out for me, I can easily sleep on that mattress *(pointing to Jeannot's mattress)*.

MAMA: No, that's Jeannot's mattress.

MARIE: Oh. Jeannot lives here now does he? I thought he was in Brussels...

MAMA: So did we.

MARIE: How come?

MAMA: We'll explain, we'll explain...

   Blackout.

ACT I

Scene 4

The table is set for twelve people, white tablecloth, flowers. Mama is dressed up to the nines. A wedding cake is in the place of honor on the table. Mama is sitting down, she's waiting. Marie is unpacking her suitcases. She unfolds some dresses and piles them up on two chairs.

MAMA: Was he unfaithful to you ?

MARIE: No, I don't think so...

MAMA: Did he beat you up?

MARIE: No...

MAMA: Did he spend all the profits?

MARIE: No... oh no...

MAMA: Did he drink?

MARIE: No...

MAMA: Didn't you get on in bed?

MARIE: Oh yes, we did...

MAMA: You wanted a child and he didn't?

MARIE: No, neither of us wanted a child.

MAMA: What was wrong then?

MARIE: Nothing, everything was fine.

MAMA: Didn't he love you any more?

MARIE: Oh yes... I think he did...

MAMA: Then you didn't love him any more?

MARIE: Oh yes, I loved him all right.

MAMA: Well then?

MARIE: Well nothing.

MAMA: Oh come on, Marie, people don't get divorced for no reason! You've got a thriving business... He's not going to be able to run the café on his own, and that café belongs to both of you.

MARIE: To hell with the café, he can have it.

MAMA: But you've got to get back the money you put into it!

MARIE: No, I'm not interested.

MAMA: *(very angry)* But for goodness' sake, what happened?

MARIE: Nothing, Mama, nothing. We were having a meal, he said "Pass the salt," he said it nicely but I don't know, I stood up, I wasn't even angry, I said "I'm getting a divorce," I went upstairs and packed my bags, and that was all.

MAMA: "Pass the salt," that's all?

MARIE: Yes.

MAMA: He asked you nicely: "Pass me the salt," and you replied: "I'm getting a divorce."

MARIE: Yes.

MAMA: *(taking her head in her hands)* How simple! And what if he'd asked you to pass him the pepper?

MARIE: I might still be there!

MAMA: What does it all depend on, eh!

MARIE: Don't you sometimes wonder!

MAMA: *(explodes, red in the face, fuming, beside herself. She stands up and yells.)* No really, are you putting me on or what? What've I ever done to the good Lord to deserve such children? You produce them just right, everything present and accounted for, five fingers, five toes, the right number of nails, with hair, with eyes that see and ears that hear, you make sure they grow and that they get sleep, day after day you manage to find enough grub for them, you work your fingers to the bone, your hair goes grey, you rack your brains to find them a good job, a good husband, you say phew, that's one of them settled, and wham! Everything falls apart in a single second simply because a guy has said pass the salt instead of pass the pepper! No, enough is enough! And your brother Jeannot busts in with the police on his heels and we have to hide him in the bathtub! What's it all mean? Can you tell me? All I can say is that you're all cracked. A bunch of crackpots!

Marie hangs her head.

MAMA: *(vehemently)* Not to mention the good example you're setting for your little sister! Who's getting married today! And there was I telling myself that's three off my hands, what a fool I was! I just hope her Gérard won't take it into his head to say pass the salt for a year or two! No, really! But at least there's Bébert, if there wasn't... He's going to be a doctor a year from now, he's as solid as concrete, we won't have slaved for nothing! But you and Jeannot, honestly! I ought to give you such a spanking! Go up to Madame Duperri's and borrow another mattress.

MARIE: Yes Mama.

Exit Marie. Mama is overwhelmed by gloomy thoughts. The doorbell rings.

MAMA: *(going to open the door)* Ah, here's the wedding party.

LAPIN: *(coming in backwards, frantic)* She said no! She said no!

MAMA: What? Who said no?

LAPIN: To the justice of the peace! She said no!

MAMA: Who? What?

LAPIN: When he said will you have so and so for your lawful wedded husband, she stood up and she said no and she marched out and you should have seen it, what a crappy mess! Bébert chased after her, Jeannot too, Gérard hadn't a clue what was going on, his parents were furious, they went for Papa and insulted him, Papa told them I'll go and bring her back hang in a sec, we both ran after them, we caught up with them at the bus stop, the bus came, Lucie jumped in, we followed, Bébert kept trying to persuade her to get off, nothing doing, I ran on ahead to tell you, they're coming... here they are...

> *Enter Lucie, followed by Bébert, Jeannot and Papa. Lucie, like a bomb, dives into the chair facing the audience.*

LUCIE: I said no, I meant no. And that's that.

> *Bébert, Jeannot and Papa prostrate.*

BÉBERT: Lucie, don't be an idiot! Come on, they're waiting for you... We'll take a taxi...

MAMA: What is going on?

JEANNOT: Don't worry Mama, we'll sort it out... She had a little tantrum, we're going back right away...

LUCIE: No, we are not going back.

BÉBERT: Lucie, be reasonable...

LUCIE: The first person to say another word about it, I'll bash his face in.

JEANNOT: Lucie...

LUCIE: Jeannot, cut the crap.

Enter Marie, dragging a mattress behind her.

MARIE: Wow, the wedding party! Yippee! Hurrah! Hi, little sister! Long live the bride! *(She runs over to her sister.)* Well, what d'you think of marriage?

LUCIE: Same as you.

MARIE: How d'you mean?

LUCIE: Except that I got my divorce before I got married.

MARIE: I don't understand...

MAMA: *(looking extremely gloomy)* Marie, go back up to Madame Duperri and ask her to lend us one more mattress. Tell her that this'll be the last we'll be borrowing, seeing that there's no one left to come back. The whole family's back now. Tell her too that in exchange I don't mind keeping her Louis XV chairs until the next election. She'll understand.

Blackout.

ACT I

Scene 5

In front of the curtain. Dismal early morning light in a street. Papa is carrying a baguette and Lapin a liter of milk. They are walking. Suddenly Papa stops.

PAPA: I went to see your French teacher...

LAPIN: Did you?

PAPA: As Mama kept putting it off...

LAPIN: So?

PAPA: So we're in deep shit, my Lapin!

LAPIN: Pretty much, yes...

PAPA: If it was only you!

LAPIN: Yes, there's also Jeannot, Marie and Lucie!

PAPA: If it was only them!

LAPIN: What else is there?

PAPA: There's me, Lapin, there's me... in deep shit... Really, I'm up to my eyeballs in it...

LAPIN: Are you?

PAPA: Where do you spend your days?

LAPIN: Well, I walk around, I swipe science fiction books and go and read them in the waiting room at the Gare de Lyon... until five o'clock. Then I come home.

PAPA: But what do you eat for lunch?

LAPIN: Well, nothing. That's why I'm so hungry in the evenings.

PAPA: Your teacher says you're crazy...

LAPIN: I know but it's not true. Don't tell Mama she said that!

PAPA: No, but we'll have to find you another high school...

LAPIN: This one's already the third... It's only private schools that would take me... but they cost a lot... Maybe when you get your raise...

PAPA: Huh! It's more like a big drop that's going to hit us...

LAPIN: Really?

PAPA: Well, yes... You know, while you're reading at the Gare de Lyon, for nearly a week now I've been traveling on all the metro lines in all directions from eight in the morning to six in the evening. I've been fired, and like you I can't bring myself to tell Mama.

LAPIN: Then you won't be getting your pay any more?

PAPA: I'll get early retirement, and then proper retirement, which means much less than my pay. There's two hundred of us in the same boat, the union put up a fight, we lost.

LAPIN: What's Mama going to say?

PAPA: I'd like to burrow deep down into the earth and go to sleep. Everybody relies on my pay, yet my tiny pay is nothing at all... You know, Lapin, this life's completely fucked up... They've squeezed me dry. The strength's gone out of me. Anyone who wants my skin can come and scrape it up; I wouldn't stop them!

LAPIN: But there's still Bébert... Bébert, he's as solid as concrete...

PAPA: Even concrete can collapse these days... Especially concrete...

Lapin and Papa walk on in silence.

Blackout.

ACT I

Scene 6

Inside the Lapin house. On the mattresses, Jeannot, Marie and Lucie are asleep. Mama is getting breakfast ready. The room is cluttered with four Louis XV armchairs. Enter Lapin and Papa.

MAMA: Sit down quick, you'll be late... It'll be ready in a sec...

Papa puts the baguette down on the table.

PAPA: Mama, Lapin and I are fed up with spending our days in the metro or in the waiting room at the Gare de Lyon, so we're telling you frankly that we're staying at home. Lapin got expelled from the high school three days ago and me I was fired a week ago. Don't get excited, there's no need to shout, we can't help it, everything's falling apart, everything's going to the dogs, it's all a dead loss, I couldn't agree with you more but we're going to end up catching our deaths out of doors all day long, so since we're eating shit anyway we might as well eat it here, at least it's warm and we're with the family.

He points to the mattresses on which Jeannot, Marie and Lucie are asleep. Papa sits down at the table and cuts himself a big slice of bread. Lapin remains standing. Mama slowly crosses the room and goes toward the front door. Lapin watches her. Papa eats in silence. Mama comes back on to the threshold with her coat and shopping bag. She opens her mouth to speak, changes her mind and goes out banging the door. Long silence.

LAPIN: What are terrorists?

PAPA: *(looking at Lapin)* They're guys that chuck bombs.

LAPIN: Where do they chuck bombs?

PAPA: I don't know, they blow up official whatsits.

LAPIN: What for?

PAPA: Because they're angry.

LAPIN: Are you angry?

PAPA: Me, I'm old.

LAPIN: Do bombs do some good?

PAPA: If ten million guys chuck bombs, then it does some good.

LAPIN: Otherwise?

PAPA: Not.

LAPIN: What does do some good other than bombs?

Papa doesn't answer.

LAPIN: The unions?

PAPA: Yes...

LAPIN: Except in your case?

PAPA: Some you lose, some you win...

LAPIN: Why aren't ten million guys chucking bombs?

PAPA: Because they hope things will work out without bombs.

LAPIN: But they don't work out?

PAPA: No.

LAPIN: Why not?

PAPA: What you don't take, they don't give you.

LAPIN: So?

PAPA: I'm old, Lapin, I've lost my strength.

LAPIN: Does Jeannot have his strength?

PAPA: Jeannot's impatient.

LAPIN: Is that bad?

PAPA: It's better to be patient and win than to be impatient and lose. *(Silence.)*

LAPIN: What d'you think Mama's doing?

PAPA: She's probably buying some grub, when there's trouble she always goes and buys some grub.

The doorbell rings.

LAPIN: Here she is!

He goes and opens the door. Enter Gérard, Lucie's fiancé, livid, frantic, his clothes disheveled. He throws a huge pile of clothes down in the middle of the room.

GÉRARD: There's Mademoiselle's clothes... *(He goes out again and comes back with a record player which he throws on top of the clothes.)*

GÉRARD: And there's her record player, a lousy record player at that... *(He goes out again and comes back with some records. Same business.)*

GÉRARD: There's Mademoiselle's records. I won't miss them much.

Lapin and Papa look at him, flabbergasted. Gérard now brings in four chairs, a table, a folding bed, some toilet articles, some books, some small storage units, some sheets, blankets, posters, cooking utensils, a radio, the pile is growing, some cushions, coats, papers....

GÉRARD: I met Madame Lapin downstairs, she didn't even say hello! Well, she can shove it, her hello... Two years of living together!

PAPA: *(conciliatory)* Oh you know, two years isn't much...

GÉRARD: It's too much.

Marie, Jeannot and Lucie begin to wake up.

JEANNOT: What's going on?

GÉRARD: What's going on is that I'm clearing out my apartment. From now on I want nothing more to do with Lucie. Nothing more, you hear me? It's over, for ever, you hear me?

JEANNOT: Well sure, considering she said no at the town hall.

GÉRARD: *(yelling, threatening)* Don't talk to me about that, huh!

Jeannot lies down again. He couldn't care less. Marie and Lucie hide under the bedclothes.

GÉRARD: *(to Papa)* Three hours we waited for you at the town hall... My parents live 873 kilometers from Paris, 873, does that mean anything to you? 873 lousy kilometers they came in their Sunday best, the hotel reserved, the wedding presents and the champagne, all to hear a little tart say "No, after all, no," and in front of the justice of the peace, what's more!

PAPA: *(embarrassed)* They've got their senior citizen discount...

GÉRARD: *(hopping mad)* You're all against me. I know you are. *(Going over to Marie's mattress)* But there's something I have to tell you my dear Lucie, and that is that it's all over between us, for ever, once and for all. Take a good look at my face because it's the last time you're going to see it. D'you hear me? You'll never see me again, never, never, never...

PAPA: You're talking to Marie.

GÉRARD: What?

PAPA: That's Marie's mattress.

Marie sticks her head out of the bedclothes and looks at Gérard.

GÉRARD: Oh, sorry... *(Pointing to the other mattress)* Is that where she is? *(Marie nods.)*

GÉRARD: *(talking to the other mattress)* Lucie, I've brought all your things and I'm afraid to tell you that...

LUCIE: I bet you've kept the cassette player... I'd stake my life on it... *(She darts over to the pile and scrabbles through it as fast as she can.)*

GÉRARD: *(exploding)* Huh, that'd be the last straw, for me to give you my cassette player, after all you've done to me!

LUCIE: Your cassette player! What a sonofabitch! We bought that cassette player with my money...

GÉRARD: Absolutely not, it was the record player we bought with your money...

LUCIE: The record player's putrid, that's why you're leaving it, and what about the cassettes? Some of those cassettes are mine... Where are they?

GÉRARD: Well, I'm keeping them seeing that I'm keeping the cassette player...

LUCIE: *(throwing herself at him screeching)* What a shithead, what a bungling ass... Fuck off... Fuck off this minute.

She rains blows down on him. Gérard defends himself like a lion, they roll over the floor. The hostilities continue on top of all the junk.

PAPA: Jeannot, separate them...

JEANNOT: Hey you two, don't fight...

He tries to separate them, and gets a kick from Lucie which sends him flying two centimeters away from Madame Duperri's vase.

JEANNOT: Shit, Madame Duperri's vase! *(He saves the vase in extremis and keeps it in his arms.)*

JEANNOT: For Christ's sake look out, you'll break everything...

LUCIE: Mind your own butt, Jeannot...

JEANNOT: Anyway, what the heck! Let them clobber each other if it makes them happy! None of my business!

He goes and lies down again, still holding the vase in his arms. The two of them go on fighting and yelling.

LUCIE: Ratbag... Asshole...

GÉRARD: Why did you say no, eh, trollop, why did you say no?...

MARIE: Oh they are so annoying... Go and fight outside, we're trying to sleep...

Enter Mama, her shopping bag full to bursting. She watches the hostilities.

MAMA: *(in a thunderous voice)* What is this bedlam?

LUCIE: *(standing up)* He swiped my cassette player...

GÉRARD: Good morning Madame, it's not true, it's the record player that's hers.

MAMA: *(pointing to the pile)* What's all that stuff?

GÉRARD: *(completely deflated)* It's Lucie's stuff that I returned to her...

LAPIN LAPIN

MAMA: *(exploding)* Oh yeah? Do you think we haven't got enough stuff here as it is? We don't live in a castle, Monsieur! We live in a room and a half. So one mattress plus another mattress, plus yet another mattress, plus Marie's suitcases, plus Madame Duperri's vase, plus Lucie, plus Jeannot, plus the Louis XV chairs, plus the four of us who already lived here before all this, that's not enough, no, he has to bring us Lucie's furniture too... Are you all insane? I tell you, I've had this family of crackpots up to here! And you all, stop snoozing! Get up, for Christ's sake, it's nine o'clock. You can't move in this dump, get those mattresses out of the way...

GÉRARD: Okay, I'm going...

MAMA: Oh no you're not. What you're going to do is stay here, damn it, and clear up all this junk, and Lucie, you're going to help him, and if you start slamming into him again you'll have me to reckon with. I don't give a shit about your squabbles. What we're all going to do now is have a big party, I've bought something to drink. *(As she says this she bangs her shopping bag down on the table and pulls out some bottles.)* We're going to celebrate all this. We're going to celebrate Jeannot's triumphant homecoming, Marie's divorce, Lucie's marriage broken-off, Lapin being expelled and Papa's unemployment, and so jump to it! *(She collapses on to a chair and bursts into tears. Everyone is filled with dismay.)*

> Mama is alone at the front of the stage, cut off by a curtain from the rest of the decor.

MAMA: Ladies and Gentlemen, life is an arrow. *(Gesture of an object passing by very quickly)* There's things I can't tell anyone, you have to realize that I'm the Mama. And a Mama doesn't show her family the worms gnawing at the foundations. But you also have to realize that I'm not your Mama, so what the hell, I'm going to get it off my chest.
I'd like to go rowing on the lake in the Bois de Boulogne one Tuesday in the autumn, Papa would be at the oars and we'd talk of love.
I'd like to buy myself a belt, fasten it in the last hole and it wouldn't be too tight.

I'd like to watch the rain out of the window one morning, and say to myself that's nice, I love life.

I'd like to believe that where I'm going the path is strewn with roses.

I'd like my mother to be still alive and worrying about me.

I wish she was still pulling a wool hat down over my head so I don't catch cold.

I know... the days of my youth are over... but when? How?

One day you wake up and they're all gone, all the people who used to ask you, "Well, how did it go?" when you came home from the big world outside.

There used to be someone you could tell about your fights in the playground, someone who'd go wild if you didn't finish your bread and butter at breakfast.

I tell you, what makes me sad isn't that Marie's getting a divorce, or that Lucie's broken off her marriage, or that Lapin's been expelled, or that Papa's unemployed and Jeannot's a terrorist... No, what makes me sad is this layer of grey plaster that's covered my whole body and my life so that no one sees me any more.

I'm the Mama who does the shopping, and Mama always has a solution for everything, because when you're knee deep in shit I can pull you out like no one else, you won't see *this* family in the gutter in a hurry!

Except that me, I'm in the mud, I'm up to my neck in it, and I stopped liking myself a long time ago.

Ladies and Gentlemen, I've been abandoned, I can confide in you, and I'd like to ask you, here and now, to take ten seconds, no, let's say seven, nobody would hold out for ten but seven's possible, and for those of you who find even that too difficult let's say five seconds, I'm asking you to take seven or five seconds to cry in your heads for me and my sorrow.

Silence. Mama counts seven seconds on her fingers.

Ah, that did me good. I'm coming back to life, you see... that was all I wanted.

Did you really cry for me? I've no idea. But just imagining that you did has cheered me up, you know. Even if it was only three out of the whole lot of you. Even if the others weren't thinking about anything, and even, I'm going to tell you, even if everybody actually only cried for themselves, well at least, for seven seconds, we'll all have been together, crying for ourselves.

Mama disappears behind the curtain, which rises, revealing the decor. There are lighted candles and hanging garlands. Everyone has had a few drinks, they're dancing to accordion or Scottish folk music, and talking and laughing very loudly.

PAPA: Mama, may I have this dance?

(He takes Mama in his arms and dances with her like a maniac. Mama stops, out of breath.)

MAMA: Oh, you're killing me Papa! That's how he swept me off my feet! They used to call him the prince charming of the dance hall! He could have made the kitchen stove dance! All the girls were after him! In heaven's name, why did he pick me?

PAPA: Because of the thrust of your hips, Mama, because of that thrust! A real tidal wave!

MAMA: He said to himself, that girl'll give me children like pies coming out of the oven, open the door and out they come, done to a turn, all warm...

PAPA: We certainly had a fine brood! Look at them... Watch them dancing... You see... *(Papa is a bit sloshed, he suddenly becomes jubilant and launches out into a violent speech, shouting first at the dancers and then at the audience.)* Keep it up, Lucie... Keep it up, Marie... What I say is they can all go to hell, all of them. I don't want to worry about anything any more. I've got beautiful children who know how to kick up their heels and who've got good appetites, what the hell do I care about all the rest? *(To the audience)* I still want to live, and what more can you ask for? I've got a plan for tomorrow. I'm going to go to the waxworks with Mama. For the day after tomorrow I've got another plan: I'm going to cook a stew for the whole family, I'm good at that. What more can you ask for? For the day after the day after tomorrow, my plan is to go to my pension office at nine in the morning with three sandwiches Mama will've made for me and I'll spend the whole day at their desks and make myself a pain in the ass, such a pain in the ass they'll never have seen anything like it. I will get every clerk to explain everything four times, I will lie down on the benches, I'll offer my beer to everyone, I'll be very polite, I'll drop all my papers on to the floor, I'll tell them I've seen a guy plant a bomb in the john, I won't leave until the office closes. I won't be doing that to get my pension. I already have my pension, I'll be doing that because it's a great plan for the day after the day after tomorrow. And on the day after that I'm going to stay in bed and sing at the top of my lungs if I feel like it. And I *will* feel like it. My word, good God, from now on I'm not going to take orders from anyone. *(Enter Bébert, carrying a cello case.)* Hello, my Bébert! Greetings my beloved son, my oldest son, my hope, come and make whoopee with us, come and dance with the living, take your coat off, leave the dead in the cloakroom!

BÉBERT: *(kissing Papa)* I'm coming...

> *He goes into the room on the right. The lights go out and silence falls in the main room. Bébert opens his cello case and takes out a Bren gun.*

BÉBERT: *(to the audience)* When I first knew her she was still young, she loved every tiny little wrinkle in my ear. I'm her oldest son, I was the first to open her loins. We don't say a lot to each other but the bond between us, no one else has it. Obviously I'm not studying medicine. What I do is smuggle these things *(Pointing at the gun)* to people who need them. A lot of people need them. I'm not sure that what I'm doing is any use, or even that it's right. All I know is that I was born to try to do something. I've still got the far-off taste of paradise in my mouth, and I know how happy we can be on this earth because I've been Mama's child.

> *Blackout.*

ACT II

Scene 1

Gérard, Lucie and Jeannot are playing cards. Lapin and Papa are reading the newspaper together. Marie is planing a plank of wood. Mama is absorbed in the preparation of a meal.

JEANNOT: What's that you're planing Marie?

MARIE: I'm making myself a shelf.

JEANNOT: And where're you going to put your shelf?

MARIE: Where d'you think? Over my mattress of course, pig face.

JEANNOT: In my opinion there isn't enough furniture in this house.

LUCIE: *(irritated, to Jeannot)* Are you playing or are you arguing?

JEANNOT: I'm playing.

MAMA: *(with her back to them)* Will someone set the table?

They all stand up and lay the table, then sit down again. Mama brings in the casserole, serves everyone and they eat.

LUCIE: *(to Marie)* Will you make me a shelf?

MARIE: Yep.

JEANNOT: Are you going to sleep here again Gérard?

GÉRARD: *(embarrassed)* Well, er, if I'm not in the way...

LUCIE: *(suddenly aggressive)* Okay you can sleep here, but if Marie makes a shelf it's going to be for my sweaters, we're separated now.

GÉRARD: *(on edge, very violently)* Who said we weren't?

PAPA: *(very calmly)* The first person to say Lucie and Gérard aren't separated will get their face bashed in.

MARIE: *(very calmly)* Lucie and Gérard are separated. They have been for two weeks.

JEANNOT: *(very calmly)* Not a shadow of a doubt.

PAPA: Gérard, would you like a little more rice?

GÉRARD: *(mollified, holding out his plate)* Yes please, thanks very much.

> *Mama helps him to rice. Silence. The doorbell rings. Lapin goes to the door. It's Madame Duperri. She stays on the threshold.*

MADAME DUPERRI: Evening everyone... Am I disturbing you?

ALL: Not at all...

DUPERRI: What?

ALL: *(very loudly)* Not at all...

MAMA: *(very loudly)* Come and sit down in one of your chairs, Madame Duperri...

DUPERRI: No... I can only stay a moment... I don't want to disturb a family reunion...

MAMA: *(very loudly)* Oh well, huh, don't worry, it looks like this family reunion will last a long time...

DUPERRI: *(suddenly bursting into tears)* Oh Madame Lapin, I can't take it any more, I can't, I can't.

> *Everyone is very embarrassed.*

MAMA: *(standing up)* There there, what's the matter?

> *Duperri collapses and cries on Mama's shoulder. Mama sits her down in one of the pseudo–Louis XV chairs.*

DUPERRI: Madame Lapin, I think I'm going to commit suicide, I can't live like this any longer, I can't, I can't.

PAPA: *(very loudly)* But what is it, Madame Duperri?

DUPERRI: Monsieur Lapin, It's a terrible tragedy, I've lost all hope, I live in unbearable solitude.

MAMA: How come?

DUPERRI: Madame Legrand, the newspaper lady, she's had her TV repaired, she doesn't want to keep mine any longer, she brought it back up to me earlier on, I won't be going down to watch the films with her in the evenings any more.

MAMA: Oh!

DUPERRI: My son never comes to see me, no one ever comes to visit, there's only two things in life I'm waiting for now—death and the bailiffs.

JEANNOT: *(in a low voice)* But at least the bailiffs furnish some sort of company... although when it comes to furnishing, it's especially the neighbors...

DUPERRI: What?

MAMA: *(very loudly)* Would you like a nice cup of coffee?

DUPERRI: I'm so upside down, I haven't had a thing to eat...

MAMA: *(in a low voice)* Lapin, set a place for her. *(Very loudly)* Well, come and eat with us then, Madame Duperri.

DUPERRI: *(sitting down at the table)* Ah, Madame Lapin, you at least are good, you are kind to miserable people...

MAMA: *(in a low voice to the rest of them, while she serves Madame Duperri)* There's not going to be any seconds, my lambs.

DUPERRI: *(eating ravenously)* You're so lucky to be able to come together like this after a hard day's work.

MAMA: *(in a low, caustic voice)* Does anyone here work? That'd be news to me... Or maybe they're hiding something.

DUPERRI: What?

MAMA: Are *you* working, Gérard?

GÉRARD: Well, actually, I'm looking for a job at the moment...

DUPERRI: What?

GÉRARD: I'm looking for a job at the moment.

LUCIE: *(irritated)* You have to scream your head off, she's deaf.

GÉRARD: *(offended)* You know, Lucie, if I'm in your way I can easily leave.

LUCIE: You've been saying that for the last two weeks.

PAPA: Stop it you two...

GÉRARD: No one likes me in this family.

LUCIE: Just bring back the cassette player then.

MARIE: Oh for God's sake shut up, that's enough of your domestic spats.

LUCIE: *(furious, very loudly)* What domestic spats?

DUPERRI: Ah no, it's a long time since there were any domestic spats in my house! Sometimes I even tell myself I miss them...

GÉRARD: Oh all right, I'll give you the cassette player, I'll go and sleep in the street!

DUPERRI: If you can believe it!

MARIE: No one's throwing you out into the street, Gérard, but I didn't leave my man just to leap feet first into a matrimonial drama, that's all.

DUPERRI: What?

LAPIN: *(very loudly)* A matrimonial drama.

DUPERRI: Ah yes, I always say that a half–starved little bird that sings from time to time is better than no bird at all! *(She sniggers.)* If you see what I mean!

LAPIN: *(very loudly)* I don't see.

MAMA: Go and get the next course, Lapin.

> *Lapin goes and fetches a dish which four apples are vainly trying to fill.*

MAMA: Here's the dessert, who'd like some fruit?

GÉRARD: I'd like an apple, if I may...

LUCIE: I'd be surprised if you got anything else!

GÉRARD: What does that mean?

LUCIE: You can see perfectly well there's only apples.

GÉRARD: Oh but, if you'd rather I didn't have an apple I'll leave them for you.

DUPERRI: May I take an apple?

MAMA: *(very loudly)* Oh come on Madame Duperri, make yourself at home, help yourself. *(Mama mutters, very quietly, between her teeth.)* There, now there's only three apples left, do the best you can with them but leave half a one for Bébert tonight.

PAPA: I don't want one.

MARIE, LUCIE, JEANNOT *and* LAPIN: Me neither.

MAMA: Great, I'll take the dish away. *(She puts the dish back in the cupboard.)*

GÉRARD: *(trying to be pleasant)* Just how it should be, a nice frugal meal.

MAMA: How d'you mean frugal? What's frugal about it?

GÉRARD: No, it's terrific, a very healthy diet, fat–free...

MAMA: Yes, it's a meal that cost 47 francs 35, it's a meal that cost 47 francs 35 for nine people, if you see what I mean.

LAPIN: He doesn't see.

DUPERRI: Madame Lapin, I'm going to ask you something...

LUCIE: *(in a low voice)* Here we go, she's going to dump her TV on us...

MAMA: *(loudly)* What's that Madame Duperri?

MADAME DUPERRI: I don't dare, you're going to say no.

JEANNOT: *(in a low voice)* No, it's her Napoleon III chest of drawers.

MAMA: *(loudly)* Tell me anyway, Madame Duperri, neighbors should always help each other out...

DUPERRI: That's true... I lent you my mattresses, didn't I...

MARIE: *(in a low voice)* Oh–oh, here come the mattresses again.

DUPERRI: You invited me to a meal... What would you have done without my mattresses, huh?

LUCIE: *(in a low voice)* The TV, plus the chest of drawers, plus a pedestal table, I'm taking bets.

MAMA: *(loudly)* That's true, what would I have done without your mattresses!

DUPERRI: Madame Lapin, I am feeling terribly blue this evening.

PAPA: *(loudly)* Oh but don't be blue Madame Duperri...

DUPERRI: No but the thing is, my morale's all shot to pieces.

PAPA: Ah, morale, these days you begin to wonder where it's gone to!

DUPERRI: Well, in a word, Madame Lapin, can I sleep over tonight?

MAMA: *(loudly)* Here? *(in a low voice)* Good God! *(loudly)* I wouldn't say no, Madame Duperri, only we don't have a bed and we don't have any more blankets...

DUPERRI: No problem, I can sleep on one of my mattresses. And I got a blanket out and put it in my hall, it only needs to be brought down, here's the key. *(She holds out her key.)*

MAMA: *(fuming, in a low voice)* Lapin, go up and get Madame Duperri's blanket. *(Ominously, staring into her plate, to the children)* I've had it up to here, I tell you, up to here.

DUPERRI: *(deliriously happy)* Why don't we make a nice cup of coffee?

In the meantime, Lapin goes to the front door, opens it and disappears for a second, then reappears walking backwards. A masked man in black comes in after him, staring him in the eyes. The sound at the table is suddenly cut off, even though they are still talking. No one sees the man in black, except the audience and Lapin, who is terrified, and retreats until he reaches the wall. The man advances on him inexorably. Lapin flattens himself against the wall, his arms outspread, turns his face towards the audience and shuts his eyes, paralyzed with fear.

LAPIN: *(yelling)* Fuck off, shitbag, sonofabitch, shut your big trap, get out...

Everyone at the table turns and looks at Lapin, astonished. We still can't hear their voices, yet they are talking, and asking Lapin what the matter is with him. The man is now bending over Lapin, he murmurs something in his ear and then, stooping a little, slowly makes his way to the door.

LAPIN: Get him, cut his throat, can't you see the vermin, there, he's there, jump him, rip his tongue out... *(To the audience)* Oh come on, can't any of you see him? He's there, he's leaving, he's dangerous, he's come to get me, stop him. *(The man in black calmly disappears. The sound returns at the table. Lapin is completely groggy.)*

ALL:
–But what's the matter with you?
–Lapin, come and sit down...
–What's gotten into you?

LAPIN: Didn't you see him?

ALL: Who? What? Are you crazy? He's having a fit!

Lapin comes back and sits down at the table.

MAMA: *(angry)* Calm down Lapin, that's enough of your nonsense, you're showing off, that's all.

LAPIN: I'm going to the can. *(He rushes into the room on the right, at the very front of the stage, and the sound at the table is immediately cut off. Lapin speaking in the direction of the balcony.)* 21, hydrogen, 21, are you going to answer, 21 I said... get a move on you bunch of pricks... If you're busy playing electrons I warn you I'll rat on you, 21, answer me you piss artists... Hydrogen! I've got other things to do, I can't stay in the can for hours on end, they'll get suspicious... Yes, it was the ethers I asked for, and make it snappy, hey shut your mouth, just answer when you're spoken to you big asshole full of ionized soup... Just because you've got a cushy job at the switchboard that's no reason to spit on people who're truly working their guts out... Yes, truly working, I'd like to see you down here in this unholy mess... you're sitting pretty up there, and we drudges, are saddled with all these filthy contacts... Put a sock in it will you, put me through to them... Ah, hi, you okay?... Incidentally, I have a hell of a time getting through to you these days, you've got a lot of idle bastards on the switchboard I can tell you... Why did you send me that rotten moronic deadhead? *(He listens.)* "Calm down, calm down" – shut up... *(He listens.)* Listen, I'll use what language I please, I live here, I've picked up the local habits... *(He listens.)* Yeah but I haven't got much time, I can do without your preaching, I ask you again why did you send me that drowned rat, that black cretin... *(He listens... and suddenly calms down.)* What? When? *(...)* Me? But why? *(...)* What d'you mean for good? *(...)* Tomorrow? But I can't say my good-byes, pack my bags right away just like that are you off your rocker? ... people don't disappear just like that on this planet... there's feelings... There's a Mama... *(He is interrupted, and listens.)* Okay okay, don't yell like that, I don't mind coming back for a while, but not tomorrow, on the next shuttle if you like... *(...)* The last shuttle's tomorrow? What about the others? *(...)* All repatriated? But why? *(He listens, terrified.)* Really? I'm the only one left? And when does it start, this turbulence? The day after tomorrow? *(...)* So you've abandoned the program? That's it we're done? We're going to leave them to swim in their warring turbulence? *(...)* They have a name for that here, it's called throwing them to the dogs. *(...)* Oh, now you're exaggerating... A bunch of bellicose, cretinous earthworms okay, but not cosmic garbage, not the dumpster of the galaxy, no, excuse me but I have to say that even so they invented music, some of them do decent things, they have Mamas, believe me, and I live with them night and day, I tell you there are things that deserve to be saved... *(...)* Not many, I agree with you there, but... *(...)* No, I haven't been contaminated... Not for a second... It's just that we had a super–program, they were actually making a little progress, and then wham you pull the plug... *(...)* The security of our agents?... *(suddenly worried)* Meaning what? *(...)* What do you know about it? Someone in the Lapin family? Who? *(...)* But something must be done *(...)* There's thousands of others, right, but these are the ones that matter to me... *(...)* Hey! If I come back you'll do something? *(...)* You'll try?... Right, okay, I'll come back. Yes. Eight o'clock tomorrow morning. Downstairs in front of the porch. I won't have much luggage with me, the Lapin family is flat broke. 'Bye. See you tomorrow. 21, hydrogen, out. *(Lapin, gloomy, returns to table.)*

MAMA: *(very gay, very loudly to Duperri)* Why's he called Lapin? Well, he was born one Sunday, on the dot of midday. He's a child of the sun, the midwife said.

PAPA: He was a sun that wasn't expected!

MAMA: You can say that again! I still wonder where I got him from! A gift from heaven! And when he came out with his cheerful little mug and his two front teeth, you should have seen the doctor's face! They'd never seen anything like it, a newborn baby with two teeth, he's an extraterrestrial, the midwife said. He'll be a genius, the doctor told me, and I said we'll call him Lapin because of his rabbit teeth. That's already his surname, they said, and what's more as a first name it doesn't exist. That's the way it's going to be, I said. He's going to be called Lapin Lapin *(To Lapin)* Eh, my Lapin?

LAPIN: Yes Mama.

Madame Duperri stands up, glass in hand. She's a bit tipsy.

DUPERRI: To our loves!

Blackout.

ACT II

Scene 2

Eight o'clock in the morning. Everyone is asleep, except Mama who's heating some milk for Lapin. Lapin is dressed. He's standing near Mama with a bag in his hand, gloomily staring at the saucepan.

MAMA: We'll go and buy you a pair of socks today, my Lapin. A new pair. How many years is it since I bought you anything new? It's not funny being the baby of the family, is it! To hell with avarice, the fun's not over yet!

LAPIN: A baguette or a loaf?

MAMA: A baguette, it's longer. Here, take the money. And then buy a croissant, just one, and don't tell the others, it's for Bébert later on, he should be here by now anyway, it's to help him forget all those guys stuffed with tubes that he spends his nights with.

LAPIN: Good-bye Mama. *(He goes to kiss her.)*

MAMA: *(pushing him away)* Be quick, my baby, I have to get their bread buttered before they wake up otherwise it'll be up for grabs. What's that bag.

LAPIN: It's papers, it's for the trashcan.

MAMA: Bring the bag back, ok... Don't sling it. Leave the door open so you don't have to ring the bell.

LAPIN: Yes Mama.

Exit Lapin.

Mama sits down and lights a cigarette. As she smokes she looks at the sleepers. She seems happy. Suddenly, the sound of an explosion in the immediate vicinity. Mama jumps. A dense cloud of smoke comes through the door. Papa, Marie, Lucie, Gérard, Jeannot and Duperri wake up. Mama runs out, shouting.

MAMA: What's going on? What's going on?

Papa in pajamas, Duperri and Jeannot rush out after her. Shouts in the distance, the smoke fills the apartment. Lucie, Marie and Gérard are sitting up on their mattresses, listening. Jeannot comes back, distraught.

JEANNOT: A bomb... Down below... Just when Lapin was leaving...

MAMA: *(off, shouting)* Lapin!

Lucie, Marie, Gérard are petrified. Duperri enters like a whirlwind and hurls herself on the television, yelling.

DUPERRI: Something's happening... Something's happening... Lapin... it's dreadful... There's soldiers all over the streets...

She switches the set on, the presenter appears and begins to speak. The TV on casters, starts to move, scatters the actors and reaches the front of the stage. The frame of the set goes flying, a curtain falls, and now the presenter is alone at the front of the stage, holding his script. A spotlight is concentrated on him.

THE ANNOUNCER: *(fixed smile)* Ladies and Gentlemen, last night some rather unexpected events occurred in the world. The international markets kind of plunged, mainly due to the dishonesty of certain barbaric countries which even though they owe a great deal to the civilized countries nevertheless made the serious and unforgivable decision to suspend the payment of their debts to us all.
But everything is going well, there's no cause for alarm.
The banks will be closed today and tomorrow, so there will be no point in trying to take money out for the moment.
All this is only very temporary.
Citizens of the male sex between the ages of 18 and 50 are requested to report to their nearest town hall where they will

be given instructions. In view of the new outbreak of purse–snatching, you are advised not to go out after nine in the evening from now on.

This is not a curfew.

There was no racing at Longchamp. There have been a few sunny spells in Epinal. Cloud over the rest of France. Last night the government changed, at present we are being led and advised by an extremely competent team, made up of the military for the most part.

Many traitors have already been arrested. A large number of prizes, which include a free trip to Acapulco, will be awarded to men or women who report any opponents to the forces of the new order.

One of the leaders of the illegal movement aiding the barbaric countries has been arrested. He is the famous Albert, who has been wanted by the police worldwide for the last ten years. HE WILL TALK! This report from Yves Lalèche.

Bébert, handcuffed, surrounded by police, crosses the stage.

MAMA: *(behind the curtain, yells)* Bébert!

Blackout.

ACT II

Scene 3

Marie and Lucie are sitting down, looking toward the front door.

MARIE: *(very loudly, speaking in the direction of the door)* Okay, we'll start without Mama, we'll take Madame Duperri's entrance. Madame Duperri, about 35 minutes after Mama has gone into the building of the forces of the new order, you go in, you ask the soldiers where the denunciations office is, they let you in at once, you go to the toilet, put on your disguise and look into every office until you find the one where Mama is. When you've found it, you go in. Start now.

No one enters.

MARIE: *(loudly)* This is your entrance, Madame Duperri!

DUPERRI: *(sticking her head round the door)* Is it me now?

MARIE: Yes, you enter.

DUPERRI: I enter, do I?

LUCIE: *(very loudly)* Yes!

> *Enter Duperri, dressed as a cleaning lady, bucket in hand. She is smiling, red in the face with shame and pleasure, and on the verge of convulsive giggles.*

DUPERRI: Good morning, I'm the new cleaning lady, *(Giggles.)* I've come to empty your wastepaper basket. *(To Marie)* So now I pick up the basket, I put it in the corridor, I put the smoke bomb in the basket... *(Giggles.)*

LUCIE: *(in a low voice to Marie)* She's going to foul it all up.

MARIE: *(loudly)* Mustn't laugh like that, Madame Duperri...

DUPERRI: *(ashamed)* Yes yes, all right. Then I go back into the office, I give the table a bit of a wipe with my duster and I creep out.

She exits on tiptoe, once again laughing uncontrollably.

LUCIE: *(very loudly)* No no, Madame Duperri, you've forgotten the most important thing...

Madame Duperri puts her head round the door, most astonished.

DUPERRI: Do I come back?

LUCIE: *(screaming)* No no, you don't come back, but you've forgotten...

Duperri is already outside again.

LUCIE: But come back Madame Duperri...

DUPERRI: *(coming back)* Do I come back or don't I come back?

LUCIE: When we do it for real you don't come back, but for the moment I'm telling you to come back because you've forgotten something very important...

Duperri is at a loss. With a finger in her mouth, she is thinking hard.

DUPERRI: What have I forgotten?

MARIE: *(prompting her)* The... dus... ter...

DUPERRI: Oh yes... Oh, I'm sorry... Aren't I stupid, I always forget the duster...

MARIE: *(patiently)* Go on then, the business with the duster.

Duperri takes the red duster out of her bucket.

DUPERRI: Then I go to the window and I wave the duster. Like this! *(She does so as she speaks.)*

MARIE: Why do you have to do that Madame Duperri? Do you remember?

DUPERRI: *(like a good child)* To let the others know that that's where Bébert and Madame Lapin are and that they're to come in.

MARIE: That's right Madame Duperri. And then you go out and light the smoke bomb.

> *Exit Duperri.*

LUCIE: I tell you she's going to foul it all up.

DUPERRI: *(from behind the door)* So what I do, I light the smoke bomb, right?

LUCIE: *(rushing out)* Yes, but not now, we've only got one!

DUPERRI: *(off)* Yes yes, but not now...

LUCIE: *(coming back)* The whole thing, she's going to foul the whole thing up I'm telling you...

MARIE: In the meantime Mama is giving them a whole lot of names and addresses of people who're supposed to be Albert's pals...

LUCIE: *(loudly, in the direction of the door)* That's you guys!

> *Gérard, Jeannot, and Papa burst in, dressed as firemen.*

PAPA: Evacuation! Fire! Everyone down to the courtyard!

JEANNOT: We knock out the officer with this *(He shows a club.)* and we grab Bébert...

> *All three go through the motions.*

MARIE: Papa, your costume's too big, no one will take you seriously... change with Gérard...

GÉRARD: *(aggressively)* Oh no, it's too big for me too...

PAPA: *(conciliatory)* It's too big for him too...

LUCIE: Yes, but Gérard's taller than you are...

GÉRARD: I see your game, Lucie, you're determined to make me look like a jerk...

LUCIE: *(quick as a flash)* Well, costume or no costume, in any case...

GÉRARD: *(choking)* Fat ass, stinky butt, whore...

LUCIE: You want me to bash your brains in?

JEANNOT: I'll strangle you, I'll strangle you! Gérard, put on Papa's costume, Lucie, shut your fat face, this is a matter of life or death for Bébert, and for us too, incidentally, you bunch of noodlebrains!

GÉRARD: *(very dignified)* Okay, I'll put on Papa's costume, and after the escape I will leave Lucie for ever. *(He sits down on a chair and cries.)*

MARIE: Can it Gérard, let's get on with the rehearsal.

PAPA: So we grab Bébert, we rush downstairs, Lucie's there dressed as a nurse and covering us with a gun, we get in the van, Marie has started the engine, and we get the hell out of there.

> *Papa, Jeannot and Gérard have been going through the motions of all this.*

LUCIE: It'll never work...

MARIE: Why not?

LUCIE: Are you kidding? With all the armed dudes that'll be everywhere, Madame Duperri who'll be farting around, Gérard who'll be...

MARIE: Are you scared?

DUPERRI: *(putting her head in)* Do I come in now?

MARIE: Madame Duperri, what are you supposed to do after you light the smoke bomb?

DUPERRI: I dive into the van that'll be in the courtyard, I wait for everybody and we get going.

MARIE: *(to Lucie)* You see, she remembers it all perfectly.

LUCIE: You won't forget the duster, right? Out of the window, right?

DUPERRI: The duster out of the window.

> *Enter Mama silently, no one notices her, she stands by the door, heavy, grey, sad.*

JEANNOT: Lucie's right, we aren't very prepared, we'll never make it, we'll all end up riddled with bullets, you, Lucie, you don't know how to handle a gun, Gérard's shitting in his pants...

GÉRARD: If I'm given a decent costume I won't shit in my pants.

JEANNOT: *(continuing without hearing him)* There's nothing to say that 35 minutes will be enough for Mama to sweetalk the officer, and even less that they'll take Bébert into that goddamn office, and as for our hand–painted red fireman's van, anyone who believed in that for a single second would have to be screwy, and Mama I don't know whether you've noticed the state she's been in since Lapin died, she can barely move, and everything depends on her...

MAMA: *(in a lifeless voice)* Lapin isn't back?

Everyone turns to look at Mama. A deathly silence.

MAMA: *(staring at the ground)* But why haven't they found his body? Not even a little toe...

Silence.

PAPA: It was a big bomb you know... it's only natural that they haven't found his...

MAMA: Have you begun the rehearsal?

JEANNOT: Yes.

MAMA: I'm coming.

> *Mama goes into the room on the right. She is having difficulty in walking, she can hardly lift her big feet. She takes off her coat, buries her face in her hands for a moment and then goes back into the main room.*

MAMA: So I get to the building of the forces of the new order, I say to the fellow on duty good morning, it's for a denunciation. I go up to the denunciations office and I wait. When the officer comes he says...

JEANNOT: Save your breath, Mama, we're going to change our plans, we'll never make it, tomorrow is too soon, we're not ready.

> *Mama sits down, demoralized.*

MARIE: Now just listen to me, Jeannot, you can do what you like but me, tomorrow, at 9:30 on the dot, as scheduled, I'm going to pick up the red van, get you all on board, drop Mama near the building of the forces of the new order and we're going to carry on as planned. If we want to get Bébert out it's tomorrow or never. And tomorrow may even be too late. They're shooting thirty people every day at the moment. *(Harshly, to Mama)* Go on, Mama.

MAMA: *(standing up)* So the officer asks me what's it about? I say good morning Monsieur it's about a denunciation, it's that Albert, I had a feeling I knew him, I only saw him for a moment on the television the other day, but if it really is him, and if I do recognize him, I can tell you where they meet and lead you to his whole gang, I've got a newsstand just underneath, I used to see them all the time. But if it isn't him, and believe me I don't want to make a mistake, could be it was just a fishing club, I'd have to see him to be sure, the prize I'm interested in is the trip to Acapulco. Then the officer sends for Bébert. When Bébert arrives the officer asks me do you recognize him and I reply of course I recognize him, I can give you the descriptions of all his pals.

Blackout.

ACT II

Scene 4

When the lights come up we are in the real denunciations office with the real officer and Mama. A soldier brings Bébert in. Bébert is half-naked, his clothes are torn, his face is swollen and covered in bruises and dried blood, he can only open one eye. His skin is in ribbons. He can barely stand. He raises his good eye to Mama.

THE OFFICER: Do you recognize him, Madame?

Mama looks at Bébert. Silence. She steps back, then surreptitiously moves to the front of the stage and speaks in a low voice. Music.

MAMA: Do I recognize him? Is that my son? That thing beaten to a pulp, covered in blood, that can only open one eye, my Bébert? Has everyone on this earth gone mad? When he was born he had a twirly bit of down in the small of his back, after every feed I had to remove a little patch of white skin from his lip, a blister, he had sucked so hard. I remember when we looked at the first hair under his arms, how we laughed, what have they done to my sons?

Mama goes back to the officer and takes in a lungful of air.

MAMA: Of course I recognize him, I can give you the descriptions of all his pals.

BÉBERT: The woman's lying, I've never seen her in my life!

MAMA: What d'you mean you've never seen me in your life! You've certainly got a lot of nerve, you filthy terrorist! Maybe you're going to tell me you're a student, a good little medical student for instance, but I know you, and his pals I'll tell you their names, Officer, and any minute now they'll be joining him right here! There's one that's called Jeannot, he's a real oddball that Jeannot, then there's Lucie, Marie, Gérard, there's one they call Papa... and there was another one called Lapin but he's dead...

BÉBERT: *(yelling)* What?

MAMA: You can see he knows them, Officer! Yes, he's dead, little Lapin, blown to bits by a bomb. Hoorah for medical studies, hoorah for the new order, hoorah for the trip to Acapulco, hoorah for our new army...

THE OFFICER: Hey, calm down Madame, let me take your statement...

BÉBERT: *(looking at Mama)* Everything she's said is a lie from A to Z...

THE OFFICER: Shut up, you.

> *He kicks him hard, Bébert collapses without a word. Mama cries out, and rushes over to help him up. At this moment Duperri enters, dressed up and carrying her bucket, as red as a beetroot, her eyes lowered like a young girl at her first ball.*

DUPERRI: Good morning, Monsieur, I'm the new cleaning lady, I've come to do your office.

THE OFFICER: What are you talking about, there aren't any cleaning women here, the soldiers do the cleaning. Your papers Madame, please...

> *Duperri raises her eyes, looks at the officer and is flabbergasted.*

DUPERRI: What on earth are you doing here?

THE OFFICER: *(no less flabbergasted)* And you?

DUPERRI: I asked you a question.

OFFICER: Er, I'm doing my job...

DUPERRI: *(looking at Bébert)* Is that Bébert?

Mama nods.

DUPERRI: *(to the Officer)* Is that your job!

OFFICER: Yes, that's my job.

DUPERRI: Take that uniform off this minute.

OFFICER: You're off your rocker!

Duperri hurls herself on him and snatches his tunic off.

DUPERRI: You filthy little swine! First you make my life a misery for months on end with the bailiffs coming to collect on your traffic violations, and now you're doing a vile job like this! I'm going to beat you black and blue...

OFFICER: Oh, cut the crap, Mom, I'll have you locked up if you don't stop it...

DUPERRI: Did you hear that, Madame Lapin, did you hear that? That's the younger generation for you! We'll see whether you have me locked up or not, you mobster! I wiped your bottom long before you could open your mouth, and now you're going to shut it. *(She deals him an almighty slap in the face which sends him flying on to the floor.)* We aren't here to enjoy ourselves. We've got an escape to do. And you're going to help us that's final. The firemen are on their way.

OFFICER: *(much enfeebled)* What escape? What firemen?

DUPERRI: We're escaping Bébert, he's Madame Lapin's son, she's my neighbor on the floor below, if you came to see me more often you'd know Bébert, and you'd never have allowed them to beat him up like that, you dope.

OFFICER: But Mom, he's a dangerous terrorist! They'll shoot you!

DUPERRI: Will you shut up? They've been good to me in that family, I lent them some mattresses, I'm living with them now and we're going to escape Bébert.

Enter Papa, Jeannot, Gérard, dressed as firemen.

DUPERRI: *(to her son)* You see, I told you! Let me introduce Monsieur Lapin, Gérard and Jeannot. Say hello.

OFFICER: *(crushed)* Hello...

PAPA: Who's that?

DUPERRI: Let me introduce my son, Hervé.

PAPA: What the hell have you done now, Madame Duperri? We've been searching for you for a decade in all the offices... The *duster,* for Christ's sake, the *duster,* we kept telling you not to forget *the duster!* How did you expect us to find you if you didn't shake the *duster* out of the window? I swear! And what's your son doing here? Who told you to bring your son here? And the smoke bomb, where's the smoke bomb? There's not the slightest trace of smoke anywhere in this dump, we look like a bunch of twerps, dressed up as firemen! I mean they'll know there's something fishy going on here...

Enter Lucie and Marie dressed as nurses, their hands up, pushed by two soldiers pointing submachine guns at their backs. One of the soldiers yells:

THE LITTLE SOLDIER: Hands up, everyone over to the wall

All obey.

THE LITTLE SOLDIER: *(yelping)* Make a move and I'll shoot. What next, chief?

HERVÉ: Shoot them all! Wipe them out!

DUPERRI: *(panic-stricken)* Even me?

HERVÉ: Especially you!

DUPERRI: *(to the little soldier)* I'm his mother!

LITTLE SOLDIER: What do I do, chief?

HERVÉ: *(hysterical)* You shoot! They're a gang of terrorists, they came to help Albert to escape...

LITTLE SOLDIER: Do we wipe out the firemen too, chief?

HERVÉ: They're phoney firemen. Shoot, no argument.

    A little voice makes itself heard.

VOICE: Hey, little soldier, are you going to kill all those people?

LITTLE SOLDIER: Who's that talking to me?

HERVÉ: I'll give you ten seconds to fire, otherwise it's curtains for you too.

DUPERRI: I curse the day when you came into my womb! You don't deserve to live on this earth, this beautiful earth.

VOICE: What have these people done to you, little soldier?

LITTLE SOLDIER: Where the hell is that voice coming from, for Christ's sake?

MAMA: Lapin, Lapin! Where are you?

VOICE: If you shoot you'll live like a dog for the rest of your days.

LITTLE SOLDIER: Shit, who's that talking to me? Can't he shut up?

HERVÉ: Fire!

LITTLE SOLDIER: Fire, fire... Easier said than done, there's ghosts here, they're stopping me taking aim.

VOICE: You won't shoot, the days when men shot each other are over, that's the new order, give me your gun.

LITTLE SOLDIER: But who'm I supposed to give my gun to? Show yourself, shit, stop horsing around, the suspense is killing me...

MAMA: Yes that's enough now, Lapin, show yourself.

The second soldier reveals himself, laughing, he's Lapin, he throws down his helmet and grabs the little soldier's gun.

THE WHOLE FAMILY: Lapin!

LAPIN: Hi, everyone! Hervé, I'm going to cast a spell on you. I'm going to turn you into a girl. That'll teach you a thing or two.

He casts a spell on Hervé, who turns into a very beautiful, very sweet–tempered girl and bursts into tears.

DUPERRI: *(rushing over to him)* Hervette! Don't cry, lambkin. Come to my arms my pussycat!

Hervette throws herself into her mother's arms. They kiss.

HERVETTE: Mommy, what a twit I was, what a numskull! Oh, I'm so happy, Mommy of mine!

MAMA: *(hopping mad)* Lapin, where've you been? I've been waiting for you for three weeks!

LAPIN: I'm sorry Mama... The bomb wasn't a bomb, it was my pals from up there, they repatriated me. I only agreed to go because they promised to stop them from killing Bébert. Once I was up there we had discussions on the stellar level and on the galactic level and we had a hell of a fight because they'd abandoned the program, they didn't give a damn about your problems and I was so homesick for you all that in the end I socked my wavelength at them and told them I was quitting. Then they had no choice, they brought me down here again for ever, and because they had promised to save Bébert they parachuted me into the forces of the new order so I could stop them killing him and here I am.

MAMA: *(looking at Lapin, to Papa)* What d'you think it is? A bad flu?

PAPA: Or the mumps? ... He never had the mumps...

LUCIE: When he had scarlet fever he got delirious like that...

MARIE: Yes but you can't catch scarlet fever twice.

JEANNOT: Acute bronchitis more likely... with a fever.

BÉBERT: *(a bit groggy)* Have to give him a eucalyptus suppository, there's some in the cupboard on the left over my bed...

LAPIN: I adore you all!

GÉRARD: Hey listen, are we escaping or are we going to take root, it's dangerous here...

LUCIE: It's true, my Gérard's right, what're we farting around for?

GÉRARD: *(his face lit up with joy)* Lucie, my Lucie, I can't believe it, don't tell me you agree with me!

> *Lucie, seriously, passionately, solemnly, plants a resounding kiss on Gérard's lips.*

LUCIE: I'm re–marrying you.

MAMA: Come on, everyone back home.

HERVETTE: *(to Madame Duperri)* Take me with you, Mommy...

DUPERRI: May I bring her, Madame Lapin?

LITTLE SOLDIER: Me too, me too... take me with you Madame, I promise I'll cover your exit, don't forget that I didn't fire. I'll be faithful to you unto death, if you leave me here they'll shoot me!

MAMA: Hang on, there were 4 of us when we started out, 7 with the return of the children, 8 with Gérard, 9 with Madame Duperri, and now that makes 11 with Hervette and the little soldier. When there's enough for 4, there's less for 11, but we'll have a lot of laughs! It's all right with me, but for the mattresses, hell, you'll just have to cope, and I warn you, you'll have to take turns doing the dishes. Lapin, come and kiss me.

> *Gérard comes back like a bomb, with two superb female soldiers who dance the polka.*

GÉRARD: All the soldiers have been turned into girls, they're sitting in the corridors, they've thrown away their rifles, some are crying, some are dancing, and there's even one that's pregnant!

ALL: Hurrah!

PAPA: Our escape is secured, everyone into the van...

> *Exit all, except Mama, who goes on dancing.*

MARIE: *(off)* Mama, get a move on!

MAMA: I'm coming! *(She dances.)* I'm staying, I like it here. I'll go home later when they've got the meal ready. For the moment I'm dancing. Oh, my poor head, it's aching, how it's aching! Dammit, here comes a monologue! They're terrible, monologues, they sneak up on you, they ripen in silence and then all of a sudden wham, your head's bursting with a big melon inside it, it's got to come out... It really *has* got to come out, otherwise you're in for a cesarean... Here it is.
To you men, I say be flexible, become round, let yourselves be

submerged in understanding, sprawl in the grass, stop being active, stay seated, close your eyes and listen to the sound of the protons dancing in the far-off galaxies, become hearers, that's to say mutes.

Let that fishlike smile come back to your faces.

Don't despair because your bellies will for ever be empty of children. Your strength lies in having filled those bellies that you will never have.

Cover your concrete houses with earth, let the grass grow on their roofs.

When we can't see you any longer, when we have curved your straight lines and no one will be able to tell whether you live in ant hills, or nests, or houses in the depths of the ocean, then the world will move differently.

When you open your hands and your treasures come pouring out of them and are dispersed over the planet like a drop of milk in a glass of pure water, then you will be able to begin to live in freedom, and the vice crushing your heads will dissolve. Your skulls will open, they'll be able to absorb energy, and then radiate it, and words won't be able to express what you feel. To you women, I say, out of pity for men, confess your understanding to them, so that they can stop walking backwards and finally launch their boat into the stream. For you understand a lot of things: like them, you have been what fills the belly, but you are capable of approaching death unafraid because you are capable of being filled. Look at them, the orphans of your potency. Teach them to melt into matter, since the division of their bodies has been denied them.

Ever since human history learned how to tell itself, men have searched on their own and women have laughed at them. They wanted to find a way without women, they were naked and abandoned, they hated women because they could see that women were never naked.

Their sadness and weakness they called strength, they built a world in their own image—sad and weak. They stole everything from you, and yet you were still not naked.

They discovered many truths, which all resulted in the curved line.

And now, women, you no longer have the right to laugh at them, for they have come close to you, more naked than ever. Don't let them get away with it any longer, don't go on sitting in the grass with your fishlike smiles, but build houses that finally resemble the universe.

Women, when any man doesn't want to see who you are, fight him with all your might. Women, those of you who still allow men to continue with their murders, may curses fall upon your heads and may you die in the gutter, because the new era can't come into being without you.

There, I've got my melon out, I can't wait to get home and see what they've done about the meal.

My love to you all. I wish you a good night.

~

DENISE BONAL

A COUNTRY WEDDING

Translated from the French by

TIMOTHY JOHNS

UBU REPERTORY THEATER PUBLICATIONS
NEW YORK

Denise Bonal was born in Algeria and began her long and varied theatre career at the age of twelve, when her family moved to Paris. From 1951 to 1971 she performed and toured with regional theaters companies, all the while perfecting her writing. Since 1971, she has led a career not only as an actress, but as a writer and teacher as well. *Légère en août* (1974) was performed in Paris, Athens, and throughout Belgium. Her prize-winning *Les Moutons de la nuit* was presented in Paris in 1976. *Honorée par un petit monument* was one of six plays selected to represent contemporary theater in Quebec in 1978, and was later presented at the International Festival in Lyons and at the Avignon Festival. It was produced in Paris by the National Theater of Chaillot in 1980. *Lit vers Léthé*, written under the pseudonym Luis Aftel, was produced at the Chapelle de la Salpétrière in Paris in 1983. *Family Portrait*, first presented as a staged reading at Ubu Repertory Theater in 1985, was produced at the Théâtre de l'Est Parisien (TEP) in 1986 and at Ubu Repertory Theater in 1992. The following year, *A Picture Perfect Sky (Passions et prairie)* also published by Ubu, premiered at the TEP in Paris. Her two most recent plays are *Beware the Heart (Féroce comme le coeur,* 1992) which was awarded the European Drama prize in 1994, and *Turbulences et petits détails* (1993), which was given a public reading at Théâtre Ouvert in Paris in 1993 and at the Avignon Festival in 1994. *Beware the Heart* was published by Ubu Repertory Theater Publications in *Plays by Women, Book Two* and given its first American staged reading in 1994. Bonal was awarded two prizes by the Société des Auteurs et Compositeurs Dramatiques (SACD), in 1980 and in 1986, and was named a fellow of the Centre National des Lettres in 1981. In 1988 she was awarded the Arletty prize for best woman playwright in the French-language theater. She taught for a number of years at the French National Conservatory of Dramatic Arts in Paris. Denise Bonal was a member of the Board of Directors of the SACD from 1988 through 1991.

Timothy Johns's translations of Jean-Louis Bourdon's *Jock,* Denise Bonal's *Family Portrait* and *A Picture Perfect Sky,* Tchicaya u'Tam'Si's *The Glorious Destiny of Marshal Nnikon Nniku,* Jean-Paul Wenzel's *Vater Land, the Country of Our Fathers,* and Bernard-Marie Koltès's *Night Just Before the Forest* have all been published by Ubu Repertory Theater Publications.

AUTHOR'S NOTE

This is a country wedding.

The set might be a large field (undulating, if possible, it's prettier that way).

Stage right, a large tree: oak, elm or willow (optionally weeping).

Stage left, a fallen tree.

People of all ages meet, greet and recognize each other.

Or not.

Throughout the play, you might see the bride crossing the stage. She's running—or she's tired—and has come to fix her make-up, or her husband is looking for her, etc.

From time to time a group of people might block our view of the scene...

The rhythm should rightfully suggest the kind of sensual effervescence which weddings provoke...

Musicians also (violinists, accordionists) could pass by, and from time to time, "accompany" a scene—just as they still do in some restaurants.

Just to say that none of this should be taken too seriously, that everything will be all right...

Also, in the distance, there might be a statue which changes its position, gets up and goes away... then comes back.

But—

The overall feeling shouldn't be that of a realistic picture of a wedding, but rather of an image in a dream... a wedding as seen through the memory, or nostalgically...

DENISE BONAL

CHARACTERS

THE BRIDE
THE GROOM
LITTLE GILBERT
GOSSIP A
GOSSIP B
ANGELA
MICHEL, *cool guy*
OCTAVE, *cool guy*
WEEPING WOMAN
MARCEL, *old geezer*
GASTON, *old geezer*
THE SON
THE MOTHER
FIRST GIRL
SECOND GIRL
THIRD GIRL
SECOND WOMAN
AGNES, *the woman in the hat*
PAUL
BENEDICTE, *Angela's friend*

LITTLE GILBERT'S MOTHER
RENAUD, *Angela's husband*
MATHIEU, *groom's father*
THE HUNGRY WOMAN
THE AMERICAN WOMAN
VINCENT
VINCENT'S WIFE
A WOMAN
A MAN
ANOTHER MAN
MARIE
JULIETTE
ROMEO
WOMAN IN A HURRY
YOUNG MAN
THE RED MAN
THE YOUNG BOY
GUESTS, ACCORDIONISTS,
VIOLINISTS, *etc.*

1

The stage is empty. The newlyweds enter on the run, then stop and kiss at length. Finally:

SHE: How much longer will you kiss me like that?

HE: Mmm, for the rest of my life...

SHE: Whoa, now! Don't die on me so fast!

> *Then, in the distance, we hear the guests growing impatient: "The newlyweds! We want the newlyweds!" The violinists are tuning up. The accordionists play a few scales... "Everyone take your seats, please!" Bottles of champagne are uncorked. Musicians begin to play. The young newlyweds rejoin the reception, they have no choice, right?*
>
> *Then, Gilbert enters, a little boy about eight, maybe ten years old, who's continually dawdling behind, forever absorbed in his electronic game... In the distance a voice cries: "G-i-i-l-b-e-r-t?!..." Finally, he in turn comes and joins the party.*
>
> *Then a group crosses the area of action, from which Gossips A and B break off.*

GOSSIP A: Isn't our little bride just the most ravishing thing you have ever seen in your entire *life?!*

GOSSIP B: All young brides are ravishing on their wedding day, and it lasts about a minute or two. The problem is getting a whole life to stand on the tip of that minute...

GOSSIP A: I think weddings should always be in the country...

GOSSIP B: Well yes, it does spare us doors...

GOSSIP A: And it is so moving to see a young couple start out on a new life under a deep blue sky, unfurled before them in all its glory, and butterflies dancing around...

GOSSIP B: God I hate butterflies... Makes me shiver just *knowing* their life lasts as long as it takes you to say "Bye bye!"

GOSSIP A: Well, they, at least, think they're immortal.

GOSSIP B: I thought I was immortal, too, until Bob left me.

GOSSIP A: Then when she repeated that last little "I do," her voice was so... it was so... crystalline and pure... that, well, it brought tears to my eyes...

GOSSIP B: That's the trouble with these damn things: they stir up all these buried memories...

GOSSIP A: And you can contemplate, yet once again, joy, in all the splendor of its youth...

GOSSIP B: Tish. When I got married I thought life would be one long, joyous surprise, that it would deepen the blue of the sky itself, that suddenly it would take off in a new direction with a glorious squeal of tires, that it would embellish my life with the colors of stained glass, and soar high above the level of mere suburbia...

GOSSIP A: What—*life?*

GOSSIP B: Yes, *life!* And all my life ever since I've kept harping on the same facts, repeating the same deeds, and see myself confronting the same old concerns, like, for instance, did I, or did I not, soap that little spot there right between my shoulder blades?

GOSSIP A: Well, if not you'd have found out soon enough.

GOSSIP B: It's as if I've lived my life between parentheses; only one of the two was always collapsing...

GOSSIP A: Oh, come now, I see you getting more and more vibrant and... petulant, with age... !

GOSSIP B: *(surprised)* What's that?... And yet so often I have these strange yearnings... and... for some time now... I've been seeing cathedrals...

GOSSIP A: Oh yes, that does happen!... But don't you see? Billions upon billions of human beings had to meet, look at one other, and finally unite so that this one young man and this one young woman could get married on this very day...

2

They go off pensively, encountering Gilbert on the way who is still absorbed in his game. Gossip A, affable as ever, makes a friendly gesture, which he fails to notice. The ladies exit. He stops...

VOICE OFF: Gilbert!

GILBERT: Yeah...

VOICE OFF: Where are you?

GILBERT: Yeah...

VOICE OFF: Come say hello!

GILBERT: Wait...

Distant laughter is heard.

VOICE OFF: Wait for what?

GILBERT: Yeah...

VOICE OFF: You hear me?

GILBERT: I can't hear you!...

More laughter.

VOICE OFF: Your very favorite cousins have just arrived, Gilbert...

GILBERT: *(to himself)* Aw, crap on 'em!

VOICE OFF: Gilbert!

GILBERT: What?

VOICE OFF: Are you coming?

GILBERT: Wait, mom. *(Playing the baby)*... I got to go make poo-poo!

> *Gilbert glances around, then sits down behind a tree and continues to play.*

VARIOUS VOICES: G-i-l-b-e-r-t! *G-i-i-l-b-e-r-t!*

> *With one hand he continues to play; with the other he gestures, in the direction of the voices, to pipe down.*

3

Angela enters. She sits down in the shade of a tree, not far from Gilbert. But she speaks to herself.

ANGELA: Thirty years ago I left the farm and still the heavy stench of steaming cow shit stays in my nostrils.
Such a tenacious memory it is, that even from this distance, even in the city, when I wake up early in the morning and see a little green, that smell comes over me.
My parents used to forget to heat the house.
So, between their bedding down and cud-chewing, I'd do my homework in the stable.
My notebooks smelled like cows.
They made fun of me at school...
But I got good grades, anyway, in spite the cows...

Gilbert looks at her. She turns her gaze on him.

Thousands of years from now I'll still remember that tranquil stench of fresh cow shit;
and by association and resemblance,
I can see again the torment of mustard poultices,
that burning lava that father and mother applied to the body of the crying child.
To hold it in place
they'd sit on either side of my bed on the burning sheets,
(that night, in the torrid arms of a stranger, the bride will come to know...)
through my tears I can see them in profile, my torture-parents.
My chest will be red and burned.
(They wouldn't dare if I were a boy).
I hate them. They don't love me. I'm an abandoned child found on the banks of a river, for sure...

She laughs sadly.

Poor souls, so sweet and so poor.
I hardly ever write to them.

There they are, sitting on the bench in the front yard, admist the odor of corn-flowers.

How are they, in their old age?

It's all so far away, yet so close.

A while ago as I passed the little footbridge, the smell of fresh cow patties came over me, the stubborn smell of a country childhood. A smell warm and nurturing...

GILBERT: *(without raising his eyes from the game)* What's a cow patty?

ANGELA: It's cow poo. Only it's not really shit, it's more like grass jam. Actually it's very clean...

GILBERT: Can you eat it?

ANGELA: No. *(Pause.)* You know when you're a kid and you're minding the herd and you find a patty that's all dried out by the sun and wind and you take a little sharpened hazel stick and gently lift up the crinkled top of the patty, and it makes a little noise like, pfft, like the sigh of a goldfish, and out comes a swarm of little flies and underneath you find, all shiny and new, magnificent tender leaves of green grass... *(Gilbert looks at her a little astonished.)*... magnificent, new grass underneath, a luminous green grass, almost like English porcelain.

GILBERT: Could you scan it? *(Angela, a little taken aback, doesn't quite know what to say.)* I've never seen cow patties, never even seen a cow 'cept in a book.

ANGELA: Hi, my name's Angela.

GILBERT: They got big teeth, like horses?

ANGELA: They don't have any teeth.

GILBERT: Yeah? So what do they do?

ANGELA: Oh, they get by okay. *(She tries to remember but really can't.)* You know, with their lower ones.

GILBERT: My name's Gilbert.

At this point there could be a sudden gust of wind and flying across the stage there might be napkins, white flowers, a woman's hat, etc.

ANGELA: Whose family are you here for?

GILBERT: Mom's a friend of the groom's. Sure is ugly, isn't he? I don't have a father.

ANGELA: Is he dead?

Gilbert doesn't answer.

ANGELA: Me, I was in Monsieur Mathieu's service, the groom's father, about ten years...

GILBERT: What kind of service?

ANGELA: All kinds.

GILBERT: What about you, you got a father?

ANGELA: I never see him.

GILBERT: So how does grass grow green underneath a cow patty, anyway, without any sunlight?

ANGELA: Well, when they get up to breathe, see, light seeps right in, right under the patties.

Angela gets interested in Gilbert's game, who explains the rules to her. A group of guests passes by. One of them is saying: "There you have it. That's just the way it is. Here we have a beautiful day and all of a sudden a wind comes up..."

GILBERT: Cow... cow. Is it bigger'n a race car?

ANGELA: Actually even taller.

GILBERT: Taller than a bus?

ANGELA: Not quite.

GILBERT: Ever see any in zoos?

ANGELA: And right above their lips, there's this little hollow spot that's so soft and smooth and a little bit moist, it feels real good to pet it...

GILBERT: They don't say anything?

ANGELA: You kidding? And you know what else? When you sink your eyes into those big wide calm eyes of theirs, you think you're never going to die.

GILBERT: 'Cause why?

ANGELA: Just 'cause... Oh, I literally could've waltzed and waltzed with my cows... only thing is, I don't know how to waltz.

4

Detaching itself from one group of guests is a couple of Cool Guys:
Michel and Octave.

MICHEL: These country weddings are idiotic. Your shoes get all
mucked up... and all this damn grass!... All you can see is green!...
And not one little spot for any real privacy!...

OCTAVE: So like I was saying, this woman was so beautiful... and
I mean so god awful beautiful... that just between us we actually called her the "Woman of Breathtaking Beauty"...

MICHEL: Hell.

OCTAVE: Alas, hell is not the word for it.

MICHEL: You were her lover?

OCTAVE: Her secretary. Actually, her biographer.

MICHEL: Guess she had a pretty full life, eh?

OCTAVE: "Biographer of the Present." I was hired to follow her
everywhere she went and jot down every last detail: whatever
she said, whatever she did, and whatever... whatever happened
to her.

MICHEL: Down to the last detail!?

OCTAVE: One day, she dropped a postage stamp and just managed to grab it before it blew away... she'd been writing in the
back yard...

MICHEL: Why didn't you catch it yourself?

OCTAVE: I was absolutely forbidden to intervene in her life, in
any form or fashion, ... but because I forgot to make a note of
the fact, I was called onto the carpet and they docked my pay...

MICHEL: You mean, you spent all day... ?

OCTAVE: "Madam woke up at thirty-two past nine this morning. She took her breakfast in bed, spilled a bit of coffee in her saucer, nearly choked on her toast. Picked up a crumb which had fallen onto her yellow silk sheet, stared at it briefly with a sort of sad amazement, then delicately placed it in her empty cup. Then, she smiled, shaking her head from side to side... "

MICHEL: My God. she must really have been a breathtaking beauty! But, mind if I ask? What about the bathroom?

OCTAVE: Same thing. See, I was only a scribe.... "Madam took a lemon-scented bubble bath"—and you'd better get the scent right!—"twice the soap slipped out of her hands. The first time, she caught it. The second time, she laughed out loud.... Wrapped herself in a mauve bathrobe"—and you *must* get that color right— "with white flowers"—*(In a woman's voice)*: 'You will note that they are morning glories'—"Madam brushed her red hair back and then, combed it down over her forehead... "

MICHEL: My God. Did you ever get any sleep?

OCTAVE: I don't believe I did.

MICHEL: But it was well paid... ?

OCTAVE: Actually, I don't remember.

MICHEL: Well, what did you talk about together?

OCTAVE: I was under orders never to speak to her.

MICHEL: And what about when she had guests over... ?

OCTAVE: I'd stay out of the way...

MICHEL: And she'd introduce you as...

A couple strolls by.

HE: And how is your dear, sweet, charming mother?

SHE: Dead.

HE: Oh, I'm so sorry!!

SHE: Dead, yes, but thank God she doesn't know it.

The couple passes by.

MICHEL: What did she call you?

OCTAVE: *(he thinks.)*... Octave. I was to touch her only in case of imminent danger...

MICHEL: And did that ever happen?

OCTAVE: Well, once, with a wild boar... *(Brief pause.)*... They were carrying their old mother, sitting in a large crate...

MICHEL: *What?*

OCTAVE: What, what?

MICHEL: *Who* was carrying their mother?

OCTAVE: Ah, so you heard about it, too?

MICHEL: No... it was you who...

OCTAVE: Next to the "Woman of Breathtaking Beauty," as we used to call her, my hearing became so acute that I could actually make out what she was on the *verge* of saying... In those days, I had incredible powers of hearing...

> *A woman suddenly appears, her hair all in a mess, agitated; she addresses Michel. This is the Weeping Woman.*

WEEPING WOMAN: Michel... Michel... tell me the truth... What happened to you? Are you hurt?... For six days and nights I've been looking all over for you, all over, Michel, even in the back rooms of bars... I loved you so much, Michel... I abandoned my country for you, I've abandoned my family, and I've nearly forgotten my own language... even my friends, Michel... I loved you even more than my poor children... So please, tell me the truth, Michel, even if it hurts... Tell me the truth... please, I beg of you... You mustn't keep me in the dark...

Michel looks at her for a long time, adjusts her collar as you would a child's, caresses her hair, and, pushing her gently away, leaves her and rejoins Octave. The Weeping Woman sits down on a tree trunk and weeps.

OCTAVE: What is the problem with that odd-looking person?

MICHEL: She is odd... She bears a strange resemblance to my first wife, so sometimes, she gets confused and thinks I'm her husband.

OCTAVE: Wait, wait a minute... the fact that she looks like your wife doesn't explain how she mistakes you for...

MICHEL: Ah well, let it alone, old man, let it alone. The festivities which accompany weddings have always driven women a little off the wall... *We* must be extremely prudent.

Angela gets up and says to Gilbert:

ANGELA: When you grow up to be a man, please, don't be so much of a "man."

Gilbert nods, all the while absorbed in his game. Angela, as she leaves, passes the two Old Geezers, to whom she nods politely.

OCTAVE: Am I right? Your first name is Michel...

MICHEL: *(relaxed)* Yes, that it is. Michel.

They exit.

5

The two Old Geezers, Gaston and Marcel, walk gingerly by, sipping their champagne. Marcel glances at Gilbert.

MARCEL: Lord Lord, we'll never see childhood again...

GASTON: Nope. That's been over and done quite a while now.

MARCEL: A guy ought to have the right—at least once in his life—to go back to his childhood, even if only for a few hours.

GASTON: What for? To be an orphan?

MARCEL: No, no, our parents'd be there, too!

GASTON: Ah, see, you want everything!... And stop goin' on about childhood so much, will you... The second one's just around the corner...

MARCEL: *(quickly avoiding Gaston's remark)* Your niece seems like such a fine person...

GASTON: You mean the bride, or her sister?

MARCEL: The bride, for chrissake!!... That gorgeous creature in all her glory! Forget about the others!

GASTON: *(coldly)* Nice... nice... yeah, I suppose, nice, in a way.

MARCEL: She has a turned-up nose... just the way I like it in a woman... not in a man, God knows, oh no! But in a woman...

GASTON: Nice... I suppose... and yet.

MARCEL: Aiyaiyai...

GASTON: And yet right there on the steps of the church, where you pose for the traditional picture, what does she do? She spots something on her husband's shoulder... a speck of dust, a hair, a dandruff flake, who knows... and with a flick of her hand... she brushes it off... just like that! *(He clumsily imitates the young woman's gesture.)* There, like that. Now, I mean, I ask you!

MARCEL: Uh-huh... So? This is a major sin?

GASTON: Oh, please!... don't you get it? At the very moment when their two images are about to crystallize into one for the rest of their lives, at that very moment when every bride is in sheer ecstasy, and her new wedding ring sparkles with all the fire of their exchange of vows, and finally, at last, she's arm in arm with the man who chose her over every other woman, and when in the eyes of the whole world she might be staring at the virile smile on her young groom's face, or considering his young and tender neck or even his bobbing Adam's apple, what does *she* do? She's bugged by a speck of dust on her young husband's tux. *(He repeats the shocking gesture.)* No, I'm sorry, she'll be bossy and possessive. "See? This man's all mine! Watch me dust him off... !"

MARCEL: *(making the same gesture, delicately)* Like... this... ?

GASTON: *(same gesture, more violently.)* Like that!

MARCEL: Ah... yes... I see.

> *A man about forty runs onto the stage, in a fit of anger, followed by his mother.*

SON: I todja awready, mama! To understand it, you'd have to crawl through the windowpane!

> *They disappear.*

MARCEL: Who was *that*?

GASTON: Don't know 'em... they're strangers... they come to weddings... and they run off...

Silence.

MARCEL: Apparently, my friend, there are now too many of us old folks...

GASTON: Too many old folks like us!?

MARCEL: That's right. And we live too long, too.

GASTON: Live too long!?

MARCEL: Personally, I never *meant* to do it, on purpose...

GASTON: Tsk... tsk... tsk

MARCEL: 'Course, there have been occasions when I tried not to die... like most people... But when I didn't smoke it was because it gave me insomnia, and when I didn't drink, it was 'cause it made me sleepy... I really didn't mean to be a burden...

GASTON: Well, I smoked. And I drank. And just like you, here I am a burden...

MARCEL: So what do they expect us to do, anyway?

GASTON: Take one guess!

MARCEL: But what can I do? Can I help it if my health has always been rock solid? I was born into a poor family that was always tired and run down, and out of the seven kids, four didn't make it. But the ones who did just can't stop.

GASTON: And me? What about me? I've been through wars, deserts, women, depressions, rationing, unemployment, every kind of flu you can name, and I'm still standing! Only thing is, it's my legs... Ah, yes, the legs!...

MARCEL: Ah, mine too. I've loved the little darlings so much, they've put me to walking for so long, that they've flat worn me down, the little gambs!... *(He laughs.)* And I can still laugh without hacking... you?

GASTON: Damn straight!

MARCEL: Which is rare at our age.

GASTON: 'Course, it's not the same laugh it used to be ...

MARCEL: That's because we don't hear with the same ears...

A woman has sat down next to the Weeping Woman and is talking to her, inaudibly.

GASTON: Ah, the days when we used to run after the bus... Used to jump up onto the rear platform... remember?... I could grab onto it on the run without messing up a single hair.

MARCEL: Yea, sure, thanks to all that Royal Crown Hair Goo!

Gaston shakes his head «no» with an air of disdain.

MARCEL: Or thanks to Baker's Cream, which they named after Josephine Baker who I once saw dance buck naked with a bunch of bananas tied round her waist, and God let me tell you, she was pure beauty...

GASTON: Was she really a Negro?

MARCEL: What they called Creole back then... So beautiful she made you want to weep... made you want to camp out on the bare ground outside her exit door...

GASTON: You ever do it?

MARCEL: Nah, too many people, not enough room.

They remain pensive, glasses empty.

WEEPING WOMAN: All of a sudden the sun has gone down—gone down just as it did when I was a girl...

GASTON: Used to be, whatever we did, there was always a woman around to reward you with a smile... Nowadays, women don't smile anymore...

MARCEL: Oh, yes they do!... Just not in our direction... *(Pause.)* And here it is already Autumn.

GASTON: *Autumn!?* This is June!

MARCEL: That's what I'm saying. We're already headin' towards Autumn!

GASTON: Whatever... in any case, what's time to us but a worn carpet?

MARCEL: Well, whattaya say let's go get some of that grub... those cakes looked pretty good to me.

GASTON: Hmm... You start off with the cake?

MARCEL: I always start with the cake... That way, you're guaranteed some!

GILBERT: *(who bursts in on the run; to the old men)* Hey, you two go all the way back to the days of horse and buggies?

GASTON: Us? Hell, sonny, we go all the way back to the days of a swift kick right in the butt...

6

They shuffle on off, and as they pass the three Girls, they turn slightly toward them, and, with a nod of their heads, vanish. The Girls snap their fingers, and swings descend from the heavens. To a tune which is not a tune, they start to swing, and taking turns, improvise rhymes.

FIRST GIRL: The Spring is leapin' in...

SECOND GIRL: And stars are peepin' out...

THIRD GIRL: The heat is seepin' in...

SECOND GIRL: And buds are creepin' out...

FIRST GIRL: The bees are bumblin' round...

THIRD GIRL: Pants are slidin' down...

FIRST GIRL: While me, I'm givin' up...

SECOND GIRL: Cats are all out howlin'...

THIRD GIRL: Gardens flat out flowerin'...

FIRST GIRL: Young men all out prowlerin'...

THIRD GIRL: But me, I'm givin' up...

FIRST GIRL: And yet, I got a nice body...

THIRD GIRL: We got three nice bodies...

SECOND GIRL: So what are we waiting for?

THIRD GIRL: Grass is not quite green enough. Sun's too humid.

FIRST GIRL: We're not gonna be virgins the rest of our lives, are we?

THIRD GIRL: Hey, like, at fifteen, the situation is still fluid.

They swing some more.

FIRST GIRL: How's Jean-Luc?

THIRD GIRL: I'm breakin' up with him.

FIRST GIRL: Not so nice, huh?

THIRD GIRL: *Too* nice. He's like always in your hair, always this or that. Want another coffee? Candy? A coke? A spin through the woods on my cool scooter?

SECOND GIRL: Ayayay.

THIRD GIRL: No, I mean like he's the kind of guy to ask you by registered mail, you know? Return receipt requested.

FIRST GIRL: Impotent?

THIRD GIRL: Wouldn't put it past him. It's like, he won't let me breathe.

SECOND GIRL: Has he kissed you?

THIRD GIRL: 'Course he has, what do you think?

FIRST GIRL: And? So?

THIRD GIRL: So... when I, like, you know, felt his tongue? All I could think of was the discovery of electricity!

> *They continue swinging in silence. Gilbert slowly walks by, still into his game.*

FIRST GIRL: Ever see any porn films?

SECOND GIRL: 'Course I have.

THIRD GIRL: They're awfully slow...

SECOND GIRL: Much too much repetition.

THIRD GIRL: They like, you know, are totally devoid of any, like, structure...

GILBERT: Way too much silicon.

He goes off under a tree, where he'll listen to the Girls. They keep swinging.

FIRST GIRL: The sap is flowin' in...

SECOND GIRL: The candles blowin' out...

THIRD GIRL: The grass is mowin' in...

FIRST GIRL: Asses pokin' out...

SECOND GIRL: Aw man, this is, like, so boring!

The two Cool Guys come back by, perhaps to ogle the girls?

OCTAVE: We mustn't forget—he put the guy's foot in the stirrup...

MICHEL: Yes, then took away the horse!

Glances in the direction of the Girls. Each of the latter gives them an ambiguous look back.

MICHEL: The thing is, of course, theirs is a generation which has no more language... All that's left to them are a few gestures whose meaning is completely beyond them...

FIRST GIRL: Relaxing in a warm, light green bubble bath with a CD of Freddy Mercury, sunlight streaming through the window, a Blue Lagoon at your fingertips, a handsome, young barechested man sitting on a dark blue stool, staring at me for hours on end, and smiling...

SECOND GIRL: And? So?

FIRST GIRL: So, like, I mean, that's something else!... Are we gonna die of boredom like this the rest of our lives?

SECOND GIRL: I'm not like really and truly *bored*. Just impatient. Two years from now I'll make love.

THIRD GIRL: Two years! That's a long time!

SECOND GIRL: The night after finals. If I fail, it'll cheer me up, if I pass, it'll be all the better...

THIRD GIRL: Got it all planned, huh?

FIRST GIRL: Got a boy picked out?

SECOND GIRL: Got one who will be, 'tween now and then.

THIRD GIRL: Does he, like, know about this?

SECOND GIRL: He'll be informed.

FIRST GIRL: Who is he?

SECOND GIRL: Simon.

FIRST GIRL: Oh, I know. The very red-haired and kinda Jewish guy.

SECOND GIRL: That's right. Kinda red-haired, very Jewish.

THIRD GIRL: He good-looking?

SECOND GIRL: Like, a cross between Robert Redford and Woody Allen.

FIRST GIRL: Intelligent?

SECOND GIRL: He's *more* than intelligent.

THIRD GIRL: That's what's so fantastic about Jews—how intelligent they all are!

> *Silence. The two women sitting on the tree trunk stand up. With her arm around the Weeping Woman's shoulder, the other says to her:*

SECOND WOMAN: Come on, hon'... let's go... you know, one day I was waiting for a call from Jacques... and I looked up. The sky was so blue, such a pure blue, such a flawless blue... I started to cry. Not so much because of Jacques... as because of that blue up above.

WEEPING WOMAN: Is that true?

> *They exit.*

FIRST GIRL: Hey, what do you say let's go hitchhiking!

SECOND GIRL: You going home?

FIRST GIRL: We spot some classy wheels... then when the guy stops...

THIRD GIRL: The second he sees us, the doors like fly right open...

FIRST GIRL: And we all go: "Hey, mister, looking for your mistress? You'll find her in the arms of your sweetheart."

SECOND GIRL: And then, we like split real quick.

> *Pause.*

THIRD GIRL: You think we're intelligent?

SECOND GIRL: We're like, just on the verge of getting to be.

FIRST GIRL: Couldn't that like maybe hurt us?

SECOND GIRL: Better believe it! We'll have to be very, very discreet about it!

THIRD GIRL: Apparently, it can actually be painful.

SECOND GIRL: Extremely. It's like, intelligence, you know, is this very painful thing. Which is why guys who are sensitive, and can't stand the sight of suffering, they wind up marrying morons...

THIRD GIRL: So? What do we do? We never get married?

SECOND GIRL: Let's hope not!

FIRST GIRL: Hey, I got it! Let's try to cry! You know, with like real hot tears to the point that we really feel the pain!

SECOND GIRL: Speaking of pain, I'd like to feel the pangs of unrequited love.

THIRD GIRL: Yeah, but for that, you really, like, need the love.

They hop down from the swings.

FIRST GIRL: *(to the second)* I'll never love a man like I love you.

THIRD GIRL: 'Scuse *me*. Maybe I should just quietly leave?

FIRST GIRL: I'd like to go back to kindergarten. Play hopscotch *(She executes a few hops.)* Straight up to Heaven! Back right down to Earth, then hop on to Hell!...

A woman in a hat and a young man enter.

SHE: Paul, you know what I would like?

Paul stops and looks at her.

I'd like you to give me a child.

PAUL: You got it!

Taking her by the hand and turning around, Paul dashes off-stage pulling her behind. The Girls, with a gesture of their hands, send the swings back up, and unhesitatingly follow them, keenly interested. Gilbert has stood up, and is alone on stage, no longer playing. What's he thinking about? The world of adults is awfully agitated! But interesting. Angela arrives. Gilbert goes over to her and listens.

7

ANGELA: It was on that morning during the first milking, with my mouth filled with mist and in the violent stench of the stable, sitting clumsily on my tripod, my head leaning against his haunch, on that sweet little triangular spot of skin that's so warm and soft you'd swear it was silk, with steam blowing out of their nostrils, and the still sleepy flies buzzing heavily about, as I listened for the loud, clear thud of the first spurt of milk against the bottom of the bucket, in my blouse pocket there's a handkerchief folded in four which I sprinkle every morning with a Cologne called "Parisian Mist," there I was, I'd just turned sixteen and I said to myself that morning: "Now that I'm sixteen years old, what am I going to do?"

GILBERT: I do that too, ask myself a lot, what am I going to do now?!

Benedicte arrives on the run.

BENEDICTE: Angela... Angela...

ANGELA: What is it?

BENEDICTE: I... don't mean to hurt you...

ANGELA: The kids!?...

BENEDICTE: But it's better that I be the one to tell you.

ANGELA: What is it! Tell me... *please!*

A woman rushes up to grab Gilbert.

MOTHER: Three hours now I've been looking for you...

GILBERT: Me too, Mom! I've been looking all *over* for you!

MOTHER: Where? Everywhere I'm not? *(She leads him away.)*

BENEDICTE: He's here.

ANGELA: Who?

BENEDICTE: I saw him from a distance...

ANGELA: Who are you talking about?

BENEDICTE: He knew you'd be invited. He might have stayed away... I'm talking about Renaud.

ANGELA: *(taking Benedicte in her arms, without looking at her, in a low voice)* He's come back.

BENEDICTE: *(softly)* Renaud?

ANGELA: Yes... he's come back.

BENEDICTE: To town?

ANGELA: Back home...

BENEDICTE: *(still in Angela's arms)* My sweet Angie... you never said a word...

ANGELA: I couldn't bring myself to...

BENEDICTE: *(breaking away)* These guys who leave home, they can't all come back at the same time... *(Silence.)* Has it been long?

ANGELA: Nearly three months.

BENEDICTE: Is it serious?

ANGELA: I have to believe it... Otherwise, how do you go on? *(Pause.)* One morning I was walking in a hurry...

8

*A flashback to the reunion of Angela and Renaud—in front of
Benedicte, who's a spectator.*

RENAUD: Hello, Angela...

ANGELA: Yes... Hello.

Pause, as they look at each other.

RENAUD: *(timidly)* Seems like you've grown taller...

ANGELA: It comes from keeping your head above water... your
neck gets longer...

Pause.

RENAUD: And the kids?

ANGELA: They've grown, too.

RENAUD: Do they talk about me?

ANGELA: I talk to them about you.

RENAUD: Are they angry?

ANGELA: They think you're at work somewhere on the other side
of the planet.

RENAUD: What about all the letters they were supposed to get?

ANGELA: *(without bitterness)* Oh sure, you would like that. Me sending a letter every two weeks from Australia with kangaroo stamps
on it and getting back in time for breakfast the next day...

Renaud, penitent, gives a little laugh.

ANGELA: *Are* you going to Australia, by chance?...

RENAUD: Why do you ask?

ANGELA: Well, those are suitcases, aren't they?

RENAUD: Suitcases they are indeed.

ANGELA: So... you're going on a trip?

RENAUD: Nope.

ANGELA: Coming back from one, then... ?

RENAUD: Nope.

ANGELA: Ah, I see. That's clear.

> *Renaud sits down on one of the suitcases.*

Tired?

RENAUD: I guess I am.

ANGELA: So, to catch some rest you drag your suitcases all around town... ?

RENAUD: In the old days, you used to catch on to everything... right off.

ANGELA: In the "old days," I hadn't stuck my head out of the water... best not touch on those "old days," Renaud... Stir them up, and they're liable to bite you...

RENAUD: Sit down, won't you?

> *Angela sits down on the other suitcase.*

Just like we used to take the train... Remember that time we left for...

Angela looks at him; he doesn't dare continue.

ANGELA: You're eating, at least, I hope?

Renaud hides his face in his hands.

RENAUD: If you want me to...

ANGELA: Yes...

RENAUD: I'm coming back.

ANGELA: Coming back?

RENAUD: Coming back home.

ANGELA: For how long?

RENAUD: For as long as you want...

Silence.

ANGELA: You want to come back home, Renaud, you've got to know why you're coming back... Because coming back, you see, is a good deal less exciting as an prospect, than leaving. When you leave, oh, well, the whole world lies before you, the air itself is made of wings, and all the farewell phrases flutter up to the sky like kites, when you leave. And even if you're hurting, it's a happy kind of light-headed hurt that's on the wing, and the freedom that greets you as you leave looks like an angel on whose generous lips you already know how to read words of welcome and big promises. But coming back to the old house, where the papers have all curled and yellowed, well, that's something else, Renaud. Coming back takes some guts, takes a lot of guts, Renaud, it takes a clear head, and it takes a heart that's cleared itself of regrets. 'Cause on homecoming day, Renaud, there aren't great surprises, no big revelations. You come back to the same old smell of the house. So yes, Renaud you've got to know why you're coming back. You've got to know with what piece of your soul you're coming back. "He with two homes, loses his mind; he with two wives, loses his soul." *(She bursts into tears and falls into his arms.)* Oh, God, Renaud, do come back, yes, do come back. Come back home. It's waiting for you and so are we. Come back without any guts or courage or clear idea or anything—just come back. We've been waiting so long for you. What I said was just out of pride and to keep myself from crying.

They stand up.

RENAUD: I was just getting fed up with Angela...

ANGELA: *(surprised)* Her name is... Angela?... you mean like me?

RENAUD: *(awkward, embarrassed)* Yeah... right... boy, was I fed up...

ANGELA: Give me one of those bags, my love.

RENAUD: What about the presents for the kids... ?

ANGELA: We'll buy some. Toys everywhere are Japanese, anyway.

RENAUD: I only ever loved you, you know.

ANGELA: *(gently)* Oh, I don't know about that... but I believe you, anyway...

> *They take a few steps together. Then Renaud disappears with the bags. Angela comes back to Benedicte. Brief pause.*

So that's how it happened.

BENEDICTE: As simple as that.

ANGELA: Just like that.

BENEDICTE: Well, then, it's good.

ANGELA: Yeah, it's good...

BENEDICTE: Did you think about him returning?

ANGELA: Not at night, as I was falling asleep...

BENEDICTE: And so life goes on, just like before?

ANGELA: Well... no. You can't just ask time to fold in on itself like an accordion. Sometimes I think we're like twin brothers on an island, waiting for the mail. But, at least he's there. And now he has to tell the kids all about Australia. I buy him all the literature.

> *She laughs.*
> *Still on the run, the Mother and Son pass by, one after the other.*

SON: I todja awready, Mama!, and I'll tell you again, to understand it you'd have to crawl through the skylight!

> *They disappear.*

ANGELA: And you... ? How are *you* doing?

BENEDICTE: Oh 'bout like a apple cart with a broken axle on a icy, mountain road in the middle of the night...

ANGELA: *(trying to laugh)* So, great!... Couldn't be better, then...

BENEDICTE: So, how about a drink.

ANGELA: Okay, but not too much.

BENEDICTE: Yeah, I say *too* much.

> *They leave , passing the two Gossips on their way, holding their plates. Gilbert catches up with Angela.*

GILBERT: The guy with the suitcases. He your dad?

> *Without answering, Angela leaves, followed by Benedicte and Gilbert. Enter the two Gossips, A and B.*

9

GOSSIP B: And the woman in violet?

GOSSIP A: That's Angela. Was in the service of Mathieu, and it's not violet, it's burgundy, for over six years. You might say she's the one who raised Mark, young as she was. It's only right she be at his wedding.

GOSSIP B: And Mark's mother is American?

GOSSIP A: Oh! And how! They say she left Mathieu—speak of the devil—only two weeks after the wedding...

GOSSIP B: Oh, my heavens! Why?

GOSSIP A: It's a bit of a family mystery... Apparently, when Mathieu went to New York to look for his wife, he forgot to bring any shirts, but had a suitcase full of books...

Gilbert runs on stage, and, feigning concern...

GILBERT: *(to the two Gossips)* You haven't seen my mother, have you?

GOSSIP A: Now who might your mother be, my dear?

GILBERT: I forgot...

He takes off. Mathieu enters with an armful of books, accompanied by Octave. The two groups greet each other and both stay on stage, separate, but together.

GOSSIP A: *(to Mathieu)* One of the happiest days of your life...

MATHIEU: Thank you for my life... *(to Octave)* If you only knew what's happening to me.

OCTAVE: Do you never go out without your library?

MATHIEU: If I stop reading, I go blind.

OCTAVE: What you've read couldn't be contained in a Mack truck!

MATHIEU: Make that five Mack trucks.

OCTAVE: You retain it all?

MATHIEU: Good God no.

OCTAVE: So?

MATHIEU: So when you come back from a magnificent beach, do you bring back every grain of sand?

OCTAVE: Who are some of your favorite auth...

MATHIEU: *(interrupting him)* Please. I read everything. I started at the age of five. I never played. I read. Never did any sports, no field trips, no politics. I read. Never played cards, chess, the horses, the lottery, nothing. I read. I read everything. Novels. Poems. Essays. Confessions. Memoirs. Travel books. (In New Guinea, they have recently discovered a Stone-Age tribe, and priests have already been sent to build a church!) Newspapers—all kinds, all stripes—reviews, magazines, studies, treatises, guides, scientific monographs, even the erroneous ones, calendars, alphabets, railway timetables (The Orient-Express stops in Venice at 6:52 P.M. for 10 minutes.) Storefront signs. "Dapper Dan's"—that's my dry cleaner.

GOSSIP B: Personally, these marriages make *me* think of death.

GOSSIP A: Please! Hold your tongue! *(She crosses herself.)*

GOSSIP B: I suppose it's because my sister died on the morning of my wedding day... Can you imagine?! The gowns spread out all over the living room, flower sprays everywhere, my mother with her brand new perm, and me, in a state you can only just imagine. We finally had to postpone it. And my fiancé, he was so thunderstruck, he couldn't get out a word, he just sat there in the hallway on the rattan sofa with his cheeks all red and his fists balled up between his knees...

GOSSIP A: How did she die?

GOSSIP B: They never found out... *and,* she was in love with my fiancé!

MATHIEU: When I go buy my croissants at the same bakery I've gone to for the last fifteen years, every morning I lift my eyes, and read: "Dave's Bakery. At the Sign of the Three Storks"... Every morning...

OCTAVE: Just to make sure one of the storks hasn't flown away...

MATHIEU: I mean I read signs to the point that I read the names of the printers who made them. I read pharmaceutical pre-scriptions, the Bible—of course—, the wording of bank notes: "Counterfeiting is punishable by life imprisonment"... did you know that?

OCTAVE: Even for small bills?

MATHIEU: The names of merchants carved in relief on their front doors, commemorative plaques for the fallen dead, traf-fic signs of all sorts, I know every route through town by heart. I know the brand names on every beer coaster, the rules and regulations of every park and garden: "Do Not Walk On The Grass. No Dogs Allowed. No Bicycles Permitted. Do Not Pick the Flowers."

OCTAVE: Ah—but do we have the right to go in?

GOSSIP B: Haven't you ever noticed? that many fathers die while their daughters are listening to Carmen at the Met?

GOSSIP A: Carmen... ? No, that one has escaped me. On the other hand, on a slightly different tack, I've got this neighbor who had an eye operation. And do you know what? With her right eye she can see all around her, and with her left eye she sees what's going on in Tokyo!...

GOSSIP B: Oh my God! With jet lag and all!

MATHIEU: The names of architects cut in cornerstones, the daily news, of course, menus of restaurants I never go to, bills of lading, the laws and statutes of the state, of course, agricultural dissertations, advice from farmer's almanacs: "Before you start working the soil, with the aim of making your work as easy as possible, first circle around the plow while holding a flashlight in your hands, some bread, and some oats..."

OCTAVE: Yes, yes, the way I always do...

GOSSIP B: And, speaking of jet lag, I know this woman who every time I meet her all she talks about is elephants...

GOSSIP A: Friend of yours?

GOSSIP B: I should say not!

GOSSIP A: Then why does she talk to you about elephants?

MATHIEU: I see a scrap of newspaper on the sidewalk, I stop and read it all, word by word, line by line until I get to the torn edge...

OCTAVE: Stooping down?

MATHIEU: No, no, standing up.

OCTAVE: What about the other side of the page?

MATHIEU: I count it among my losses.

OCTAVE: Doesn't it make you thirsty, all that reading?

MATHIEU: Good God yes! You're absolutely right!

OCTAVE: Your spread here is magnificent...

MATHIEU: Oh, you think so? And yet if you only knew what just happened to me...

They go off.

GOSSIP A: What does it mean? This dream I have every night, that I'm looking for a bed to sleep in... ? Uh oh, watch out, here come those two old geezers. Quick, let's get out of here!

The Gossips exit.

10

The Geezers enter. One of them is holding a tray filled with dishes and drinks. The other holds a parasol. Apparently they're heading for the tree-trunk, to sit down.

MARCEL: First they prolong our lives and then they blame us for it!

GASTON: Prolong our lives! Prolong our lives! What's it mean to prolong the life of an eighty-year-old man? Now, at forty, that's where they should start prolonging lives! Right on the cusp of your fortieth year for ten years straight on, now you're talking progress! But at our age? What's the use? We don't walk, we shuffle, we eat only soft food, hear only dimly, and we don't even want to bathe anymore. And women? Those lovely, hairbrained, wanton sluts, the piss-ant snivelers...

MARCEL: Piffling drivelers is more like it...

GASTON: Whatever!... With their big bright strawberry mouths and cruel bouncing buns, lemme tell ya, they're systematically turning their backs on us. Have you noticed? Women these days? We only see them from the rear!

MARCEL: That's 'cause they walk faster and get ahead of us!

GASTON: Yeah, well, they've been trying to get ahead of us for years!

MARCEL: Personally, if they gave me ten more good years, I wouldn't say no!

GASTON: Good God what on earth for?

MARCEL: Listen, between the ages of twenty-five and forty-five, I fathered two children, planted three birch and two apple trees, built a house, learned Spanish, designed my best friend's garden, and made love a thousand times, made love in winter right in the snow...

GASTON: Love, oh frostbitten love...

MARCEL: Made love every other which way you goddamn please. Bought three cars, one brand spanking new Renault and three used. And guess what: the Renée stunk!

GASTON: Ren*ée* ? What's this? Back seat flashback?

MARCEL: I said Ren*ault.* Just watch what you... hear. Hear me? Read Proust, too. Marcel, that is, same name as me.

GASTON: The whole enchilada?

MARCEL: And, I perfected a three-day cure of the common cold, and made my company a pile of dough on it...

GASTON: *What?!* You were in public education!

MARCEL: Then left that for a lumber company. Cheated on my wife only four times in my life—in body, that is, never with my heart.

GASTON: Hmm, just where is it you locate your heart?

MARCEL: Visited Egypt, and even took part in archaeological digs. Had two dogs, each one dumber'n the other. And, I wrote articles...

Gilbert runs on stage. Same attitude as before.

GILBERT: Has anyone seen my mother?

GASTON: No. Have you seen mine?

Gilbert runs off.

MARCEL: In-depth articles for the union trade paper.

GASTON: Yeah, so?

MARCEL: So, if I could do all that in the space of twenty years...

GASTON: Listen you poor dumb coot, you couldn't sell Mickey Mouse at the door of a nursery school, today!

MARCEL: Seems to me, pal, sometimes, old age isn't much agreein' with you...

GASTON: Old age doesn't agree with anyone...

> *The bride and groom pass by on the run. He catches her and kisses her at length. The bride finally pulls loose and the chase is on once again.*

MARCEL: Damn, that was good... even if it didn't work... sure was good! What I hate is that sometimes, I lose my balance!

GASTON: Me too. Lose mine, too.

MARCEL: I cannot understand why they haven't invented the portable banister yet.

GASTON: The portable... banister.

MARCEL: Yeah, banister. You remember what a banister is, don't you?

GASTON: And... uh... you'd carry it around with you.

MARCEL: Of course.

GASTON: What for?

MARCEL: To hang on to, dumb one!

GASTON: And the banister would... hold up how, exactly?

MARCEL: Ah, well, you see now that's the whole point of the invention, isn't it. Listen, if I knew how to make it hold up in the air, I'd have perfected it a long time ago. They'll find a way, someday. Hell, they've done better. They'll unfold it, lay it down right next to you and... there you go!

GASTON: And just who's gonna use this contraption?

MARCEL: Who? Us, that's who... And children. And the sick. And the drunk. The blind. Expectant mothers. People with casts! Come on! No more crutches! Give me my banister!

> *He mimes a man holding on to a banister as he walks, chuckling to himself.*

11

And now the entire group gathers to dance, accompanied by musicians: violins, accordions... And suddenly the Hungry Woman appears. She will address the entire group, but nobody pays much mind.

HUNGRY WOMAN: Love me... Please love me... You can see how bad things are with me... Stop, just for a second... Look how short life is, how little, how tiny, no sooner do you get here than it's already too late... It's now or never! I'm kindhearted... You can lean on me, cling to my hair, my calves, I'm top quality!... My health is unblemished! I can open doors, no problem there. I put away my things at night, before going to bed. I don't talk in my sleep. I walk downstairs without looking at my feet. I wear rayon shirts, like silk, but cheaper. I can draw dogs sitting down and gazing into the distance. But I can do without wearing a nightshirt... I've taken up piano again. Right now, I'm on "Largo" by Dvorak. *(She plays a little on an imaginary piano and we hear it... The wedding crowd stops and listens, as if at a concert.)* It's a little long, but so beautiful! *(As soon as she addresses the crowd, they resume their dancing.)* I don't cry. I almost never cry. That's one of my best features. I am a golden opportunity. You might even say, I'm a unique opportunity. But put aside all the dividends and profits and losses and obligations and all the hairsplitting. Put all that aside, and just love me! Just turn your head a little this way. That'll do for a good start. I cut my own hair. I give a good massage. So quick, love me. Quick, quick. Because quick, the time it takes to say it is already in the past. Love me, you won't regret it. I am completely ready to be the happy wife of a man who wants to be happy.

But the wedding crowd continues to dance, without worrying about the Hungry Woman.

MATHIEU: When I went to New York to find you I was crazy about you.

AMERICAN WOMAN: I was crazy, too. Crazy to follow you.

MATHIEU: You're the one who called me.

AMERICAN WOMAN: Who forced you to believe me?

MATHIEU: If only you knew what's happening to me...

AMERICAN WOMAN: I'm not interested.

MATHIEU: What does interest you?

AMERICAN WOMAN: Strange men and their thighs...

MATHIEU: Our only good moments are when we fight...

AMERICAN WOMAN: And not even! Your poundings are starting to lose their punch...

They go off, dancing together. First Girl and Michel:

FIRST GIRL: You dance, like, say forty years ago!

MICHEL: Meaning?

FIRST GIRL: Meaning, your style is the Inflated Crotch!

MICHEL: *(disconcerted)* And you... your style... ?

FIRST GIRL: Me, I dance to dance. *(She lets him go and dances alone, looking at him.)* And you know? Really and truly? I feel a lot less dumb than in your virile arms!

She rejoins the crowd. He remains a little hesitant and while he prepares to rejoin Octave, he is prevented from doing so by the Mother-Son couple, dancing together.

SON: If I told ya once I told ya a hundred times, Mama! To comprehend it you'd have crawl through the windowpane!

They go off. Michel finally rejoins Octave.

MICHEL: And? Your "Woman of Breathtaking-Beauty"?

OCTAVE: It was an insanely hot day. She's taking a nap and gives me the day off. The house is huge... In the barn I discover some notebooks which, like mine, recount the acts and sayings of... (He stops.)

MICHEL: By the way, what *was* her name, anyway?

OCTAVE: I can't reveal it... Everyone in the world has heard of her...

MICHEL: All of a sudden you're pale.

OCTAVE: Each notebook—and there were six of them—is written in a different hand. And each one stops abruptly, right in the middle of a sentence. Sometimes, even, the pen has skidded to a halt admist a clot of inkstains...

MICHEL: You got out of there just in time.

OCTAVE: You think I would've met the same fate?

MICHEL: Let's dance!

OCTAVE: Together?

MICHEL: Why, ashamed of me?

OCTAVE: No...

> So Michel makes up an oriental dance in which two men dance face to face without touching. Then they go off, while Gilbert appears, dancing with the Second Girl.

GILBERT: Later on, I'll get married to you...

SECOND GIRL: If I say so.

GILBERT: I'll make you a baby. I know how, too. I've seen it in the movies...

They go off. The two Gossips appear, dancing together.

GOSSIP A: Before that, I used to go and spend my vacation there...

GOSSIP B: Did you get tired of it?

GOSSIP A: For some time now, the doors of the barns and the houses have been opening all by themselves.

GOSSIP B: Too many drafts?

GOSSIP A: You install locks, then padlocks, then chains, then steel bars across the doors... No use. Softly, without a sound, the doors open...

GOSSIP B: What is it, black magic?

GOSSIP A: Out in the snow, in the blazing sun, over the dead leaves of autumn, doors will simply open, just like that, wide open...

GOSSIP B: And the people who live there... ?

GOSSIP A: Many villagers weep... many go away, leaving houses behind them in a high wind... Some leave in the middle of a meal... and you can still see the table set and a napkin draped over the back of a chair...

GOSSIP B: Personally, I hate doors... so!

GOSSIP A: Sometimes the cat stays behind... you can see him there... the house is all his.

GOSSIP B: I have said it many and many a time: "We ain't seen nothin' yet!"

They go off, dancing.

12

A young man leaps out of the group to address them all.

VINCENT: Stop! Stop! All, of you, you see that beautiful woman there who's smiling all the time and never suffers? Take a good long look at her underneath her stylish hat...

HIS WIFE: Vincent... please... stop it... will you? What's gotten into you?

VINCENT: Take a good look at her because she is *the* Cold-Hearted Woman in person! She loves to sit in off-beat cafés, in the dark of back rooms where the shining gold of lager mixes with the light of advertisers' ashtrays.... Take a good look at her, friends, but don't smile at her. Don't ever smile at her!

HIS WIFE: Vincent... you're crazy...

MAN: The guy's drunk!

WOMAN: It's the heat out here!

VINCENT: Come out here in the light and show yourself. Come out of your shell!

> *A woman steps forward beautiful, calm. She is wearing a summer hat which is a milliner's glory. She faces without fear or defiance the looks from the crowd.*

WOMAN: On an occasion like this, one should control oneself...

VINCENT: Don't smile at her. For if she returns your smile, you're a goner. She'll go away. She'll leave your arms as soon as she's happy. She always goes away at the end of the story.

HIS WIFE: Vincent, let's go... you're not well!...

> *Vincent pushes his wife away and addresses the woman in the hat:*

VINCENT: Ten years already separate you from now. But I would've recognized you with leprosy and buried under a dung-heap! Thirty years from now I would've recognized you through poverty, total destitution, bald and stinking and filthy and without a hat!

WOMAN: Somebody do something, quick! Before something happens!

VINCENT: I was young, not even twenty. I wanted to become the greatest painter of my generation. Picasso came first, then there was me. I was crazy in those days, I was drunk, delirious, happy, and desperate. My mood changed daily. I had fire in my body, and at night I could hear my own blood beat. I used to dream I fed on my tubes of paint...

HIS WIFE: No one cares here, Vincent.

MAN: Another artist. They're all crazy!

VINCENT: I wanted to paint plaster grey-skies filled with skin-less women...

MAN: Oh yeah, no doubt about it, this guy's insane...

ANOTHER: Which doesn't mean anything!

A THIRD: Painting like that? No thanks...

VINCENT: One morning...

WOMAN: Here he goes...

VINCENT: It was the morning of the Cold-Hearted Woman. I walked into my favorite café. It was going to be a sunny day! I ordered a coffee. Then I raised my head and sitting there right in front of me, was she. She gave me a smile...

WOMAN: It happens to everybody!

VINCENT: She was wearing a black velvet hat, with a big white rose.

MAN: This is some kinda routine for weddings and banquets?

VINCENT: She stayed in my arms, stayed in my bed, for a year. I painted like a madman. Larger and larger canvases. I loved her like a madman. She'd laugh. She'd laugh at night and in the mornings too. She was the happy woman. A year later to the day, on the 15th of November, she left. Gathered up her blouses, her hats, and left without a word. Without a scribble. So if you feel like it, go ahead: spit right in her face!

> *Vincent's wife falls into a faint. People rush to her and carry her away.*

MAN: There you go. He's even deeper into it now...

WOMAN: What a story. Completely devoid of interest.

MAN: One thing's true. She does have a beautiful hat!

> *As the crowd disperses, a small round table is revealed in the distance, where two people are sitting, completely motionless.*

MAN: Who's that?

WOMAN: The bride's parents.

MAN: Why aren't they dancing?

WOMAN: Dancing? They aren't even *moving*...

MAN: What's the matter with them?

WOMAN: They're bored...

MAN: Why?

WOMAN: Because they're marrying off their daughter.

MAN: But it's a celebration!

WOMAN: Do you have a daughter?

MAN: No!

WOMAN: Well there you go.

>*They go off.*

13

The three Girls return.

FIRST GIRL: The sight of a marriage in white, I mean it's right in your face...

SECOND GIRL: What a nauseating exhibition of virginity at the moment of sacrifice...

THIRD GIRL: Personally? I think people ought to get married in the nude. That way, all the fat pukes at the wedding can have their fantasies at their fingertips...

SECOND GIRL: I'm never getting married. Makes me think of bullfights...

FIRST GIRL: How come my father went all the way to America to get my mother?

THIRD GIRL: To have you...

FIRST GIRL: They never stop fighting...

SECOND GIRL: Mine fight too.

FIRST GIRL: The other night? I heard the blows from the other end of the house... My mother was screaming... and crying like a little girl... I kept saying to myself: "Oh shit, tomorrow's Sunday and I gotta see her at breakfast with her eyes black and blue and her face bashed to a pulp... What am I gonna do?"

THIRD GIRL: Didn't she come down?

FIRST GIRL: She came down the next day in a magnificent, new dressing-gown, beautiful, calm, radiant. Now I don't like her as much as I used to...

SECOND GIRL: Mine have always screamed and shouted and

fought. I always hide under the covers 'cause when I hear my mom's screams, I'm afraid the neighbors are gonna come... When she gets really miserable? she comes into my room and crawls into my bed, she cries into my arms and all over my t-shirt!

THIRD GIRL: What do you say?

SECOND GIRL: I tell her: "Leave him. Let's just get outta here. You have a skill. We don't need him. Finally, we'll have some peace and quiet, the two of us together. I'll protect you." One night, I even told her I'd do all the cooking.

THIRD GIRL: What does she say?

SECOND GIRL: As soon as she's in my arms, she sleeps like a baby. As for me, it's another sleepless night.

THIRD GIRL: Battered moms are like kids...

SECOND GIRL: Even un-battered they're like kids.

THIRD GIRL: So, like, why do they get married?

FIRST GIRL: So they can have daughters like us.

SECOND GIRL: Well, I am never going to get married, and that's final.

FIRST GIRL: You got that right. What do you say, all of us, let's all marry each other!

SECOND GIRL: What about home?

THIRD GIRL: Hey, I live alone.

FIRST GIRL: Huh? How's that?

THIRD GIRL: My father's a lawyer, my mother's a judge, and they don't have enough time for me between work, parties, conventions, bridge, you get the picture. So like they bought me this studio, and they send me a check, every week. I get by.

SECOND GIRL: Wow, I like that idea.

FIRST GIRL: Isn't it hard?

THIRD GIRL: It's like I have my radio... some pals... my cat... and I'm not the only one living like this, either. Eveline? Her parents got a divorce and decided it was better not to kill themselves in the custody battle... And Jacqueline, the red-head with the great big eyes? Well, she ran away one time, so to spare themselves the pain of looking for her again, they bought her a room on the other side of town... They say like in the old days, when a girl wanted to run away, the whole family got out their shotguns. Nowadays, they buy her luggage... So, now, at least, we don't need to leave Home Sweet Home full of tears and a lot of sweet sorrow.

SECOND GIRL: Is it true that the only time your dad doesn't have a book in hand is when he's beating your mom?

FIRST GIRL: I used to always see him with his arms full of brochures he'd read as he walked along. He goes to the bathroom with two books, one under his arm, and the other in his hand which he devours without looking up.

SECOND GIRL: How's he manage to pee?

FIRST GIRL: Many are the man and woman who have tried to figure that one out...

THIRD GIRL: My cousin told me once, and this was at a wedding almost as crummy as this one, that the bride ran off with the best man.

SECOND GIRL: Alas, things like that only happen once!

THIRD GIRL: Hey! Let me show some of my latest magic...

And she starts to perform some neat tricks for the two other Girls.

14

Benedicte enters drunk and desperate, talking about herself.

BENEDICTE: Poor girl, lives all alone in a big old bed full of snow
   and jagged rocks,
   she walks through streets where the lights flicker out,
   eats fruit that explodes into glass shards,
   her skirts fall away and her nudity's paraded before streetwalkers
   at night she screams,
   in the morning she's attacked by snakes and daggers...
   he did the right thing to leave, you did the right thing.
   Look at the woman you once loved so much,
   your one and only, the woman you cried for, the woman you'd
   die for,
   look at her, she who was your glory and your fate,
   the girl you carried through tempests in your arms,
   through fires,
   just look at her, look at her now,
   look how ugly she is, look at her charred and stinking flesh,
   her cloven feet, her scabby thighs,
   her fingernails bitten to the quick,
   her pickled innards,
   her sex sewn tight forever.
   You did the right thing to leave, my love, because she's mean,
   she's ravenous, she's odious, and sad oh, so sad!
   If only you knew how sad, sadder than a stray dog
   lost in a storm,
   sadder than a mist over the ocean
   in the still of a night when a father has died
   without a word...
   it's gone forever... the love of a life... which transformed the world
   gone forever...

Angela enters.

ANGELA: Benedicte... oh my dear Benedicte...

BENEDICTE: Things fall apart... why not me too...

ANGELA: We'll pick you up, put you back together.

BENEDICTE: Look how fat I've gotten.

ANGELA: I see fat ladies all over, wearing their belts high up on their bellies, and guess what—they're all laughing.

BENEDICTE: All I've got is a belly full of tears ... *(She cries.)*

ANGELA: That's it, go ahead and cry... since your tears aren't over yet...

BENEDICTE: I prefer my terror to God himself standing right in front of me. And I prefer my own hell of a hundred thousand foul mouths, because that's where I live with *him*. He could disappear into the Amazon jungle and I'd still be living with him, with screams and questions and all, but still "with him"... he doesn't know it, poor guy...

ANGELA: He knows.

BENEDICTE: How's that?

ANGELA: For men who leave, there's always a lingering eye in the back of their minds, following them...

BENEDICTE: For my wedding... did I have a bouquet of fresh flowers?

ANGELA: Freesia, roses, and lilacs...

BENEDICTE: Yes... you remember, don't you? Was it a nice day?

ANGELA: Just like today.

BENEDICTE: Oh yes... yes... a beautiful day... when he slipped the ring on my finger, his eyes were filled with tears...

ANGELA: Men cry once in a lifetime...

BENEDICTE: Well, I've cried everywhere. In streets, buses, elevators, closets, airplanes, in my coffee, in oceans, in chests of drawers, and into telephones. *(She laughs.)* I can't figure out how mine still works!... *(Pause.)* You know what was hardest of all? Two pillows on the bed. And the napkin ring, with his name on it... Is he here?

ANGELA: I haven't seen him.

BENEDICTE: Alone, or with someone?

ANGELA: I haven't seen him.

BENEDICTE: I can hear him laughing in the crowd...

ANGELA: No, no.

BENEDICTE: I have something in my purse... It makes me want to throw up... He doesn't have the right to look at me... You tell him that...

ANGELA: He's not here.

BENEDICTE: Go tell him it's not me... who's here!... *(She bursts out laughing.)* ... which is why my purse is so heavy...

ANGELA: Okay, so now I'll ask. What's in the purse?

BENEDICTE: Four months after he left, I found three rolls of film in a drawer... each with thirty-six exposures...

ANGELA: Give'em here.

BENEDICTE: What if I find out something even more horrible?—I know it's all over, it's all ruined... I know that. But what if a monster were to come up and spit horrors in my face?...

ANGELA: We'd kick his head in.

BENEDICTE: I think I'm going to throw up...

ANGELA: Come on... Give me the purse...

Angela leads her away.

The three Girls, who had stayed at a distance:

FIRST GIRL: If you wanted, you could be a pickpocket.

THIRD GIRL: I already tried...

FIRST GIRL: And?

THIRD GIRL: I spent the night in jail.

SECOND GIRL: And? So?

THIRD GIRL: Now I'm taking courses.

They go off.

15

Vincent is taking photos of the receding Girls, the tree, a leaf on the ground, etc. Marie enters, walking slowly. She's used to being alone.

VINCENT: Hey, Marie, my lovely... did they leave you all by yourself?

MARIE: I left myself all by myself.

VINCENT: Well, I'm glad you came, anyway... Everyone's happy to see you again. *(Pause.)* How are you doing?

She answers with a shrug and a smile.

VINCENT: Holding up alright?

MARIE: Well, hanging in there. Time drags on and on... but I'm hanging in there.

VINCENT: And finances?

MARIE: I'm working at home.

VINCENT: And you're making ends meet?

MARIE: Life's a little easier in the country.

VINCENT: Have you been able to see him?

MARIE: Last November I did... the third visit in eight years...

VINCENT: How is he?

MARIE: His teeth are almost all gone, and he's lost all his hair.

VINCENT: Did you stay down there?

MARIE: Three days...

VINCENT: How are his spirits?

MARIE: Well, they still won't give him paper and pen. He tells me he's memorizing a book which he'll end up getting out someday...

VINCENT: Don't they let him write to you?

MARIE: One letter a month. One page only. His writing's so tiny it takes me days to make it all out. Which is good. Keeps me busy. *(She laughs.)* We have our own secret code for the love stuff.

VINCENT: You did the right thing to come, Marie... it took some guts... but doesn't this upset you just a little?

MARIE: What?

VINCENT: This crowd... all these emotional tugs...

MARIE: Rest assured: I don't understand all of it.

VINCENT: I was pretty ridiculous while ago, huh?

MARIE: You'd told me about that woman... She's beautiful, isn't she: an angel in a hat.

VINCENT: Well, we're all mad... They'll probably find the bride swinging from this tree in the morning...

MARIE: Hush that talk.

VINCENT: But tell me, Marie... What do you do down there, all by yourself?

MARIE: I get up every day at six, make my coffee, sit down and drink it at the end of the table by the window, where, on a nice day you can see the hillside. I think about him, down there. Down in his hole. When it's time for the guards to toss him a piece of bread. After that... I try to imagine what's happening in other houses. A man lights a fire in his fireplace. Another guy is making hot chocolate for his pregnant wife. Schoolchildren are eating their toast. Lots of dogs, happy 'cause the house is finally waking up... A man wonders how he's going to sit on his tractor, with that boil on his ass. A young girl is waiting for the mail to come. Not for the mail itself, but for the mailman. The owner of the newsstand who is raising his iron window gates still doesn't know that in the newspapers they publish the list of pardoned criminals.

VINCENT: Someday it'll be Jacques's turn.

MARIE: I doubt it. He'd have to renounce his principles, and approve of tyranny. He's already refused twice, I suppose he'll refuse again...

VINCENT: Did you meet any of the others?

MARIE: Yes. They'll testify to the torture and humiliation... But he, he won't get out.

VINCENT: But... what about *you*, Marie?... You!

MARIE: I haven't made love in eight years... I don't even remember when...

VINCENT: By all means, don't forget *him*, but... for heaven's sake do something for your*self!*

MARIE: A shy young girl is sitting on a bench. It's Spring. The mimosas are in bloom. A young man sitting next to her puts his hand on the girl's right knee. The girl pretends to be interested in the white wisp of cloud left by a jet plane... he'd really like to put his hand between her thighs... but who knows? Yes?... He does it. And I squeezed my thighs together, pinioning his hand for life... The white wisp from the jet vanished... Even then, he was already militant... We were both seventeen years old... (*Silence.*) What are you painting these days?

VINCENT: Oh, my lettuce heads.

MARIE: Ah, yes, your lettuce.

VINCENT: Heads of lettuce dangling by a string... and yet you can see, in all that frizzy detail, the heart of the thing. Get it?... *(He laughs sadly.)* The lettuce is staring you right in the eye...

MARIE: Stay with me a little.... I'm going to leave quietly... but all of a sudden I feel a bit awkward...

VINCENT: How are the girls?

MARIE: Beautiful. I talk to them about him, and they listen, but not as well as... They're all busy planning ski trips with their buddies... *(Pause.)* Up until now, they've never been bothered by their family name... Everyone in our little town has been so kind to us... But in a few years... they won't be from this country anymore... where they were born...

    They exit.

16

Octave and Mathieu return, the latter with a plate on top of his books.

MATHIEU: Good Lord, do you have any idea what's happening to me?

> *Octave points to his full mouth; he can't talk. Gilbert flies by on the run, and clumsily bumps into them, spilling champagne.*

It doesn't leave a stain, anyway, you little shit!

OCTAVE: Who's that?

MATHIEU: Little bastard has no father! You know what just happened to me? Last night I was in the bookstore where I often stop on...

OCTAVE: Last night, an unseasonable fog drifted in, reeking of mucilage...

MATHIEU: I pick up a book at random. It's called: *A Life Like Any Other.* And I start to flip through it, reading here and there... Slowly my chest begins to tighten...

> *Octave is choking on his food... He's coughing frantically.*

MATHIEU: *(pounding Octave on the back)* This book tells the story of my life right down to the last detail.

OCTAVE: *(still coughing)* Didn't hear you...

MATHIEU: You alright? *(Octave nods yes... Mathieu waits till he catches his breath.)* The book tells the story of my life right down to the last detail.

OCTAVE: Oh, I suppose we all find ourselves in a novel at one time or another. Every one of us little Bovarys has found his basket of apricots, at one time or another.

MATHIEU: I'm not talking about apricots! Sure, all lives resemble each other: we're born, we break down, we die, sure... It's the details which differentiate us. For example, at the moment I was born, a storm uprooted an oak tree in our backyard. My mother delivered me into this world amidst the noise of falling timber. Trivial, you may say. But it's in the book! During my first communion, I was in love with a little girl, during the ceremony I turned around to give her a smile and I set fire to the robe of a communicant in front of me. You can imagine the panic, with firemen inside the church! And the slap in the face! Right? It's all right there in the book. Everything, down to the tiniest detail, it's all contained in the book. Events. Conversations. Delicate bowels. Friendships... mistakes... hidden motivations... favorite drinks.

OCTAVE: Am I in it?

MATHIEU: I was in love with a little girl with a hunchback. Not exactly common; nevertheless, there it is. And, everything I've read!

OCTAVE: Everything you've read? Damn... I hope they included a dictionary.

MATHIEU: The first time I kissed the woman who was to be my wife, I was so ecstatic, so transported, I lost my balance and nearly dragged us both onto the rails in front of an oncoming train. And one day as I was putting a necklace around my mother's neck, I bit her... no one else ever knew that!

OCTAVE: Why did you bite her?

MATHIEU: They explain it all in the book. My deepest secrets are revealed in it...

OCTAVE: And what do they say about me?

MATHIEU: You know that my wife went back to America a week after we got married...

OCTAVE: I didn't...

MATHIEU: Well, she did, and the whole world knew about it.

OCTAVE: Okay...

MATHIEU: After she left, to avoid any potential conflicts with my mother, who was living with us, over the management of the house, I hired a little maid, named Angela... straight off the farm.

OCTAVE: Ah yes, the one dressed in burgundy?

MATHIEU: Not burgundy, violet. Anyway, four years later, my wife wrote me—there were some mistakes in her letter, and the book notes them—begging me to come get her in New York... I never should have gone... but that's a whole other story...

OCTAVE: I'm very curious to know why you bit your mother.

MATHIEU: Buy the book and read it.

> *Angela enters, as a young girl. The following takes place with Octave as spectator.*

ANGELA: You called me, Monsieur?

MATHIEU: Angela, have you ever been to New York?

ANGELA: I was born down in the Valley.

MATHIEU: Yes, of course, Angela... With your permission, I'd like to take you there... No, no... don't worry... my intentions are completely honorable... Now, now, let's stay calm, both of us... It's just that... one should never stir up the gods hovering over our heads, with their hands in their pockets... *(Aside, to Octave)* I can't imagine where I came up with that phrase—as pretentious as it was ridiculous! *(Turning back to Angela)* If you want... I bought you a ticket... we're supposed to leave tomorrow... but it can be very very cold over there... so I bought you a 100% pure wool overcoat and a little green hat, also pure wool. What do you say?

ANGELA: Thank you very much, Monsieur... But I don't quite understand...

MATHIEU: It's just that something wonderful has happened to me... I'm completely overwhelmed by it... I just have to have someone to talk to about it, otherwise I'll burst... In the plane, if I fall asleep, you wake me up... so that I'll know this isn't all a dream... *(He starts to cry.)*

ANGELA: I understand... Go ahead and cry, Monsieur... I really think these tears will never come back to haunt you...

MATHIEU: *(to Octave, aside)* Not bad for a girl from the Valley, eh?

ANGELA: And as soon as Monsieur falls asleep, I'm to wake him up?

Angela fades away. Mathieu and Octave are together again.

OCTAVE: How in the world does somebody as young as she is get away with dressing in burgundy!

MATHIEU: Violet. And that scene? It's all in the book, word for word!

OCTAVE: You must find the author.

MATHIEU: Published anonymously.

OCTAVE: Can they do that?

MATHIEU: Oh yeah. Instead of the author's name on the title: three little stars.

OCTAVE: Well when was it published?

MATHIEU: It went on sale yesterday.

OCTAVE: And I really am in it?

MATHIEU: Yes, goddammit, I've told you a million times!

OCTAVE: But tell me now, what really is the problem here?... It's actually rather nice to be able to hold your whole life in your hands. And apart from those close to you... who will know it's you?

MATHIEU: I haven't told you all of it. On the very last page of the book... the author writes that I buy a book which tells the story of my life...

OCTAVE: Mm... I like it.

MATHIEU: Don't you think that's a sign that my life ends there...?

OCTAVE: Ah, but wait for volume two!

17

The three Girls pass by, arms around their waists. They do a little dance, in their way. Next come the two Old Geezers. The Girls disappear. Mathieu and Octave disappear in turn.

MARCEL: *(staring off at the girls)* God *damn* could I ever get it up in my day... And I mean *up!* I mean a helluva lot higher up than horizontal!

GASTON: Oh come on, now, old man... just keep it plain and simple!

MARCEL: I really would like to know how many I've had in life... hard-ons, that is... just no telling... may as well count the stars in the sky...

GASTON: Even stars flicker out.

MARCEL: Hell, I still get it up...

GASTON: In your dreams, you old coot...

MARCEL: I beg your pardon. The sun rises. I can feel it cooking up something through the window blinds. I hear the news man rolling up his window guards, and me, without getting up from bed, I get up my own way...

GASTON: Hey, tell it to the National Academy of Science!

MARCEL: I see guys like us all the time, strutting around with a pretty girl on their arm.

GASTON: Sure. Their nieces... or maybe you mean very *rich* old guys.

MARCEL: It's true, the very rich and old are a lot less old than the poor are at the same age... *(Silence.)* How did we manage it, anyway?

GASTON: Manage what?

MARCEL: Manage to make it all the way to this age.

GASTON: Well, from Mondays through Saturdays through...

MARCEL: No, but I mean what else?

GASTON: And from one Saturday on to the next...

MARCEL: Uh-uh... No, there's some kind of mystery here in this survival success. What we had in us was a whole network of diverse desires which gave out a heat... a power... to our lives. The heat of molten metal!

GASTON: Whoa, boy, calm down now... do you really...

MARCEL: Really now, just remember: In other ages we were Chieftains, the Pillars of the Temples, the Faces Carved in the Rock.

Gaston laughs sardonically.

People would form alliances with us, offer us their allegiance. Ask *us* the necessary questions. Our very shadows would be sought. No one would dare embark on an adventure without first consulting us... Divines would project our futures... A little different, I'd say, than coasting from one Saturday to the next!

GASTON: All so that nowadays we're nothing but a couple of broken down old farts, that everybody wants to be rid of once and for all.

MARCEL: Hey, you got a little piece of old age stuck up your craw, buddy? *(Silence.)* Were you good looking, once?

GASTON: Why, can't you tell?

MARCEL: Sure can. Only thing is, winter doesn't tell the whole story of summer.

GASTON: Well, I was very good looking. I always wore silk ties, had a good sense of humor. Every Sunday I'd get up at the crack of dawn and jog along the edge of the woods...

MARCEL: And now you've got knees as shaky as mine.

GASTON: I loved money and love women, women with lots of make up!

Passing by with their arms entwined, are Romeo and Juliet.

JULIET: Romeo, Romeo, forget all these nightingales and larks and ladders... Now's the time to love me as I love you, because you are the very first love of my life and that's all that matters for the rest of time. You must love me as hard as you can. That's all, that's all you have to do.

ROMEO: What about our parents, Juliet?

JULIET: What parents? Romeo, it's too lovely a day not to be caressed.

ROMEO: You're right, Juliet. Embrace me!

They run away.

MARCEL: Hey, that was mighty good... even if it had to go wrong... damn good.

GASTON: What *isn't* going to go wrong is what they're in the process of inventing.

MARCEL: Oh? What's that?

GASTON: My son is working on a project with the Department of Overpopulation. They're going to build a city under the sea.

MARCEL: What, to study the ocean?

GASTON: No, for us.

MARCEL: I'm not studying any ocean, not at my age.

GASTON: Here's the thing. If you want to empty the cities of all the old folks who hang around in the streets and cafes and sit on the choicest park benches and overburden the hospitals and live in apartments that are too big for them, old folks who bring in no money for the State and who lounge around doing nothing and are totally unproductive, well, then it's true that from an ethical as well as a sociological point of view, the submarine city is a wonderful solution...

MARCEL: Maybe, but count me out.

GASTON: Don't worry, nobody'll ask your permission!

MARCEL: Your son must be a real funny guy!

GASTON: Real cities under the ocean, with avenues bordered by plastic palm-trees, shops, movies, hospitals of course, free shuffleboard, public toilets, even swimming pools... *(He laughs.)*

MARCEL: And just... us?

GASTON: Just us. With our nurses and air-conditioning.

MARCEL: I don't believe it...

The two Gossips pass by.

GOSSIP A: He's so attached to that woman that whenever he can't find her, he thinks *he's* the one who forgot to come.

GOSSIP B: I understand perfectly.

They sit down on the tree trunk.

MARCEL: This is some kind of a joke... Let whoever wants to, go. Not me... And the sun? What about the sun?

GASTON: Why not the moon?

MARCEL: You always have been a grade-A bullshitter.

GASTON: Someday you'll get a form letter telling you to pack your bags.

MARCEL: What about my cat? She *hates* the water.

GASTON: Every now and then, great big shiny elevators playing old waltzes will bring you your terrestrial grandchildren...

MARCEL: I'm going home.

GASTON: So soon?

MARCEL: Got to get a shot from my nurse.

GASTON: A young one!... meaning maybe another one of your famous "horizontals"...

MARCEL: So what are we supposed to see out the windows?

GASTON: Water. Water, waves, a few storms, some seaweed... and water.

MARCEL: Forget old folks homes! You're talking aquariums here!

He moves away slowly. The two Gossips get up.

GOSSIP A: Poor thing... she was a great singer in her own country. Then she got in with the boat-people. Raped seven times, thrown to the sharks, fished out again, and now she lives here, and works in an office. On her way to work on the subway she does knitting. Knits these tiny little wool squares which she tacks together for quilts. Poor thing. Can you imagine?... She was a *singer!*...

GOSSIP B: Hmm. Those quilts... how much does she sell them for?

They go off.

18

The wedding party, in a snake dance, carries away Marcel. Vincent comes to snatch away the Woman in the Hat from the dance line.

VINCENT: You were ashamed of me back there.

AGNES: No, not at all. I liked your outburst a lot, in fact. Excellent theater...

VINCENT: So. Now that time has waved its magic wand, tell me: why *did* you smile at me in that café?

AGNES: You really want to know?

VINCENT: Is it painful? *(Pause.)*

AGNES: That morning, in the courtyard of the hospital, I was waiting for some test results. The doctors weren't very optimistic. I looked at the trees, and said to myself: "When these leaves begin to change, where will I be?" Then I saw a young intern cross the courtyard, his bright blue insignia sewn onto his white shirt. He looked like a teenager. Never again would I feel a man's lips pressed against mine. I wished lightning would strike me dead on the spot. But, as you recall, it was an exceptionally sunny summer day. I made a bet with myself: if the results were negative, I'd give a year of my life to the first man who looked at me. One year wasn't very expensive... not for a whole life in return...

VINCENT: So, you betrayed me from the very first glance.

AGNES: As I left the hospital I walked with my eyes lowered. I stepped into that unfamiliar café with my eyes on the ground. There were other men there; I could hear their voices. But it was you to whom I gave my joy and gratitude for being alive...

VINCENT: Too bad for that.

AGNES: Not really. We laughed a lot together.

VINCENT: That black velvet hat with the big white rose...

AGNES: Yellow. Yellow rose.

VINCENT: Huh?

AGNES: Do you still paint?

VINCENT: Of course I do. Lettuce! I hang them in restaurants. Customers eat their Romaine without looking at mine... Better that way.

AGNES: Cézanne had his apples... you, you've got your lettuce.

VINCENT: *(not taken in)* You got it...

AGNES: Kiss me... *(He kisses her long and deep.)*It was white.

VINCENT: *(looking at her lovingly)* Agnes, figure out a way, will you?... for me never to see you again... my one and only...

> *Agnes goes away. He remains all alone, wondering why he's there. Should he run after her? But he doesn't budge. Too late... he insists on hurting himself. So he walks over to the tree stump and sits down.*

Three heads of lettuce to the buck... and to round off the day.

19

ANGELA: *(entering)* On the threshold of that house where I was born, I can still see them.
Standing upright, as if for a photograph,
All their clothes are plaid.
My father's mopping his neck with a big handkerchief rolled into a ball.
He looks at me as if I were about to melt.
My little sister has a runny nose—not from crying—just naturally runny.
My mother is holding her belt buckle with both hands.

They say good-bye without opening their mouths.

I don't cry.
I don't look back.
I have just enough time to get to the bus.
The road's on an incline, the gravel crackles beneath my feet.
And already I hear the engine revving up.

Through the window,
I can see our donkey, he's not eating, he just stares into space.
I won't ever see him again, ever.

Won't ever see Whitey, who always gave me her milk without complaint.

Only when the train has slowed down, do I cry.
Because a hen, next to a pond, was drinking by throwing back her head,
like they all do.
She was a red hen drinking all alone,
looking up at the sky.
And I cried and I cried and I cried.

I understood then that I had gone beyond my family to the other side.

To the other side of my years.

When the conductor came by, I noticed he'd forgotten to button a button on his crotch,
Then, my tears stopped all by themselves.
It was already Autumn.
The sun, the trees, and the hens, all had the same color.

I was sixteen.

When I got to town, it was as if I was inside a burning building.

On the run, as usual, Mother and Son enter.

SON: I toldya and I toldya and I toldya, mama! Can't you get it through your thick skull? To find out you'd have to squeeze through a keyhole.

MOTHER: So go ahead. Squeeze through.

SON: It is not possible to squeeze through a keyhole!

MOTHER: Oh! So what's the answer, then, Bobby sweet!

SON: Shit! Shit! Shit! Shit! Shit!...

They exit.

ANGELA: I write to them so rarely. They don't even know why they've lived. The fields where as a little girl I used to bundle up the hay have all gone fallow. Down by the shallows where we used to fish craw dads, the brush is so thick with thorns you can't get even through. All the kids have left home. My brother's a mechanic, my sister's with the post office. My folks don't even look up at the sky to check the weather anymore. They couldn't care less which way the wind's blowing. Now they wonder how come they sowed and plowed and worked the soil so long and hard, and tell me the soil feeds itself... that good, rich earth that never ends. At night my mother and father watch TV. Do they even speak to each other?

Gossip A and Michel pass by.

MICHEL: You are certainly very active for your age.

GOSSIP A: But you don't know how old I am...

MICHEL: True. But you seem a lot less old than I would say you are...

They walk on.

ANGELA: Of course, I think about them... Sitting there in their plain plaid. But little by little... I can't bear to anymore. They're starting to shrink... I see them getting littler and littler. Sometimes they even sit down on a shelf with their legs dangling over, on each side of a sprig of parsley... I can't accept that, you can't just accept seeing your family perched on a shelf like that... It scares me, but toward the end of this summer, I'm going to go see them...

A few wedding guests join Gossip A and Michel. Suddenly Gossip A trips and falls flat on her face. The others rush to her, and help her up.

MAN: *(the one who helped her up)* Did you trip and fall?

MICHEL: Are you alright?

A MAN: What did you slip on?

MICHEL: Nothing.

GOSSIP B: *(to Gossip A)* What on earth did you do?

GOSSIP A: You say that as if I did it on purpose!!

WOMAN: I think we should call a doctor.

GOSSIP A: No, no...

A MAN: Let's have a look at your knee there.

GOSSIP A: *(showing him)* But you know, I didn't have too much to drink... Oh! my stocking...

> *Slowly things quiet down. As Gossip A dusts herself off.*

GOSSIP B: *(to Gossip A)* Have you ever noticed? Women fall down a lot more than men...

GOSSIP A: I have noticed... When we're young we fall into their arms... later on, we fall all alone...

> *The group of guests shows its appreciation of her wit. Then the crowd disperses.*

ANGELA: And two years later, with the country far behind me, after a seven hour flight to a city of glass and steel stretching toward heaven and Monsieur Mathieu in the arms of his beloved American, there I was clutching a fistful of dollars. It was starting to snow. Trying to figure out their value, I take the green bills, one by one, and study them. All of a sudden, there on the face of one of them, I see my name written in red ink: "Angela." "Angela," on an American dollar bill!? With a note below: "To Angela, on rue des Pommes, I still love you and I'm waiting for you!" Signed: "Renaud," followed by an American telephone number. Renaud. Can it be the boy who delivered groceries to Monsieur Mathieu's—sugar and honey and tea and bottled water slung on his left shoulder? We'd hardly said a word to each other. Lots of smiles, but the ice never broken. Here I was in the middle of the miraculous! Over the phone, I say: "It's me, Angela." He gives me an address and a rendezvous. I have this old postcard of that spot in Washington Square, below a sort of Arc de Triomphe. Tough to find, but I manage. There I am, standing right in front him...

Some of the guests pass, talking among themselves. The Weeping Woman finds herself next to Octave.

WEEPING WOMAN: They have nothing left. No water, no electricity, no heat. They have nothing left to eat. And when winter comes they'll burn what's left of their furniture and books... they'll eat their pets...

OCTAVE: Please, I beg of you... not here!... not in the middle of the party... !

WEEPING WOMAN: Where then. *Where?*

OCTAVE: Somewhere else...

WEEPING WOMAN: You see these children disfigured by terror, children sick and weak leaning against the walls of burnt out huts. There's no more hope for the people over there... they're killing themselves. So they don't miss, they stick the barrel in their mouths and pull the trigger...

OCTAVE: Please... please... not here... not now...

WEEPING WOMAN: When then ?

OCTAVE: I don't know... Tomorrow... later... whenever you want!

WEEPING WOMAN: Then we'll all be sleeping on a bed of snakes!

OCTAVE: *(absently)* Whatever you want!

They separate.

20

Angela and Renaud, at some distance from one another. Snow now begins to fall, but only over the two of them. All around them both, the sky remains summery and bright.

RENAUD: There was a snowstorm in New York. The city was deserted. Pigeons lay dead in the snow drifts. And I was running to meet the love of my life, at eighteen... Finally she came... my secret, my stubborn girl... From a distance I spotted her green hat...

ANGELA: I recognized him. Recognized the way he walked. I hadn't forgotten him at all... I was happy already...

RENAUD: She was so little in New York. Nobody could've looked any littler in the New York snow. I could've held her in my hand... which is why she bowled me over... She smiled at me—who knows, maybe even laughed. With that turned up nose... and almond eyes... and already, she was happy! All of a sudden I felt tired. I could easily have lain down in that snow and fallen asleep... she wasn't, after all, so little, nor New York so big!... But there it was, this thing that had come upon us... this thing without a name... and with miracles, everything is determined in advance!

Now they're facing each other, with the snow coming down on them.

RENAUD: So... it's you... Angela?

ANGELA: Of course it's me... who else would I be?

RENAUD: How did you manage to... find me?

ANGELA: When Monsieur Renaud writes his telephone number in America on a dollar bill and Mademoiselle Angela reads a note on it that intrigues her... *(She shows him the dollar bill.)*

RENAUD: Yes... yes... that's my red ink alright.

ANGELA: I don't know about the ink, but it certainly is the words... Couldn't Monsieur Renaud have found a somewhat less... chancy way, of expressing his feelings?

RENAUD: Well, I mean... that is...

ANGELA: Yes...

RENAUD: What I mean is... I sent that dollar bill... in Paris... last year! For Christmas...

ANGELA: In Paris?

RENAUD: That's right.

ANGELA: I never got it...

RENAUD: It must have gotten lost...

ANGELA: *(laughing)* It didn't get lost at all!

> *The Mother and Son pass by on the run, very close. Angela stares at them, amazed.*

In New York?

RENAUD: *(to himself)* It was the snow that did it... and her green wool cap, which was already completely white... *(To Angela)* Are your feet cold?

ANGELA: Not at all. Why?

RENAUD: You seem to be dancing...

ANGELA: It's just the joy, which seems to find me on the tip of my toes... If you wish, you can kiss me... *(And, on the tip of her toes, it is she who kisses him.)*

RENAUD: Even in the cold, your mouth is warm...

Benedicte enters.

BENEDICTE: What did you do with the film?

ANGELA: Leave me alone...

BENEDICTE: You destroyed them, didn't you, just to be mean!

ANGELA: I can't talk to you now. I'm in New York with Renaud. We were just about to get engaged... *(She laughs.)* In the snow!... See you in a bit, Benedicte...

> *Benedicte moves away from the circle of snow, but remains present, listening...*

RENAUD: I'll be back soon.

ANGELA: Promise?

RENAUD: Promise. *(To himself.)* We were already engaged. I was on the edge of a cliff, and I jumped. I'll come back, Angela...

ANGELA: How many dollar bills are there in the world? Billions?

RENAUD: Yeah... billions...

VOICE OFF: Angela!... Come on!... They want to take a picture...

ANGELA: *(pointing to her dollar bill)* I'll take this one over all those billions...

> *And Angela goes off, backpedaling, waving good-bye with her hand as if at a train station, departing on a long trip.*

21

Renaud and Benedicte are strolling together. It's toward the end of the day.

RENAUD: She had that dollar bill framed. It's right at the head of our bed, a little yellow with age...

BENEDICTE: Good. It deserves it...

RENAUD: You know what? Our little Angela in the snow on Washington Square? She was a mistake.

BENEDICTE: You mean, you didn't love her?

RENAUD: How was I to know that two Angelas lived on rue des Pommes? That Christmas night, I was feeling so sad and lonely, I sent my secret love two dollar bills. One of them said I wanted to see her. And the other, which she was supposed to return with her answer. But the Angela I loved never bothered to answer... And the dollar with the red ink, flew away...

BENEDICTE: Flew right into the hands of the wrong Angela, who came to that rendezvous...

RENAUD: Quite a chain of coincidences, I'd say... She had to have left the farm at sixteen... had to come to work on rue des Pommes, from whence Mathieu, in his erotic madness, had to whisk her away to New York and give her a roll of bills which, in her peasant prudence, she had to look at one by one!

BENEDICTE: Was she in love with you, before New York?

RENAUD: *(gestures to indicate he doesn't know.)* And one Angela hid the other. Apparently, the odds were one in three billion that dollar bill get into her hands. I don't even know what a billion is... Have you heard of any bottles tossed into the Pacific washing up at the feet of young maidens on the Adriatic coast, lately?

BENEDICTE: No, but we all believe in it.

RENAUD: You know what? I loved my mistaken Angela as if I had chosen her over all the women in the world. Because she is a jewel...

BENEDICTE: But you ended up leaving your jewel, one day...

RENAUD: Because twelve years later, I found the other one, without even looking for her. All of a sudden my mistake hit me over the head—and in the balls, for that matter. And I had to claw my way back through time and space to find myself intact once more, in front of my old flame...

22

A pack of guests comes up, whence disordered snippets of speech are heard.

A WOMAN: *(to Vincent)* So, you're the guy who paints heads of lettuce?

VINCENT: That's me, the lettuce-head man...

A MAN: This champagne really is rather mediocre...

A WOMAN: I had my cat put to sleep. She'll never be petted again.

ANOTHER WOMAN: Same for me, nobody pets me anymore.

GASTON: Oh, so there you are! How'd it go with the nurse?

MARCEL: What nurse?

A WOMAN: The day I turned thirty I looked in the mirror and I said to myself "you're gonna look just like your grandma... "

THE OTHER: And, so?

WOMAN: That's exactly what happened.

WOMAN IN A HURRY: I'm always on the run. I make lists then I forget them, 'cause I'm always in a hurry and I forget everything. Even my father! I forget his voice. I forget his eyes. I can't even picture him anymore. *(She starts to cry.)*

A MAN: Can you imagine? There she is, watching TV, and she sees two cops dragging her dad away!

A YOUNG MAN: In my building, there's this young girl learning to play the piano. Well every time she sits down to play I have the distinct feeling that I'm about to lose my fiancée.

THE SON: *(to his mother)* Oh yeah, right! Now it's all my fault!

WOMAN IN A HURRY: You run, you run and you run and you never tell your father you love him... then later on... you forget all about him....*(She sobs.)*

THE OTHER WOMAN: Don't worry... It's the champagne makes you cry...

WOMAN IN A HURRY: My father *loved* champagne!

GOSSIP B: *(to Gossip A)* And I am saying to you that in her house you run across animals with their hair completely messed up!

A MAN: And now? She wears glasses to go to sleep.

ANOTHER MAN: The stores were filled with straw hats... and what happens? War breaks out!

THE WEEPING WOMAN: I was lying in my bed with the window open, and I said to myself: "What a blessing, for once, to hear planes which aren't bombers."

23

The three Girls enter.

FIRST GIRL: Our grandmothers were scared of getting pregnant, our mothers of forgetting the pill, and us? All we've got is death to be afraid of.

SECOND GIRL: No thanks, that's fine... thanks... No, no, I don't need a bag...

FIRST GIRL: So, the first time I see my boyfriend pull out that little translucent Christmas stocking, what do I do?

THIRD GIRL: Pull out some knitting.

FIRST GIRL: No, but really. Where do I look?

SECOND GIRL: Close your eyes.

FIRST GIRL: And? Think about what?

SECOND GIRL: Think about another boyfriend.

FIRST GIRL: You just can't be expected to make a commitment like that in life, without a *little* experience...

THIRD GIRL: Well, that's just the thing! If you look at the whole picture it isn't very pretty. When they're thirty they're too old, the ones our age are little twerps and the twenty-year olds are looking around somewhere else...

FIRST GIRL: Well that's the trick. To put ourselves somewhere in that somewhere else.

SECOND GIRL: My sister? She's like nineteen and very pessimistic. What she says, is "Either they're married or they're queer. Otherwise, the minute you go, like "Hey, let's see each other tomorrow?"—they like split and you never see 'em again."

FIRST GIRL: You know what scares me. What if I don't like it *at all*.

THIRD GIRL: Is that possible?

FIRST GIRL: Better believe. My father has this friend? She walks out into the street in her nightgown one night, this is like on her wedding night...

SECOND GIRL: What, she forgot something... ?

FIRST GIRL: She was screaming stuff that was pure gibberish. She'd lost her mind.

THIRD GIRL: What about her husband?

FIRST GIRL: Entered a monastery.

THIRD GIRL: Aw, parents tell you tales that fit their own fantasies... Mine say they knew a couple who did it so much they died of it, the both of them.

SECOND GIRL: At the same time?

THIRD GIRL: Well that, I wouldn't know.

FIRST GIRL: Hey, at least that's going out with style!

SECOND GIRL: Better than dying of boredom. That's what scares me most. What if I have to spend the rest of my life bored shitless? Sunday nights they ask my mom "How come you look so down?" and she says "Oh, it's just the start of my Monday morning look." Sixty of them, sixty odd women taking orders from some nearsighted creep with a bow tie. My mother says: "One Monday we ought all of us to come to work in mourning, all sixty of us, with black veils over our faces just like the old days."

SECOND GIRL: You know my brother? He went with a whore.

FIRST GIRL: And what happened?

SECOND GIRL: He *says* you hardly have time to notice a thing. And of course now he examines himself all over the place to see if he's caught something...

THIRD GIRL: Of course, there's nothing in any of that for us...

Silence.

FIRST GIRL: And of course, later on, with our diplomas neatly folded in fours and spread out over our alabaster knees, what are we going to do when unemployment's taken over half the country? Hmm?

Silence, as they seem to think.

THIRD GIRL: We'll split hairs...

SECOND GIRL: Whip butter till it cries uncle...

THIRD GIRL: Hide the hen with the golden egg in a Swiss chicken coop...

SECOND GIRL: For that matter, what's that stuff all over the hands of the innocent?

THIRD GIRL: We'll never bathe twice in the same bidet.

SECOND GIRL: The early bird gets the worm, so we'll never go to bed.

THIRD GIRL: To get rich, I'll build up a pile of debts.

SECOND GIRL: And we'll pull the devil's tail till he gets it up!

Now they start to pretend to swing on the swings as they did before in reality.

FIRST GIRL: What if we took those two old geezers who've been shuffling around out here for so long, what if we took 'em out behind the bushes and slowly took off our clothes? Don't you think they'd kick in a little pittance for us?

SECOND GIRL: Maybe... if they didn't kick the bucket first...

FIRST GIRL: Didn't you ever have, like, *any* experience with a boy... which taught you something?

THIRD GIRL: Oh sure. Like one day I was sitting next to a guy who was all excited... When he ran his hand under my skirt, the moment he felt my pubic hair, he sneezed...

Singing is heard in the distance. They listen, then depart.

24

Night has fallen. Stars are out, as well as party lights. Angela and Benedicte enter.

ANGELA: I had the pictures developed.

BENEDICTE: All three rolls?

ANGELA: Uh-huh.

BENEDICTE: And, what are they like?

ANGELA: I haven't looked at them.

BENEDICTE: *Don't* look at them. Keep them. Throw them in the garbage. Burn them.

> *Angela starts to align photos on the ground as if playing a game of solitaire. Benedicte moves away a little so as not to be tempted to look.*

ANGELA:
1. Here's one of you, sitting at your desk.
2. You, looking straight into the camera, as if asking a question...
3. You, with a faint smile, index finger pointing upward...
4. You, thinking, chin in left hand...
5. Here, you're filling out an application...
6. Running your hand through your hair...
7. You're looking for a piece of paper underneath a stack of files...
8. Here's the cat, sitting on your papers...
9. Here you're gesturing as if to say "I don't know."
10. You on the telephone...
11. Refilling your pen...
12. You have a cold and you're writing with a Kleenex under your nose.
13. Rubbing the corner of your eye...
14. 15. 16. Three shots, all the same... amazed... amazed... and amazed

17. You're bundling up some colored wrapping paper.
18. Night, under lamplight, you're writing...
19. You're sticking a stamp on a letter...
20. You're smoking a cigar.
21. Here you are with eyes closed, possibly sleeping...
22. Oops, this one's blurry—you moved...
23. The cat again, and you talking to it...
24. Here you're crying, you can see the tears...
25. Sharpening a pencil...
26. Your mouth is open as if you were calling somebody...
27. You're using an eraser...
28. Sealing a letter...
29. You, getting up from your chair and looking out into the street...
30. Here you're wearing glasses...
31. You're looking in a dictionary...
32. You're eating a cookie while you write...
33. You're scratching your head and frowning...
34. Here you're gluing some sheets of paper together with Elmer's...
35. You're wadding up some sheets paper...
36. You're putting a rose into a glass...
37. You're nibbling on your left index finger...
38. Can't see you, your hands are over your face...
39. You're opening your mail...
40. You, smoking... we can see the cigarette smoke
41. You, laughing, mouth wide open...
42. Here's one of you playing with your rings...
43. Here, you've hurt your left hand...
44. Your hair is longer here, and you're twisting a lock of hair...
45. You're wrapping a package...
46. You're drinking some seltzer...
47. You're filing papers into a folder...
    OOOPS!

BENEDICTE: What is it?

ANGELA:
48. It's not you!
49. You're wiping your glasses.

50. You're looking through some drawers...
51. You're wearing a hat...
52. You're dusting your desk...
53. Here you're coughing...
54. You're dialing a telephone number...
55. You're cold and you're writing with a wool scarf around your neck...
56. You're writing with your glasses propped up in your hair...
57. The cat's on your paper, you can't write...
58. You're writing...
59. Writing...
60. Writing...
61. You're putting a flower in a letter...
62. You're reading a paper...
63. You're standing beside your desk and all we see are your hands...
64. You're yawning...
65. You're taking a pill...
66. Here you're rubbing your hands together...
67. You're recording a message on your answering machine...
68. You're tired, your head is resting on your right shoulder...
69. You're standing in front of your desk, looking for something...
70. You spilled a cup of coffee... or is that tea?
71. You're attaching a memo to your lamp...
72. Doing nothing...
73. You're counting on your fingers...
74. You're talking to someone behind you who's out of sight...
75. You're cutting out a newspaper article...
76. Staring at the ceiling...
77. You're tearing up a check...
78. You're writing, and with your left hand you're pinching your lip...
79. You're drinking a glass of whiskey—I can see the bottle.
80. You're smiling in front of a stack of books...
81. You've laid out all your pencils on your writing table...
82. You're reading a book of Eluard's poems...
83. Oops, blurry again.
84. Head's in your hands, only your mouth is visible...
85. You're clapping your forehead as if you just remembered something...

86. You've put your head down on your desk...
87. You're drawing a straight line with a ruler...
88. You're smiling...
89. You're polishing your desk...
90. Eating an apple...
91. Looking at your watch...
92. You're wearing a turtleneck... we can only see half your face...
93. You're stretching, arms extended...
94. You're sticking out your tongue...
95. You're mad... and scowling...
96. You're looking through a magnifying glass...
97. Your hands are clasped behind your neck...
98. You're putting on lipstick without a mirror...
99. You're clapping...
100. With two fingers pointing to your temple, you're feigning suicide...
101. Your hands are clasped and resting over your mouth...
102. You're writing, while with your left hand you seem to be saying good-bye to someone...
103. You've got the cat on your lap, his head is resting on the edge of the desk...
104. You're licking an ice cream cone...
105. Writing...
106. Writing...
107. Writing...
108. You're laughing with your hand pressed to your chest...
One hundred and eight photos of your face, observed with loving care...

BENEDICTE: Yeah...

Benedicte seems on the verge of fainting.

ANGELA: What is it?

BENEDICTE: Tell me. In these photos, am I in profile?

ANGELA: No, they're taken from the front...

BENEDICTE: From the front...

ANGELA: Each and every one, from the front, definitely...

Benedicte starts walking... slowly... then turns and comes back to Angela.

BENEDICTE: My desk is about two feet away from a window which I never open... How is it... How can it be... 108 times... without me ever noticing?

ANGELA: From the house across the street?

BENEDICTE: You're even drunker than I am... Angela... I live on the ninth floor of a building... which overlooks a little playground for toddlers...

All of a sudden she laughs uncontrollably.

ANGELA: You don't understand... But still, it's a wonderful present.

BENEDICTE: *(brutally suspicious)* Are you sure that's me, and not some other woman in those photos... sitting at my desk while I was out?

ANGELA: Oh sure, it is another woman. She just has your face.

BENEDICTE: Let's go get a drink... since he left... I seem to be thirsty all the time...

25

They are stopped by the wedding party, which is returning. Everyone is a little tired, now, and is dancing softly. The night is dark. A man emerges who seems to be still young.

THE MAN: Go ahead and laugh... laugh that laughter of disenchantment that shakes you from head to toe. Go ahead and laugh, because you think the old world is finally slaughtered. I will not betray the ardor of my youth, I will not betray the color red. Red as the red blood shed so the world might change. Red as Spain, being flayed alive, red as Vercors, or the mountains of Greece, and red as the red meat my father ate once only every two weeks, red as a paid day off, red as the blue sea finally seized, red as the lily of the valley on the first day of May, mounted on my father's shoulders as he sings "Of the past, let's make a clean slate," with my mother holding his hand and singing too in her tiny voice, and red as the rushing waters wherein Rosa was thrown, red as a hard hat's lunch pail, and red as my Big Chief notebook wherein my father and I learned about the circulation of the blood, the arrest of the King at Varennes, and the arrival of the potato in Europe, and red as that baby carriage hurtling down the steps, and red as teachers of old who used to teach Civics and Geography, red as the teacher I am, and red as the summer when I spied an earthworm and asked him, "So, brother worm, what have you done with *your* fiancée?," and the radio announcing the murder of Allende, and red as my father's tears that very day... It was a failure! A complete failure on exactly that side where the red was reddest! And where it was less red, it was also a failure! It has all caved in like the heavens on the heads of the Gauls! But who dares to say that red no longer has the right to be red because fools have confused it with blood? Go ahead and laugh, I will not betray hope, nor those who have died for the color red, nor the living still alive, and just to show you that red still exists and still flows on from the source...

He takes out a knife and... is he going to commit this spectacular suicide? Who knows... because the young bride runs to his side...

BRIDE: Antoine... Antoine... Please... don't give up hope... another woman will come along... she'll love you and you'll love her... give yourself a little more time and things will be fine... And life *is* wonderful!...

> *The young man looks at her in amazement. This woman just doesn't get it, does she? And so with a shrug of his shoulders, he sadly goes away.*

26

Little Gilbert runs on.

GILBERT: Come here... come here, all of you! They're gonna auction off the bride's garter belt!

The whole wedding party takes on a new life and exits joyously. Remaining on stage, dreamy and disconcerted, the First Girl. A Boy approaches.

BOY: I've been noticing you since this morning... I think you're...

FIRST GIRL: ... ?

BOY: I mean I think you're... really great...

FIRST GIRL: Yeah?

BOY: Can I see you again?

FIRST GIRL: ...

BOY: Like, maybe, tomorrow?

FIRST GIRL: Where?

BOY: How about Resistance Plaza ?— by the fountain...

FIRST GIRL: I'll be there.

We hear the cries of bids at the auction... and the sound of music.

∾

SIMONE SCHWARZ-BART

YOUR HANDSOME CAPTAIN

Translated from the French by

JESSICA HARRIS
and
CATHERINE TEMERSON

UBU REPERTORY THEATER PUBLICATIONS
NEW YORK

Simone Schwarz-Bart was born in Guadeloupe and educated in Pointe-à-Pitre, Paris and Dakar. In 1959, she met André Schwarz-Bart (winner of that year's Prix Goncourt for his novel *The Last of the Just*) and collaborated with him on her first novel, *Un plat de porc aux bananes vertes* (1967). She has since gained worldwide recognition for her two novels: *The Bridge of Beyond (Pluie et Vent sur Télumée-Miracle)* which won the "Prix des lectrices de *Elle*" (1972) and *Between Two Worlds (Ti-Jean L'Horizon* 1979). Ms. Schwarz-Bart's most recent work is a six volume encyclopedia, *Hommage à la femme noire,* published by Editions Consulaires in Paris. This unique project traces the history of black women from ancient times to the present in a series of striking portraits. *Your Handsome Captain (Ton beau capitaine)* is Simone Schwarz-Bart's first play. Having premiered in Guadeloupe, the play was acclaimed at the International Festival of Limoges in October of 1987 and went on to be a Parisian hit at the National Theatre of Chaillot in December 1988. It had a successful career in the US as well. First presented in a workshop production at Hunter College's Little Theatre in March 1988 by Ubu Repertory Theater, *Your Handsome Captain* was given a fully staged production at Ubu Rep in October-November 1989, which was revived in March 1990 at SUNY/Albany. The play was also staged in November 1988 at Brown University in Providence, Rhode Island. Finally it was presented in French by Ubu Rep at the Florence Gould Hall in New York, in May 1990. Simone Schwarz-Bart's work, including *Ton beau capitaine,* is published by Editions du Seuil in Paris.

Jessica Harris is a writer living in New York City. She teaches at Queens College and specializes in Senegalese theater. She is co-editor of *La Vie Ailleurs* (Harcourt Brace), a collection of French texts from the Caribbean, Africa, Quebec and Europe. She has published six cookbooks.

Catherine Temerson, Ubu literary manager for over 10 years, has translated Jean Claude Grumberg's *The Free Zone* and *The Workroom,* and co-translated Denise Chalem's *The Sea Between Us* as well as Maryse Condé's *Tropical Breeze Hotel,* all published by Ubu Repertory Theater. She has also translated short stories, films and radio scripts and is the author of *Hollywood: petite histoire d'un grand empire* and *Plaisir de jouer, plaisir de penser: conversation avec Charles Rosen.*

Your Handsome Captain, in Jessica Harris and Catherine Temerson's translation, had its American premiere in a workshop production at Hunter College, Little Theatre, 68th Street & Lexington Avenue, New York, NY 10021, on March 14, 1988, as part of the Ubu International Festival produced by Ubu Repertory Theater.

Director . . . . **Seret Scott**
Set and Lighting Designer . . . . **Jerome J. Hardeman**

CAST

Wilnor . . . . **Stanley E. Harrison**
The Voice . . . . **Sheila Gibbs**

Your Handsome Captain, in Jessica Harris and Catherine Temerson's translation was given its first fully staged production at Ubu Repertory Theater, 15 West 28th Street, New York, NY 10001, from October 24 through November 19, 1989.

Director. . . . . **Françoise Kourilsky**
Set and Lighting Designer . . . . **Watoku Ueno**
Costume Designer . . . . **Carol Ann Pelletier**
Composer . . . . **Henry Threadgill**
Musician . . . . **Wayne Kirton**

CAST

Wilnor . . . . **Reg E. Cathey**
The Voice. . . . . **Sharon Mac Gruder**

Produced by **Ubu Repertory Theater**
Françoise Kourilsky, *Artistic Director*

"[...] Thanks to the simplicity of the theme and the quality of the direction and acting, this sweet and poignant play loses nothing in the translation. [...]"

—Kim Ives, *The Guardian*, November 15, 1989

CHARACTERS

WILNOR BAPTISTE, *a Haitian farm worker, a tall, thin man about thirty years old. The part could be played by a white actor in makeup, or wearing a mask that is flexible enough for the audience to visualize the movements of his lips; in which case the actor's body should remain white.*

A RADIO/CASSETTE RECORDER

SET

Interior of a small one-room Creole shack. There is a stool in front of a soap box, a mattress on the ground, a gas burner in a corner with some dishes and silverware, a bottle of rum, a pair of shoes. A suit hangs on the wall with a shirt and tie, and a small plastic-framed mirror. A radio/cassette recorder is on top of the soap box. The shutters are open and it is night.

STAGE DIRECTIONS

An imaginary space, like the one in the Noh theatre, for example, is created through music and dance. Traditional Haitian dances are choreographed in such a way that they become balletic. These dances have a dramatic function; they express the different moments of an individual drama rather than a collective state of mind. They can be regarded as an additional language that the main character has at his disposal. This more or less secret means of expression is common in the Caribbean. Music also plays its part. Often, the sounds that are heard in the play—human voice, drum, or band—come directly from the soul of the character. These are auditory illusions reproduced onstage and, in some cases, a synthesizer will be necessary. Sometimes the same song can be real (it comes from the cassette); sometimes imaginary.

TABLEAU I

It is nighttime. Footsteps are heard. A door opens. Someone bumps into a piece of furniture.

WILNOR: Watch out friend! This country is precious, fragile. Even the sky here is made of china; so don't go breaking these good people's furniture.

Creaking is heard. A gas lamp is lit. A black farm worker appears with a machete in his hand and a burlap sack. The man takes a large envelope from the sack, opens it slowly as if to take out a letter, and removes a cassette tape which he holds up.

The plane had a good flight, thank you. And I received the cassette the same day Brother Archibald arrived. Thank you. Thanks be to God. *(He gives a small laugh.)* Wilnor, my dear, I want to tell you that nothing belongs to you here, not even the grass on the road, not even the wind. *(He gives another small laugh.)* And if you really want to know, the only thing that is truly yours... *(He raises the cassette up to eye level.)* is this, old friend, this.

He sits on the stool, inserts the cassette into the tape recorder and turns it on. Noises, laughter, children's voices, and a cock crow are heard. One senses there is a whole little circle of people gathered around the tape recorder. A woman's voice is heard chasing everyone out. Complete silence follows. Finally, this same female voice begins to sing.

THE VOICE:

Moin n'aime danser, moin n'aime chanter, *(etc.)*

The song is lively and the voice happy, mischievous and high-pitched. The song stops and the woman's voice begins again.

Hello! Hello Wilnor, Wilnor Baptiste. As soon as you hear this voice, you'll know that it's Marie-Ange speaking to you. I kicked all my people out of the shack, including the rooster, and now we're alone, you and me. You over there and me here, you here and me over there. It's all the same. Wilnor, tell me, how are you? Really, how are you? I have so many things to tell you that my tongue has all dried up. As the old saying goes, "Man is not alone on earth; he has neighbors." So before beginning my little speech, I should first send you some greetings, shouldn't I? It's proper, the custom, the accepted thing. *(The delivery quickens.)* Your father and mother are well, thank you, *(The "thank yous" are long and ceremonious, breaking the rhythm.)* and they send their hellos. Your sisters, Lolotte, Finotte and Grenotte are well, thank you; they send their hellos. All of the relatives, friends, and in-laws here are well, thank you, and they send their hellos. Good news from all our exiled ones around the world: Grenada, the Dominican Republic, Puerto Rico, and the rest of the group; they are well and say hello. *(One clearly hears that the woman is out of breath. She begins again at a more normal rhythm.)* Yet, unfortunately... Oh God, I can't avoid telling you your friend Petrus has... drowned. He was lost at sea and vanished along with thirty other souls who were trying to reach America on a raft. Old Mama Petrus, when she heard the news, blood blocked her throat and she fell to the ground gasping like a sperm whale. We thought she was dying, completely done for, and all night long we checked her breathing and placed compresses on her. But just imagine—it would actually be funny—we'd have had a good laugh but for your poor friend at the bottom of the sea; just imagine, the next day, she was alive. Well, barely alive, but alive. And when asked how she was feeling, she replied peevishly, "I'd have slept well if I'd been left alone." *(She laughs stridently, then begins again in a normal tone.)* Wilnor, how are you? Tell me, really, how are you? In the last cassette you sent—was it three months ago? Three months already?—You say you're as fat as a prize pig and living in a large house with pillars, a big front door, and so many electric light bulbs that you're floating among the stars. I don't want to contradict you, Wilnor—may the Blessed Virgin forgive me—but the man who delivered everything to me... thank you for the money, Wilnor, thank you for the huge pile of gifts... that young man told me that our exiled brothers in Guadeloupe don't live in large houses with pillars and big front doors, but, with all due respect, in chamber pots. He might have been saying that to be funny; but it worried me, Wilnor, it worried me. And when I asked him how you looked, at first he didn't want to answer. Then he told me that you had changed a lot, become skinny, melted like a candle. That you now looked like a little shriveled-up black man. Shriveled-up outside and shriveled-up inside. Shriveled-up, shriveled-up, *(She gives a short sob.)* shriveled-up. *(She sobs.)* He might have been saying that as a joke, too, but it worried me, Wilnor, it brought me grief. And that same night, I had a dream. First I saw myself at the river washing your flannel shirt; you know, the gray one with the red stripes, the pretty one. And suddenly I realize I'm washing your body, *(Pause.)* your living body. *(Pause.)* You are all flat inside the shirt, Wilnor. Your head and your hands stick out; your legs, everything, flat. Flat as a newspaper picture. You try to slip away and I want to hold you back—but you melt between my arms and soon there is nothing inside the shirt, Wilnor. It's empty... empty... *(The man stops the cassette and grumbles.)*

WILNOR: A woman really needs a man. I no sooner leave that even her dreams go haywire.

> *The man gets up, puzzled, and goes to look at himself in the mirror hanging on the wall. He puts on the white shirt and tie and reappraises himself in the mirror. Finally, he squares his shoulders.*

No doubt about it, a woman really needs a man.

> *The man returns to the soap box, sits down and presses the play button of the cassette recorder with a confident air. At first there is silence; then, after a few long seconds, the woman's weak voice rises into crescendo, punctuated by the rhythm of light hand clapping.*

THE VOICE:
        Moin n'aime danser, *(etc.)*

> *This time she sings the entire first verse. Finally, the woman continues.*

Wilnor, Wilnor. Today is February 2nd, 1985. It's been ages since I first sang this song for you. Remember, you often used to say that was what convinced you to tie the knot—a winged woman who sings like a dragonfly despite the tons of sorrows dragging on her skirts. And then you left; you went away to earn a wayfarer's daily bread. But you—whose soul was always full of marvels— you wanted daily bread, the whole loaf, and more. You spoke of striking it rich; you dreamed of buying land by the river and a cow. Every night you dreamed of that. I could hear you. And I got to like your dream. I could see the land. I could see the cow. I even milked that cow. That's why I let you get on that plane, Wilnor. *(Pause.)* The years have gone by. *(Pause.)* I have wanted for nothing, nothing since you left. My stomach has not been empty and I've never gone barefoot on Sunday. No, you always have known how to come up with enough money, good money, and to send it my way. But now they tell me you're becoming all shriveled-up and that's why I beg you on my knees, come back. Come back, my dear Wilnor, even if it's without the land, without the cow.

Pause. One hears rapid breathing on the tape, then the voice continues with a small laugh.

Wilnor, I wish I were a boat sailing to Guadeloupe. Once there, you'd climb inside me, you'd walk on my decks, you'd place your hands on my frame, you'd explore me from stem to stern. And then you would set sail and I would take you to a country far, far, far away. *(Pause.)* On the other side of the world, perhaps, where people don't look at you as though you were less than nothing, dried-out coconuts. Wilnor, is there no country on earth where we Haitians can work and send a little money home from time to time without being reduced to formless gusts of air? *(Pause.)* Wilnor, handsome captain of my ship, if my letter reaches you in the morning, I wish you good morning, and if my letter reaches you in the evening, I wish you... *(She concludes in a sweeping, ceremonious tone.)* good evening. *(Pause.)* Your tape recorder wife, *(Pause.)* Marie-Ange.

She clears her throat uneasily and then continues.

By the way, you might wonder why I left you with no news for three long months. This is exactly, the very thing, I wanted to speak to you about today, and I realize it's the only thing I didn't talk about. But what do you want my dear? Sometimes there are certain words that choke you, that stick in your throat like fish bones. I'll try again tomorrow... God willing.

Black out.

TABLEAU II

The lights come back up and show the man standing in front of the soap box, paralyzed with amazement. Apparently he stopped the tape while the theater was dark and now he looks at the machine suspiciously as if he doesn't dare restart it. His finger is poised tentatively over the play button as though it might burn him.

WILNOR: If it's bad news, waiting a bit won't matter. If it's good news, it will only be better.

He takes three steps toward a rum bottle on the ground, then suddenly seems to stumble and to catch his balance with one arm holding onto an invisible rope stretched in the air. A few measures of ti-bois music are heard which seem to come from the sky. Wilnor stumbles to the left again, then to the right in time to the ti-bois music and, while hanging onto the invisible rope, he circles around the bottle and comes to a stop with a blissful look on his face.

It seems, according to what they say at home, that the African gods invented the drum to give us consolation, while the black man invented rum, which isn't bad either, God knows! *(He brings the bottle to eye level and sizes up its contents.)* Patience is at the bottom of the bottle. *(He takes a large swig.)* At the very bottom. *(He takes another large swig.)*

With the bottle held against his chest, he returns to the box, hopping humorously in dance steps as though pursued by the light music of the ti-bois. He then sits on the stool and very carefully presses the tip of his finger down on the play button.

THE VOICE: Wilnor, about the story that stuck in my throat yesterday, you remember? I realize, finally, that there was no such point in making such a fuss about it. So much wind for so small a ship, so much mousse for so little chocolate. On thinking about it, *(She gives a small laugh.)* the story is rather funny. *(She gives a small forced laugh.)* It's about the money, the big sum you sent me three months ago with your friend from the village of Raizailles. I don't know if he's a close friend of yours, but if you see him again—which I doubt, since he left for Miami—you can tell him for me he's a big rascal. *(She gives an indignant sigh.)* One fine morning, Monsieur showed up at my door wearing a red jacket, a yellow tie and a tie pin that wasn't that bad at all and was even quite pretty. In short, a beautiful tie pin. He introduces himself, gives me all your gifts honestly: the blouse, the handkerchiefs, the box of goodies, all the soaps and perfumes, the perfumed soaps, everything. But then, imagine, the big good-for-nothing, as he was giving me the money—your hard-earned money—he changed his mind and let me know that he would give me nothing, nothing at all unless I gave in to his wishes. My God! As she goes through life, a woman can say that she's seen it all. Finally, he gave up, but not without trying. The animal tried everything and more. *(She laughs and laughs.)*

WILNOR: But what is this story...? Wait! Wait!

THE VOICE: *(playful)* Imagine—speaking of money entrusted to handsome young men who come rubbing the beautiful bills under your nose, your wives' noses—this time you won't be able to stop laughing; you'll really laugh. There's this lady from Port-au-Prince, a grand, pious lady, with a soul as pure as spring water, truly someone exceptionally moral, whose husband has been picking oranges in Florida for years. They say that from picking so many oranges, he's become an orange tree himself, he can be seen over there, standing all day long at a crossroads, holding out his branches to the passersby, his fruits up for grabs, ready to be plundered and devastated. They say this as a joke, naturally. *(She gives a small appropriate laugh.)* But, to get back to my story, one day, the woman from Port-au-Prince receives a visit on behalf of her husband: a handsome young man wearing a jacket... but who cares how he was dressed? A young man bringing her money and the kind of gifts wives usually get from husbands who work in America's orange groves. That's where the story becomes funny. *(Pause.)* Really funny. *(Pause.)* Suddenly, she is moved, so deeply moved on seeing the young man, she has the impression that he's bringing her some of her husband's world, some of his scent. She looks at the eyes which had seen the absent one. *(She gives a small sob.)* She touches the hands which just the day before, just yesterday, had touched the absent one. My God! *(She gives a small cry.)*... Finally, she's completely confused *(She sighs.)* and ends up in bed with the young man. *(She sobs.)* But, in reality, it's her husband. *(Pause.)* Seemingly with the young man, but in reality lying by her husband. Do you understand, Wilnor? Do you understand? *(She gives a small sob.)*

> *The man shakes his head without understanding. There is a long silence, then the woman's voice is heard again.*

Do you understand, Wilnor?

> *The man is bewildered. The voice continues in a whisper.*

Do you understand? *(Pause.)* Wilnor, I know you. I know how sensitive you are. Nevertheless, stop shaking your head and figure it out. Take time to think. What times—what world—do you think you're living in, my poor friend? This is earth, Wilnor, and on earth everything is whirlwind and smoke. There are none of the straight, wide lanes of heaven. So I beg you, stop shaking your head and figure it out. Take time to think, to weigh things. Don't make me say all the words. *(There is a pause and then the voice continues in a certain tone.)* Wilnor. *(She pauses again, then continues in another tone of voice.)* Wilnor. *(The voice becomes aggressive for the first time.)* The fact is that the woman from Port-au-Prince, the one who found her husband's scent on the young man, the one who became all mixed up, lost in happiness to the point of confusing everything in her head... *(The voice breaks.)* That woman is me.

WILNOR: You?

THE VOICE: He joked exactly like you, Wilnor. The same way. And his eyes reminded me of your eyes. His hands reminded me of your hands. It was you I held in my arms. It was only you that I welcomed in my bed.

WILNOR: *(cutting her off)* Enough!

THE VOICE: It was you. It was only you in my bed, enjoying my body.

WILNOR: Enough I say! Tramp! Enough said! Enough lies! Enough truth! Enough everything! Enough everybody! Leave me! Leave me alone! *(The man stops the cassette violently. Silence. He takes a few faltering steps forward.)* Enough, gods, enough! *(The faltering steps turn into a dance—small hops to the side like the Lerose. He raises his arms as though he were hovering in the air.)* Enough angels! *(A drum begins to beat, sharply at first, pulsating, then its rhythm changes with the introduction of the entire band, while a deep bass voice slowly utters the following words, with great majesty but, nonetheless, with secret melancholy.)*

BASS VOICE:
Moujé, moujé é o, *(etc.)*

The man dances now with eyes closed. Little by little, darkness falls on the stage, transforming it into night and silence.

TABLEAU III

The lights come up. The man opens his eyes, looks around him, stunned, with his mouth open. He returns to the soap box. He is out of breath as though he had been running. Halfway there, at the sound of a ti-bois, he suddenly jumps to the left, then to the right, with arms out horizontally. Finally, he approaches the radio/cassette recorder and hesitantly turns it back on.

THE VOICE: *(strangely serene)* Wilnor, handsome captain, today is March 17, St. Valentine's day. Noon in the heavens, but more like midnight on earth, suddenly. *(Pause.)* Today is the day that our road comes to an end, that our food burns up, that the roof of our shack blows away. *(Pause.)* And since we are going to separate—don't deny it, you've already made up your mind *(The man nods his head with approval.)*—I must tell you the rest of the story... Because there is more, Wilnor. I must tell you properly, until all things have been said, finished, wrapped up and sealed in a shroud. The first time that your good friend came was Monday, January 2nd, St. Eustache's day. I thought of you on seeing him and I gave in after he threatened not to give me my money. He came back Saturday, January 7th and I thought of you again. Then I thought of you Monday, January 9th; Wednesday, January 11th; and Tuesday, the 17th, and that's all. That day your image fell like a mask from his face and I chased him away. I told him to clear out. I've seen nothing since then. *(Pause.)* I tried every-thing to weaken my stomach. *(Pause.)* Finally, I lost half my blood and they took me to the hospital. *(Pause.)* But the child didn't leave with my blood. It didn't leave, Wilnor; it didn't. *(Pause.)* Farewell. *(There is a long silence, from which the woman's voice emerges like a challenge, livelier tan ever, very high-pitched.)*

Moin n'aime chanter, moin n'aime danser. Aye, aye, aye.

The voice breaks.

Aye, aye, aye.

WILNOR: Ha! Ha! Ha! What a woman! *(He repeats her words, still with the same surprised, almost admiring tone.)* I thought of you the 7th of January; I thought of you the 9th of January; and the 11th of January I also thought of you! Ha! Ha!... And from thinking of me, she got a big belly!... That's really taking a man for a jackass!... For the king, the emperor of jackasses, since jackasses first began raining down on earth! What a woman! Ha! Ha!

> *He is completely stunned. Clearly he hasn't yet completely gauged what is happening to him. He gets up and takes a few steps. The sound of the ti-bois can be heard, very slowed, to which the man responds by an even slower, lingering attempt to dance, one step to the left, one step to the right. Then he raises his hands to his temples and says calmly, still surprised.*

What a misfortune!

> *The ti-bois starts up again, more and more tensely; then there are three well-sounded drum beats while the man turns around as though stung by a dart and stamps in time to the drumbeats.*

That tramp! All of my money went to her, all of my sweat. But now I am going to live, live what is called the good life. Oh yes! What a relief! *(Drumbeats are heard. The man twirls around and stops with the drumbeat.)* All my money! *(More drumbeats are heard. The same movements are repeated. He speaks in a mocking tone.)* Money! Money! *(Slight pause.)* Money! Money! Money! *(The drum stops with a sharp beat.)* No, not all my money.

> *He goes to the mattress, raises a corner and frantically scratches at the ground with his hands. He removes a bowl containing a sheaf of bills and, with a somber air, places it next to the radio/cassette recorder. He removes the bills and scatters them in front of him. He speaks bitterly.*

No, not all the money.

> *Suddenly, trembling with contained violence, he seizes the radio/cassette recorder and raises it as though to smash it. When he speaks again, it is in sugary tones.*

Dear Marie-Ange. When you hear this voice, you'll know that it's Wilnor speaking to you. Wilnor Baptiste answering you. O.K.? *(Pause.)* My dear, thank you for having thought so much about me, about me personally, Wilnor Baptiste, the king, the emperor of suckers. I've thought about you a great deal too. Why hide it from you any longer? Since arriving in Guadeloupe, I've thought about you a great deal. With all these beautiful black women in ruffles and flounces and all of these jazzy mulattoes buzzing around you like mosquitoes from morning til night. Gorgeous, beautiful like the rainbow, if you really want to know. That's what the women are like here, Marie-Ange. Especially since I have a house with pillars and a big front door. They like that—I can't help it—they like to come to my house even though I'm only a Haitian. I'm their black man, the black man's top black man, if you want to know, Marie-Ange. At first, I used to take sitz baths from Monday morning to Saturday night because I wanted to keep my promise to you. And then I fell into the pit; I fell under the spell just like you. Their eyes reminded me of your eyes, their scent became your scent, do you understand Marie-Ange? Do you? Ah yes, that's how it is when separation sets in, when boats drift apart, when airplanes begin to roar, their engines full blast. A man's body cries for a woman's body, a woman's body cries out for a man's and that's what the Good Lord wishes. Separation is a vast ocean and more than one person has drowned in it, O.K.? O.K. Other than that, all is well, thank you, thank the Lord. See, I have everything I need here, the only missing thing is a car, a small four-wheeled car that spits fire. Motor cars—the women here love them, there's no denying it, they love them. *(Pause.)* With a car, I would think of you even more. Farewell. *(His voice cracks.)* Wilnor. *(Dissatisfied with his tone, he shakes his head and tries another one.)* Wilnor. *(He is still dissatisfied.)* Wilnor. *(He nods his head with approval and then seems dissatisfied again. Tense, with knitted brows, he searches for inspiration then speaks, suddenly.)* What do you want my dear Marie-Ange? Man is a rat; woman is a rat. Neither one is worth a damn. O.K.? O.K.

His hands have now left the cassette; he's straightened himself up in his seat and is staring into space.

The biggest jackass ever under the stars. *(He laughs.)* But all of this is very far away. *(He gestures.)* Very far away.

> *As though called up by the gesture, one hears the first note of an extremely joyous Creole quadrille coming from afar. The man changes attitude. He listens and seems more relaxed. His shoulders move; his hands twitch; his teeth shine. Suddenly lively, he stands up and does a few dance steps while the quadrille takes shape under the caller's strong guiding voice.*

Take your partners, *(etc.)*

> *He dances the quadrille with three invisible partners. Sometimes he gaily echoes the voice of the caller. At other times (five times) the music stops as though sliced by a razor and the man goes through the motions in complete silence, but at a very slow pace as though in a slow-motion tape. During those moments, he calls out a few words which are also distorted, drawn out, put through a synthesizer. The words and phrases which he will call out successively during the five musical pauses are the following:* 1) "Tramp!" 2) "Leave me alone I tell you." 3) "Life, O.K., life; but where is life, where is it?" 4) "Oh the beautiful black women in ruffles and flounces." 5) "The jazzy mulattoes." *After each of these fragments, the quadrille starts up again as before. Therefore, there are five stops and five starts. But suddenly the music and dance come to a definitive stop and, cut off in mid-movement, he finds himself standing on one foot, facing the audience, his joyful features transformed into a strange mask of pain, eyes closed and mouth half open. Blackout.*

TABLEAU IV

The man has stopped in a position resembling that of a winged creature. He looks at his "wings," glancing to the left and right.

WILNOR: What a beautiful quadrille! A bit more and I would have flown away.

He slowly lowers his raised foot to the ground, which he scrapes lazily once or twice.

The earth.

He turns his neck in the direction of the radio/cassette recorder. Pause.

Poor Marie-Ange, after all.

He takes a step toward the radio/cassette recorder.

Poor, poor Marie-Ange.

He sits down, shakes his head with a subtle smile, and finally makes a declaration to the cassette.

Actually, I lied to you. I lied to you, my little bird. *(He gives a small laugh.)* Since I've been in Guadeloupe, if you want to know, there's never—it's strange to say, funny—there's never been another woman at my house. *(He gives a small laugh.)* Every evening that the Good Lord sends, I take my cold sitz baths and sometimes I even take them during the day. I fill up my basin and sit in it. Also, when I can, I immerse myself in the stream for hours and hours. To sleep, I put compresses between my thighs, and I have a basin of water ready at the side of the bed in case I wake up. Sometimes, stretched out in the darkness, like this, *(He stretches out his arms.)* I have the feeling that it's swelling. It feels like balloons between my thighs. I feel as if I'm going to fly away. And, then suddenly, it happens. I fly, I fly away, I rise up very high in the night, *(He gives a small laugh.)* attached to my two balloons.

The man is seated. Pensive, he makes a series of "philosophical" sounds in the back of his throat and, smiling, shakes his head, astonished at everything that's happened to him in the course of his life. He will continue to smile this way throughout the following monologue until the word "promptly" is first pronounced.

Actually, as for the money, about the money, I also lied to you, I didn't tell you the truth. *(Pause.)* Not the whole truth. *(Pause.)* I send you my savings, true, but I don't send you the savings from my savings. I put those in my piggybank, in my jar.

While saying this, he seizes a bill which he holds to the flame of the lamp's gas jet. As he continues speaking, he will gradually burn all the bills spread out on the soapbox and some of the ones which have fallen on the ground.

A jar that I bury at the foot of my bed to anchor and stabilize me; *(He gives a small laugh.)* because of certain dreams, bizarre beyond belief; dreams which carry me to stranger and more foreign lands, farther and farther away; and I'm afraid that one fine morning I'll no longer be able to find the way back. That's why I sleep over my little jar of money, which I bury under my feet. *(He gives a small laugh.)* Right under my feet, so they'll get the idea and know the road back when I'm dreaming in a faraway land. *(He gives a small laugh.)* You see, it amounted to quite a few bills in the end. Some were for a veranda that I wanted to have built at the back of the house when I got back, so that we could sit outside and enjoy the cool air when we would be quite old, thin as leaves, stretched out and consumed with joy. Others, maybe, might have been for the couple of goats that I'd envisioned in my head, along with the cow. Some were for enameled dishes. Some were for a white dress with matching shoes; for a radio/cassette recorder that we would own so we wouldn't have to rent one and we could listen to all the cassettes of all of these years—all the years on cassette. And some were for nothing in particular, simply in expectation of a dream, a fancy, a whim that we might one day have at the end of all those years, while we would be out enjoying the cool air, for example, out on the veranda that I would have had built the day after my return, promptly.

The last bill has gone up with the word "promptly" which he repeats without smiling. He looks at his fingers full of ashes.

And now that's it?

The woman's voice can be heard coming from very far away, distorted by a synthesizer so that each syllable is infinitely drawn out, almost unrecognizable, nearly reduced to the sound of a musical saw, but still, if possible, with a poignant dramatic accent.

THE VOICE:
> Moooooin n'aaaaimmmme chaaaaaanter
> Moooooin n'aaaaimmmme daaaaaanser...

Elbows on the soapbox, the man has covered his face with his hands as though lost in thought. One hears the woman's voice again, closer, still distorted by the synthesizer, but in an intermediate pace that is midway between the extremely slow preceding pace and the normal pace. The tonality has also changed, become "neutral" midway between the infinite sadness of the slow pace and the woman's "normal" gaiety.

> Mooin n'aiime chaanter
> Mooin n'aiime daanser...

This time the man raises his head slightly and spreads his fingers apart in front of his eyes. The woman's voice takes off like a rocket: lively, high-pitched, terribly alive, at the normal rhythm of the song which she sings to the end for the first time.

> Moin n'aime chanter
> Moin n'aime danser, (etc.)

In the middle of the song, the man extends his hand hesitantly and rests it on the radio/cassette recorder. He caresses it tenderly, and continues to do so after the song ends, when he begins to speak again.

WILNOR: Marie-Ange... *(Pause.)* When I read your cassette, for an instant, one brief instant, I almost doubted you. *(Pause.)* For one instant. *(Pause.)* Fortunately, I've always been appreciated by those in heaven. That's my good fortune, that I'm appreciated by those who live on high. And here I was believing without believing, doubting and not doubting, when all of a sudden I heard your voice right here at my house, your voice coming and going just like in bygone days, and suddenly I saw the light: it came to me! It may have been a kind of gesture, an act of mercy from St. Anthony of Padua. Or perhaps it was a god from Guinea, Legba, oh yes, or Damballah Ouedo, or perhaps Erzulie Freda Dahomey, the good, dear, one. I don't know who it was, I don't know, but I've always been appreciated by those up there. And suddenly I saw the light, bright and clear, oh yes, as though I had an electric light bulb in the middle of my throat. *(He places his hands on either side of his throat, mimicking the radiating light.)* There. *(Pause.)* And now I see, I know, I understand. To tell you the truth, it's happened to me, to me, too. I've often been mystified, just like you, Marie-Ange. I'm watching one of their women go by in the street and all of the sudden it's as though I had you in front of my eyes, Marie-Ange. And that's it, that's what separation is all about, Marie-Ange. And if that woman headed my way, it wouldn't take much urging to put her in my bed, right in my house with the pillars and the big front door. That's it, that's exactly it. Ah yes, separation is a big ocean, which muddles everything; it shakes things up like a cupful of dice. You start seeing with your ears, hearing with your eyes and feeling with your hands things that are very far away, while the things nearby that surround you, you notice no more than a puff of smoke. Marie-Ange, sometimes funny things happen to me, really funny things. Some days when I see the women trotting up the road in front of me, the cute little black women with ruffles and flounces, and all those jazzy mulattoes, I feel a blow to my stomach as though it were you; I feel a sudden painful blow and then I feel light, so light, I fly away as if I were being carried off by two balloons, ouaaye! *(He corrects himself.)* One balloon.

> *He seizes the bottle, takes a swig of rum and solemnly smacks his lips in a show of self-confidence. He continues with quiet majesty.*

One more word, a small bit of advice. Be sure to rest now throughout the days that God gives us. Don't trouble your soul, if you want the child to come into the world with a good start. Chew your food well, keep your heart joyful, and drive all that ugliness out of your sight so that he won't be born with a crooked nose or mouth. Remember, I want that child as beautiful as an angel. *(He puffs himself up menacingly.)* Do you hear me? *(He reassumes his air of calm majesty.)* If my letter finds you in the morning, I wish you good morning; if it arrives in the evening, I wish you good evening.

> *He has crossed over to the little mirror hanging on the wall. He glances at himself and concludes.*

Your handsome captain, Wilnor.

> *But something in the mirror bothers him. Hastily he removes his shirt and tie and remains bare-chested. Finally, he speaks again, in a less self-confident tone.*

Your handsome captain... .

> *He stops. The phrase seems to overwhelm him. He brings his hand to his mouth, hunching and shaking his shoulders in a smothered laugh.*

Your handsome captain?

> *The music of the ti-bois is heard. He dismisses it with a gesture, like a temptation. But it starts up again, accompanied by a drum which shakes the man and inspires a bitter kind of dance involving desperate-looking gestures. Suddenly, the drumming and the man stop simultaneously. Feet spread apart, arms dangling, he tries again.*

Your handsome captain?

> *The drum starts up again, more forcefully, in a faster and faster rhythm, drawing the man into a dance that's at the same*

time very brief and very violent. Then everything stops short, as though sliced by a razor, except that the man has his arms raised in the air and they seem to be twisting, trying to climb higher, while his face has become like a mask. Blackout. The question is heard one last time in the night.

Your handsome captain?

∾

FATIMA GALLAIRE

YOU HAVE COME BACK

Translated from the French by

JILL MAC DOUGALL

UBU REPERTORY THEATER PUBLICATIONS
NEW YORK

Fatima Gallaire studied literature in her native Algeria following independence, at a time when few Algerian women were pursuing a college education. She continued studying in France where she obtained a degree in film studies. Bilingual in Arabic and French, she spent many years trying to integrate the two languages and cultures. She has written poetry and short stories as well as twenty plays treating traditional North African themes and contemporary issues. Her work has been translated into English, German, Swedish, Russian, Uzbek, Spanish, and Hebrew. Her first play, *You Have Come Back (Ah! Vous êtes venus... là où il y a quelques tombes)*, translated by Jill Mac Dougall and directed by Françoise Kourilsky, was given its world premiere by Ubu Repertory Theater as part of the 1988 New York International Festival of the Arts and was originally published in the first volume of *Plays by Women: An International Anthology*, in 1988. Treating the theme of religious intolerance, the play remain tragically pertinent today. Other plays include: *Le Fou de Layla (Majnoun Layla)*, adapted from the novel by André Miquel and based on Arab legend, produced in Paris in 1987 and performed at the 1988 International University Theater Festival in Casablanca; *Témoignage contre un homme stérile* premiered in Metz in 1987, published in Paris by the French journal *L'Avant-Scène* and in Jill Mac Dougall's translation—*Madame Bertin's Testimony*—by Ubu Rep in *Monologues*, in 1995; *Les Co-épouses, La Fête virile, Au loin, les Caroubiers* and *Rimm, la Gazelle,* all published by Editions des Quatre-Vents, Paris. Fatima Gallaire has received two major awards honoring her work as a whole: the 1990 Prix Arletty and a 1994 award from the Académie Française.

Jill Mac Dougall has been active in theatre research and production, in translating plays, and in teaching in Europe, Africa, and North America for over twenty years. In addition to her translations for Ubu, she has translated works for New Dramatists, the Centre des Auteurs Dramatiques in Montreal, *Women and Performance,* and *Canadian Theatre Review.* Her translations published in the Ubu Repertory Theater series include *The Eye* (Zadi Zaourou), *The Girls from the 5 and 10* (Abla Farhoud), *Lost Voices* (Diur N'Tumb), *Burn River Burn* (Jean-Pol Fargeau), *The Crossroads* (Josué Kossi Efoui), *That Old Black Magic* (Koffi Kwahulé), *The Orphanage* (Reine

Bartève), *Game of Patience* (Abla Farhoud), *You Have Come Back* and *Madame Bertin's Testimony* (Fatima Gallaire). Jill Mac Dougall holds an M.A. in Theatre Arts (University of Quebec at Montreal) and a Ph.D in Performance studies (NYU). She is currently teaching theatre and acting with Pennsylvania State University.

You Have Come Back, in Jill Mac Dougall's translation, had its
World premiere as part of the First New York International Festival
of the Arts at Saint Clement's Church on June 21, 1988.

Director ....Françoise Kourilsky
Set Designer ....Phillip Baldwin
Lighting Designer ....Michael Chybowski
Costume Designer ....Carol Ann Pelletier
Music and sound by ....Genji Ito

CAST
(in order of appearance)

The Old Man ....Thomas C. Anderson
Lella (Princess) ....Blanca Camacho
Nounou (Lella's old nurse) ....Frances Foster
Badia/Khadija ....Carmen Rosario
Aicha/Cherifa ....Cherron Hoye
Abla/Zahra ....Laurine Towler
Hadda/The Elder ....Rajika Puri
The Maboula (The Mad Woman) ....René Houtrides
The Slave/The Angry Woman ....Sharon McGruder
The Cripple/The Male Elder ....Waguih Takla

Produced by **Ubu Repertory Theater**
Françoise Kourilsky, *Artistic Director*

[...] Set in contemporary Algeria, Fatima Gallaire-Bourega's *You Have Come Back* follows Lella, a princess who has returned home, after 20 years in France, to bury her father. Despite warnings from her 103-year-old nurse, an omnipresent howling madwoman, an old slave, and a crippled man, she remains calm, sweet and trusting in the face of gruff village elders who finally beat her to death for having married an uncircumcised man. In the Islamic world, where even Benazir Bhutto enters an arranged marriage, the issues Gallaire-Bourega raises are pressing and complex [...].

—Alisa Solomon, *The Village Voice,* June 5, 1988

[...] Gallaire-Bourega, Algerian-born but now a Parisian, presents a remarkable sense of mood and locale in *You Have Come Back.* [...] The play almost has the quality of dance as Lella, settling into her old house, assisted by her former nursemaid, now 103, greets veiled women friends and eventually is forced to confront the black-garbed female elders, who will mete out her terrifying destiny. [...]

—William A. Raidy, *The Star-Ledger,* June 30, 1988

[...] An exotic, drum-driven nightmare about the death grip of Islamic law on a Westernized North African woman, [*You Have Come Back*] throbbed with the author's love and hate for the repressive culture in which she grew up. [...]

—Sylviane Gold, *The Wall Street Journal,* July 26, 1988

[...] *You Have Come Back,* Fatima Gallaire-Bourega's first play, is a study of the surface machinations of bigotry, of how those who nurture a community's traditions become destroyers when an alien culture intrudes. [...] The Algerian-set play was a rare sampling of the sound of a Middle Eastern woman's voice on an American stage. [...]

—Donna Kipp, *American Theater,* September 1988

AUTHOR'S NOTE

It is my first visit to New York. I have just stepped off the plane from Paris and I am in the pleasant haze of jet lag. Catherine, the messenger from Ubu Theater, drives me straight to a rehearsal. It's in Manhattan, in a building with bay windows, was it the second or the third floor? Catherine opens the door and marvelous "youyous" rise up to greet us.

I am transfixed with joy. Through my drowsiness emerge figures from Algeria, a few women veiled in black, their hands to their mouths; my ears ring with their song of welcome.

There is Nounou, my old nurse, looking at me with that mischievous smile I know so well. She is slightly stooped, just as I remember her.

And there is Princess—myself—I see her standing among the others... discrete and modest in her lovely robes. Perhaps I am gazing into a mirror?

"Come in, Fatima, come in."

For a few sublime moments, I was a little girl. What a rare privilege to travel back to the past, to the place of my childhood, to meet again all those I had loved, my nurse, my first friends.

I didn't know theater could perform such miracles.

I enter the room, but I can't hold back my tears. I weep with emotion. Why should I deny myself?

I stayed in New York for three weeks and I spent many hours at rehearsals of my play, *You Have Come Back,* directed by Françoise Kourilsky, but this first impression of being an actress in my own life persisted.

It was both poignant and magnificent.

During my stay I could appreciate the dedication the American actresses brought to their work. Without ever getting bored, I spent entire days listening to them work in a language I do not understand. I never failed to admire the persistency of these young women to repeat my text over and over until they had found exactly the right intonation, exactly the right gesture or the traditional dance step for the scene.

Their passion was completely reassuring. I knew right away it would be a fine production.

I must mention that Françoise's direction is quite remarkable. A blend of gentleness and firmness, and a constant concern with the authentic.

She frequently asked for my opinion and criticisms, but I could only express my satisfaction.

It did not even disturb me to change my pace of work. I usually write early in the morning and stop at noon to rest. In Paris I still cling to that pleasant Mediterranean custom of the sieste. After a mid-day halt the return to work is easier, lighter.

Well, I had no siestes in New York and I don't regret this.

The very brief pauses allowed in the rehearsal schedule forced me to adapt to a new rhythm and to stay alert all day. I could thus speak to the actors through an interpreter and learn what they expected of me as their playwright.

The whole Algerian community of New York was present at the premiere. They enjoyed the show which went beyond a theatrical production... It was a veritable journey.

FATIMA GALLAIRE

CHARACTERS

LELLA, *Princess*
THE OLD MAN, *Family retainer*
NOUNOU, *Lella's old nurse*
THE MABOULA, *The Madwoman*
FOUR YOUNG WOMEN:
    HADDA, *Lella's poor cousin*
    BADIA, *Lella's former schoolmate*
    ABLA, *Lella's childhood friend*
    AICHA, *Lella's former schoolmate*
THE SLAVE
THE CRIPPLE
FIVE OLD WOMEN:
    THE ELDER
    ZAHRA
    CHERIFA
    KHADIJA
    THE ANGRY WOMAN
THE MALE ELDER

SETTING

The play takes place in the courtyard of a traditional Algerian home. The time is the present.

PROLOGUE

Total darkness. Silence. The sound of footsteps climbing stairs is heard—two sets of footsteps, one light and even; the other heavy, tired, staggering. The breathing that accompanies the steps is audible, amplified to fill the darkness. The voice of an old man is heard. He is trying to catch his breath.

OLD MAN: What an idea... arriving in the middle of the night like this. As a surprise. For who, huh? Poor Princess. You've learned little about the world... about people's ingratitude... but... What the devil did you put in this to make it so heavy?

He is answered by the juvenile and joyful voice of a young woman.

LELLA: Presents!

The two voices alternate, his increasingly grouchy, hers increasingly cheerful.

OLD MAN: Presents. You haven't changed. Still so completely generous, so completely crazy. Tell me... oof, this is heavier than hell, I swear...

LELLA: Poor man.

OLD MAN: Tell me now, how did you manage to survive over there where people count and measure... Presents. Always in the clouds, far from the hard facts of reality. That must explain how you can give away so much happiness.

We hear the sound of an object falling and breaking.

LELLA: My God, what... ?

OLD MAN: Let's stop a minute.

The footsteps cease.

LELLA: Nounou used to leave candles here. I'm sure that was her candlestick that I hit.

OLD MAN: Nounou... My dear girl, your Nounou never comes this way now. You forget how old she is. They even say she's lost her wits, poor soul.

LELLA: I know, I know, old Father... but give me the time to get there and catch my breath before announcing any more tragic truths.

OLD MAN: I just wanted to tell you she's gone back to live in her hovel at the edge of the village. Most would have given their eyeteeth to live in this house but she wouldn't hear of it. She said she didn't want to sleep with ghosts. Old as she is, her mind's a little off... Shall we go on?

LELLA: I'm ready.

The footsteps begin again.

OLD MAN: I think we're almost there.

LELLA: Do be careful. The last steps are the steepest.

OLD MAN: Oh, don't worry about me. I'm not afraid of heights. It's only on flat ground that I lose my balance. *(He laughs.)*

LELLA: Ah, ha. So, you're still at your old, extravagant ways.

OLD MAN: What else is there left to console me?

LELLA: Has your drinking tainted your heart? Or prevented you from acting at times like a saint?

OLD MAN: Ah, Princess, I've had too much fun to be a saint.

LELLA: Wait, I've found something. Maybe a candle.

OLD MAN: So, at least we will live through the night... tended by a small flickering light.

LELLA: Saintly old man, is it in your power to find a light?

OLD MAN: That's what I'm looking for.

> *He sets the heavy suitcases down. We hear the sound of a match being struck, which illuminates a large courtyard surrounded on three sides by the walls of the house. The match goes out.*

We're here. Let me put your suitcases near the door. Come on, you're on the last step. I'll find another match.

> *They step into the courtyard. His breathing sound labored— like a forge.*

LELLA: Poor man, I've exhausted you.

OLD MAN: Don't move. *(He lights a match.)* There... can you see?

> *The candle flame reveals a man and a woman. He is a big man with very dark, wrinkled skin, wearing simple clothes. She is a young woman of medium size, wearing Western dress. They apparently have nothing in common except a mutual affection. Both look at each other and the surroundings, moving back and forth and murmuring exclamations of discovery. All around is the silence of the night. Two suitcases stand in the middle of the courtyard.*

LELLA: Yes... nothing... nothing has changed. It's exactly as I remember it.

OLD MAN: Well, stone stays pretty much the same, you know.

LELLA: *(indicating a bare trellis overhead)* But the arbor?

OLD MAN: Nothing's grown for years. No water. Nobody to tend to it. Well, here you are.

LELLA: Thanks to you.

OLD MAN: Thanks to me, true enough. Who else would have come on this crazy expedition in the middle of the night?

LELLA: Oh, where are my manners? Let's sit down. Please have a seat.

The old man sighs with relief and sinks down on the stone step leading to the rooms of the house.

OLD MAN: To tell you the truth, I wouldn't have done this for anyone else; driving out in the middle of the night—it's pure madness.

LELLA: You know the way better than any taxi driver.

OLD MAN: No doubt about that, but it isn't the pot holes in our roads that are the greatest dangers.

LELLA: What then?

OLD MAN: Robbers, my child, robbers.

LELLA: What robbers?

THE OLD MAN: Highway robbers! The roads are crawling with them.

LELLA: My Lord!

OLD MAN: Oh, please, I'm not your Lord.

LELLA: *(bowing in courtly fashion)* My Lord. Are you sure you're not exaggerating? You haven't been up to your old extravagant ways? You didn't have just a little glass of wine before you came to get me?

OLD MAN: Who's friendly enough around here to offer me a glass of wine? I have to buy it by the bottle and God knows it costs enough. I swear I haven't touch a drop.

LELLA: Well, you have brought me here safely, despite the pot holes and the robbers and I can at least offer you a glass of water.

OLD MAN: Water? Where do you think we are? There's no water at his hour, not here. No water or anything else... But there's a bit of the night left to rest. Take the candle and go to the far room. Maybe there's a mattress that hasn't been completely devoured by the moths. I'll wait here for the sorceress. At dawn, she'll come with water.

LELLA: You still call my nurse "the sorceress?"

OLD MAN: What nurse? She never nursed anyone, as far as I know.

LELLA: She tried to.

OLD MAN: I tried to be a good Moslem when I was young. Where has it got me? What do I look like?

LELLA: A poor but good Moslem.

OLD MAN: Yes, when I'm sober. You see me now, calm and content, but it's your kindness that makes me this way. I am so happy you are back. Oh, I know I'm not laughing... I've forgotten how. My heart is so full of bitterness... How can I expect to enter the paradise of Allah?

LELLA: Old friend, are you blaspheming?

OLD MAN: Ah, no! I would never do that in your presence, never... You're the only one... the only one who ever understood me.

LELLA: It just occurred to me... you don't chew tobacco anymore?

OLD MAN: Lord, yes. You've made me forget everything. *(He draws out his pouch and begins chewing.)* It's not as good as it used to be.

LELLA: Old man, tell me.

OLD MAN: What?

LELLA: You don't think I'm ungrateful, disrespectful, monstrous?

OLD MAN: Princess, Princess, why these shocking words?

LELLA: My father has been dead for three months and I've not come.

OLD MAN: He wouldn't care. He said you'd buried each other years ago; may God have mercy...

LELLA: I know. But sitting here like this, with his grave freshly dug, I keep looking for signs of grief and I feel nothing.

OLD MAN: Do you think he did? He lived a privileged life and died with no regrets.

LELLA: So, it's as it should be. Since the day I left twenty years ago, he did everything possible to prevent my return... unless I begged his pardon. Which I would not do, so I didn't come back. I missed my mother's grave more than my father's face. I saw her buried when I was a child and I haven't gotten over that.

OLD MAN: She was a saint.

LELLA: I know how much you worshipped her.

OLD MAN: It's almost daybreak; you should get some sleep. Go on, now.

LELLA: Will you stay here for the rest of the night?

OLD MAN: I'm not crazy enough to leave you here alone. Early morning prayers will begin soon. I'll wait here. As soon as the sorceress comes, I'll leave.

LELLA: I'm sorry I have nothing to offer you.

OLD MAN: The house has been empty for so long. You've come back and given me the joy of seeing you again. I didn't expect it and I want nothing more now. Go to bed, Princess. Here, take the candle.

LELLA: I don't need it. I can find my way in this labyrinth that I still love.

A woman's voice is heard, clear and tense.

VOICE OF MABOULA: *Berber ala dorrok.*

LELLA: What's that?

OLD MAN: That? Just the Madwoman; your neighbor, the Maboula, don't you remember?

LELLA: You mean she's still alive?

OLD MAN: She's no older than you. You were born in the same year.

LELLA: I guess you're right. But it seems her madness would have worn her out by now.

OLD MAN: Far from that! When she has real fits and starts raving at the market place, it takes at least ten men to restrain her.

VOICE OF MABOULA: *Berber ala dorrok.*

OLD MAN: She's singing for you. She knows you're here. She wants to comfort you. Go now. Good night, Princess.

LELLA: Good night.

The flame of the candle dies as the sky progressively lights up. The muezzin's call to prayer announces dawn.

PART I

The light of dawn intensifies. The set is the same but the silhouette of the old man sitting on the threshold has changed to that of an old woman (Nounou). She wears a traditional dark dress. She waits patiently. The sounds of the waking village are heard: birds chirping, a car starting up somewhere, a distant call. Lella appears quietly at the doorway behind Nounou, who lifts her head and stays motionless a moment, her face radiating joy. They embrace in silence and then separate to look at each other. They hug each other again. Lella is laughing and sobbing, Nounou wipes away a tear, then the words burst forth. The two women turn in the courtyard, talking to each other, thanking the heavens, laughing, crying. In the following dialogue their voices intermingle.

LELLA: To see you again!

NOUNOU: You have come back! You are back! God has looked on me! You are back.

LELLA: *Haou jit.* I have come.

NOUNOU: *Haou jiti.* You have come.

LELLA: *Haou jitek.* I've come back. *Haou jitkem.* I've come back to you.

NOUNOU: *Haou jitini.* You have come back to me. *Haou jitine.* You have come back to us.

LELLA: *Ouenti jiti.* You also have come.

NOUNOU: *El Hamdou lilleh!* Praise be to God! He has heard me; me, the old woman, the sorceress. He has let me live long enough to see your dear face again. Heart of my heart, back again, flesh of my flesh. Have you come back to bury me?

LELLA: Nounou, you're eternal, solid as a rock. No, I haven't come to bury you, may God hear me. And you know death is close to us all: the old and the newborn, to the woman who's just given birth and the man in good health. You are perhaps the one who will bury me.

NOUNOU: Never! God would not allow that. I have known the injustice of burying those dear to me and some younger than I. I have had my share of sorrow. I gave your mother her last bath and her mother before her. I brought them up, just as I did you. My eyes have turned dry from having cried too much. I shed my last tear, a tear of joy at seeing you. That is my last. I can go to rest now. Thank you for coming to hold my hand. It is not fear that makes me jabber like this. I so wanted to see your dear face before returning to my creator.

LELLA: Nounou, you're still sturdy. You're not even a hundred yet.

NOUNOU: Yes, I am. I am one hundred and three and I still have all my wits.

LELLA: I have children now, you know. Wouldn't you like to meet them?

NOUNOU: I have often dreamt of your twins. I wore the last of my eyes out looking at the pictures you sent. I have seen them so often in my sleep that I know them as well as you, believe me. Do you know how much I love them?

LELLA: Soon you'll be able to see them.

NOUNOU: No, I will not see them. There are too many forces working against that, too much hate and evil around us. Child of the child of my child, just to think you have children of your own overjoys me. On this blessed day, I have held you close again, something I so hoped for although it seemed hopeless. But you must listen to me now...

LELLA: But listen to me...

NOUNOU: Listen to me, you hear? You must leave. Do not ask

me why, that is how I feel it. Bury me today and then leave.

LELLA: You are going to make me laugh in a most disrespectful way. What is all this talk of burial? I have come to pay my respects to my father, the *Hadj* who has gone to meet my mother. That's all. I have no wish to bury anyone.

NOUNOU: Light of my life, do not leave me behind again. I am too dry and useless. I have drained my strength praying for your return. I have no more reason to live. I have a right to die.

LELLA: It's true, at your age, dying is right.

NOUNOU: Do not leave me here alone.

LELLA: I won't leave you here.

NOUNOU: May God hear you.

LELLA: I'll take you back with me, back to what is now home to me, on the other side of the sea. I have a big house there; your place is there, waiting for you.

NOUNOU: Sweet adorable child, you are now raving worse than me. It is not a new start I need but a quiet end. I am so tired that if you allowed it, I would let go right here and now. Strange and troubling sounds have reached my ears and I am afraid to interpret them. Too many people wish to harm you. You have stayed as pure as the gold that surrounded your childhood but people are evil, foul, spiteful. Be careful. Do not linger here. Close these dry eyes and be on your way. Promise me you will.

LELLA: Nounou.

NOUNOU: Promise.

Cries rise from the street; the voices of the Young Women are heard.

LELLA: That's for us, I think.

NOUNOU: Here I am chattering away and I have not even thought to feed you. It is disgraceful, I am forgetting my duty. The water must be back on now. We will greet your guests and then I will prepare the tea... No, first you must get ready. *(She stands back to look at Lella.)* Lovely child... you are so beautiful. I am the color of earth, you are the color of life. Go, put on your finest clothes, a royal dress for a royal occasion. As your oldest relative, I order you to dress and show both friends and enemies who you really are: our Princess.

> *Lella goes inside to dress. Nounou moves to open the door. The door leading to the stairs and the street will remain open for the rest of the scene.*

> *The Young Women who enter are entirely veiled in white. As they cross the threshold, they withdraw the veils from their faces. Their dresses, semi-traditional, are brightly colored. Only one stands out because she is not veiled and wears a tattered and drably colored dress under a shawl. This is the Madwoman, the Maboula, as she is commonly referred to.*

> *The group is composed of childhood friends and neighbors, those who had left the village to marry in town, cousins of various degrees, poorer women seeking a meal and a blessing, and sick women hoping for a miracle.*

> *The emotion, the tension and the volume of speech will rise as the morning progresses.*

> *The guests enter the courtyard where rugs and cushions, worn but of still vibrant colors, are laid out. The scene is visually and musically spectacular.*

> *Nounou presides over the arrangements of the party. She settles the guests comfortably, according to a secret and subtle hierarchy. She calls out to a young neighbor from the top of the stairs, asking him to fetch cakes, candy and lemonade. An immense round table is set up in the middle of the guests, who are seated on the ground.*

Hadda, a poor cousin with only one eye, has been given the task of watching over the Maboula. The Madwoman is calm for the moment but there is a wariness of her erratic behavior.

Stunning in her traditional dress, Lella appears in the doorway. She is greeted by cries of joy and hoots of admiration. After numerous embraces, bows, exclamations, thanks to Allah, laughing, cooing and crying around Lella, the guests sit in a demi-circle which will remain agitated. There is a festive atmosphere that invades the scene. It might be Thursday, eve of the Holy Day, and it is summer, the wedding season. Music floats in from the village. The women continue to talk all at once, savoring their pleasure.

YOUNG WOMEN:
Rabbi chef lina!
Rabbi kbir!
El Hamdou lilleh!
How wonderful to be back.
Little has changed.
Here again.

LELLA AND VOICES: *(mingling)*
Lella, you have come home. *Haou jiti!*
I have come back, yes.
Lella, we have come.
You have come! You are here!
Haou jiti! You have come back to us.
Haou jitou! You have come, all of you.
Haou jimek! We have come.
The lovely, the saintly, the gentle one is here again.
Here we are! Together despite the years.
This is a blessed day, a beautiful day.
Lella! God has seen us.
Princess, you are still our princess.
We are not alone.
The French people cannot love you as we do.
Do they know what love is?

LELLA: One of them loves me.

VOICES: And he has managed to keep you over there. Then he must really be a man. Do the French spoil you as we do?

LELLA: One of them does.

VOICES: Ah, this French one who loves you and spoils you is some man. Has he made you forget us?

LELLA: If that were true, I wouldn't be here. I remember everything. I remember everyone.

BADIA: So, tell us all about it.

LELLA: Before I tell you about my new country, I want to talk about this one that I have missed so, even in my sleep. What is your news? Tell me everything about those I love and those who no longer love me.

BADIA: Princess, Lella!

LELLA: Yes, Badia, tell me. You have the honor of being the first to speak.

BADIA: It's true I had the honor of splashing in the same pond as you, Lella. We were hiding, of course; the waters were forbidden to the girls. Do you remember?

LELLA: Happy memories will never leave me.

BADIA: You remember the green pond? It's still there, as dangerous as ever.

LELLA: Dangerous as ever?

BADIA: That's what I tell my grandchildren. Because I am, at forty, a grandmother.

LELLA: It stands to reason, my friend and sister. You were married twenty years before I was. Your grandchildren are as old as my children.

BADIA: Lella, you cannot imagine how the village has changed.

LELLA: The little I saw of it last night gave me that impression.

BADIA: When I say change, I mean for the worse.

LELLA: I feared as much.

BADIA: Yet I have stayed here. I was well married, you know. Do you remember the student from the technical school who was so shy? I used to meet him secretly in the evening.

LELLA: What I remember is I was terrified you'd get caught!

BADIA: You were so well brought up and obedient at that time. Daring came late to you.

LELLA: True, I'm a late bloomer.

BADIA: The more luscious the fruit. But I am quite happy with my lot and so are my daughters. They're married, too. I look after their children.

LELLA: You've always cared for others.

The Madwoman jumps up suddenly.

MABOULA: *Berber ala dorrok.*

NOUNOU: Keep her quiet! Why is she here, anyway? She does not recognize a soul.

HADDA: Put a plate at her feet. She will quiet down if she eats something.

Hadda forces the Maboula to sit down. Seeing the pastry, the Madwoman becomes calm. Nounou moves around the group, offering tea, coffee and treats. All the women nibble as they continue their conversation.

BADIA: You know, Lella, a lot of our school friends have moved away; not as far as you, but still... too far to be here today. They married and left for Annaba, Constantine, Bejaia, Jijel, Blida, Algiers... *(She adopts a jocking tone.)* But none were as fickle as you, going so far from us.

LELLA: I know, I crossed seas and mountains but I also crossed centuries and that hurt very much. I was full of wounds I thought would never heal until I met this man.

WOMEN: *(in chorus)* Praise be to the Frenchman. May God watch over him.

LELLA: Sisters, it's true. I have found a pleasant companion and... a wonderful lover.

The women burst out giggling. They rock and shake with laughter as they repeat "a wonderful lover" in different tones of complicity.

MABOULA: Bravo! Bravo!

NOUNOU: Hadda, make her eat some more. May she choke on her cake.

LELLA: Nounou, why try to be so mean? You really never knew how.

NOUNOU: If it were up to me, you would already be on the airplane; and me, at peace in my grave.

BADIA: Ever since we heard you were coming, all she's talked about is going to the cemetery and staying for good. She begged us to have her grave ready when you arrived. But no one in their right mind would do that. It's blasphemous to prepare the tomb of a living person.

NOUNOU: I am not saying a word. I am too busy with my hands to chatter.

ABLA: May I speak now?

BADIA: Yes, go on. You've so much to tell. I have had my say. Everything is going well for me, thank God.

ABLA: Princess, with your permission...

LELLA: Abla, have you forgotten we ate from the same bowl?

ABLA: Princess, your simplicity is admired even by your enemies. You mean that you ate from my wooden bowl and I ate from your fine dishes, painted with fruits and flowers. You always treated me as your equal, poor as I was, and I almost believed it. Some say today that I am too proud.

LELLA: That doesn't matter. How have you been, Abla?

ABLA: I have become accustomed to hunger. My husband never really had a decent job. All I have I give to my children. I married late, like you, and I had twins, like you.

LELLA: So they told me. I have brought them some clothes. And I've brought each of you a little present. Nounou will pass them out later.

VOICES: Ah, Nounou, the good sorceress!

NOUNOU: Sorceress, indeed, silly little birds. I have never opened a tomb to steal the nails or the hair off a body.

VOICES:
Lord, nor have I!
Me neither.
We would never do that.
Not even as a favor?

LELLA: That's enough! Abla, please go on.

ABLA: I can't really complain. I survive and my children get a decent meal from time to time.

LELLA: Do you remember my mother?

ABLA: How could I forget her? She fed me all through childhood, all the time she was alive. She was a saintly woman; her heart was like her face, pure and beautiful.

LELLA: Your words are like honey to me. And what of your elder sister?

ABLA: Poor Sessia! She's on her fifth marriage.

LELLA: Widowed four times?

ABLA: If it were only that! No, repudiated four times.

LELLA: I thought that repudiation was banned. If the husband remarries, doesn't the wife have the right to stay on if she has children?

ABLA: According to law, yes; although there's a big difference between what they say and what they do. But Sessia's case is special because she was actually divorced by our father, so to speak. He arranges the marriage and then, as soon as he has an argument with his son-in-law, he comes to fetch her, leaving the children to the husband.

LELLA: So this is his fifth son-in-law from one daughter?

ABLA: Exactly. And poor Sessia has strewn a dozen children around the country and she will probably never see them again. At this moment she seems happy in her new home. Her husband is a gentle sort but Sessia is already scared because Father has started demanding this and that and she doesn't know how long her husband's patience will hold out.

LELLA: How she must suffer in silence. I'm sorry she isn't here today.

ABLA: Just to hear you were coming, Sessia cried for joy. She was here for a wedding last week but couldn't stay. She asked me to give you a kiss for her.

LELLA: Please send her my blessings. *(She turns to another woman.)* Aicha, what have you got to tell us? You've been dying to speak.

AICHA: Many good things. I married in the city, on the coast. You remember I always wanted to live near the sea. Anyway, they had claimed I was sterile.

LELLA: I'd heard that. When a woman has been badly cared for, they often say she's sterile. And they never think of the husband.

AICHA: My womb was closed for nine years. After nine years of waiting I had a son. Allah rewards the pure of heart.

LELLA: Yes... so they say.

AICHA: And I am expecting another his fall. Perhaps I will have ten more, just like my mother.

LELLA: Bless you.

NOUNOU: We are going to run out of pastries! And it's almost time for lunch.

LELLA: But Nounou, we haven't stopped eating. Why are you worrying about lunch?

NOUNOU: No one will ever say...

LELLA: No one can say that we don't feed our guests, that we don't stuff you in this house, I know. A question of honor. Send the boy to the inn. Ask him to bring the best meal there is. Nicely spiced.

VOICES: *(in chorus)*
  God bless you.
  God bless you and keep you.
  She has come back. She is here. And so are we.
  We embrace and we laugh together.
  Blessed day.

> *Nounou goes to the door to issue the order and comes back muttering.*

NOUNOU: And the hour of prayer is approaching.

VOICES:
  God will forgive us.
  We will let the hour go by.
  We will pray twice as hard this evening.
  This is the time for our coming together.

LELLA: Nounou, do you need any help?

NOUNOU: No, everyone stay put. I do not want any hysterical girls under foot. And they have come to see you, not to get in my way, these little magpies.

VOICES:
  Pay no attention to harsh words.
  Nounou hides a heart of gold.
  Nounou, show us a little dance.
  Today is a day for rejoicing, not for grumbling.
  Show us how to dance.

> *One woman pulls out a tambourine and begins to beat the rhythm. The group applauds and joins in. The Maboula stands up and begins to dance.*

LELLA: Somebody stop her. She's going to fall down.

> *The Madwoman abandons her body to the dance, swirling faster and faster to the frantic beat of the tambourine. For a moment,*

only the violent music, the tambourine, the increasingly rapid steps of the Maboula and the clapping of the women is heard. The dance reaches a crescendo and the Madwoman falls to the ground, unconscious. Hadda rushes to her side and lays her gently on the cushions, using her shawl as a pillow. There is a moment of silence.

LELLA: What can we do to help her?

NOUNOU: She got what she wanted. Let us hope she will sleep through the rest of the day at least. Sometimes she collapses like that for two or three days. Just go on with your conversation.

LELLA: So, Aicha, finish your story. How did you manage to survive nine years of a barren marriage?

AICHA: Through my mother-in-law. She was a Godsend. From the start, she adored me. Do you know her?

LELLA: No, but I've heard of her.

VOICES:
So have I!
I saw her at a wedding.
I saw her at a funeral.
She lives near my aunt.

AICHA: Well, you must have heard how fat she is. She's enormous, big as a whale. She's so fat she can hardly move. She only goes out in a car and does nothing in the house. Her only son is her pride and joy. When it was time to find him a wife, she started looking for a rare pearl, hard working, cheerful, respectful, efficient, excellent cook, someone who would wait on her hand and foot and, of course, a virgin. Who else answered this description but me? The ideal daughter-in-law who treats her like a queen and who has never failed her through the years, who entertains her love and her gluttony. Do you think she would give up all that, this paradise on earth, simply to have a grandchild within the year? She waited patiently, waited and prayed.

LELLA: Prayed?

AICHA: Prayed for days on end. She didn't get any thinner but she kept praying just the same. And God answered her prayers. God and the healer we finally consulted. I underwent a treatment that opened my womb. And my mother-in-law loves me more than ever.

> *An unearthly wail interrupts the narration. The Maboula awakes, thrashing and crying and freezing the group with terror.*

NOUNOU: Hadda, give her a blow and knock her out. Let us be rid of this wailing.

HADDA: *(holding out her empty hands)* How should I knock her out?

NOUNOU: Take the tambourine.

VOICES: *(in chorus)*
Oh, no. That's for dancing.

> *The Madwoman cries out again in her half-consciousness.*

MABOULA: *Berber ala dorrok.*

NOUNOU: Here, take the soup ladle.

HADDA: But I'll kill her with that.

NOUNOU: So, kill her.

HADDA: A fan. I'd rather have a fan.

NOUNOU: Who has a fan? A heavy one.

> *The Madwoman continues to howl intermittently. There is some confusion and muttering in the group as the women search for an appropriate object. The sun is rising to its zenith. A few noises from the outside penetrate the atmosphere. At last, a girl appears*

with a brightly colored fan that she hands to Hadda. Hadda, poised with the fan, observes the Maboula.

HADDA: She seems to be quieting down.

NOUNOU: Hit her!

Hadda hits the Madwoman with the fan. Each time the Maboula cries out, Hadda hits her until she is quiet again.

LELLA: Can we go on or must we kill this poor woman?

NOUNOU: The blows do not hurt her. That is all she understands. She is used to it.

LELLA: So, let's go on. Hadda, it's your turn to speak.

HADDA: Princess, I have little to say. All is well.

LELLA: My little cousin, still so fragile, still so discreet. How is your old mother?

HADDA: *(laughing)* Still old and still as mother as before. Wait till she hears you have come back!

Steps are heard on the stairs, then a knock at the door. Nounou goes to the door and brings back a magnificent royal couscous. The guests cluster around the table as the dinner is ceremoniously served. Glasses are filled with lemonade and buttermilk. The Madwoman sits up but does not partake of the meal. Instead, she rocks back and forth, hums or laughs alone. Sometimes she lets out a howl and receives a blow with the fan that silences her. The other women eat with pleasure.

LELLA: Why can't this poor madwoman, who is my neighbor, also speak?

OTHERS: Leave her out of this. She is nothing but a bother.

LELLA: She doesn't bother me. I am not a stranger nor an enemy. There is nothing to be ashamed of. I love her as I love you all... Do you think she recognizes me?

BADIA: Of course she does. She knows you're here. She stayed awake the whole night waiting for you. She was very agitated and only fell asleep after you arrived.

LELLA: I heard her screaming last night.

BADIA: To tell the truth, she was very upset to hear you were coming. As usual, she fears a calamity.

LELLA: When the mad speak of a calamity, it's best to listen.

VOICES:
  What is this about?
  Today is a day for fun.
  For eating and dancing.

BADIA: Why worry about a crazy woman who screams and rocks herself?

LELLA: This crazy woman senses things more keenly than any of us. What does she talks about when she raves?

BADIA: She has spoken of your inheritance, your father's legacy.

LELLA: What legacy?

BADIA: She says it cannot be accepted. She keeps repeating that... Lella, this couscous is delicious. Eat and enjoy it.

LELLA: Is it money?

BADIA: I don't think so. Or that and something more.

> *Steps are heard on the stairs. A woman, veiled in black, appears at the doorway and rushes to throw herself at Lella's feet.*

FATIMA GALLAIRE

LELLA: Stand up, whoever you are, sister or mother. What is your name?

SLAVE: I am your slave.

LELLA: I have no slaves.

SLAVE: I was your slave before you were even born.

NOUNOU: She is one of the old servants of your grandfather. She looked after you at your birth when I was ill. I recognize her by the tattoos on her arm.

LELLA: Then come rejoice with us. Rise, lift your veil and eat with us.

SLAVE: Never. I can neither stand nor eat in your presence.

LELLA: *(amused)* Well, excuse me for asking such a silly question, but just what have you come for then?

SLAVE: To protect you with my life.

LELLA: Protect me from what, old Mother?

SLAVE: From all that threatens you on this fatal day.

LELLA: May I at least see your face?

SLAVE: You know my face. It is inscribed in your memory.

LELLA: You keep evading me. If you are my slave, what can I ask of you?

SLAVE: Anything you wish is my command.

LELLA: Then stand up immediately and remove your veil. If you are ready to die for me, I must see your face.

SLAVE: Princess, please think before you speak.

LELLA: I have. Rise. Remove your veil.

The Slave rises slowly. The women wait in anxious silence.

LELLA: *(pointing and commanding)* First, turn around so that all can see you. Now, uncover your face.

The Slave executes the orders slowly. The women let out a collective gasp. The Slave's face is smeared with ashes. The Madwoman lets out a howl and rises. She begins rocking back and forth in a strange dance that the Slave joins in. The other women enter the Maboula's litany, singing and clapping their hands. They create a strange, disturbing music, a lullaby filled with wildness. Only Lella and Nounou do not join in, witnesses of this impromptu and disquieting performance. The two dancers reach a crescendo and then fall slowly to the ground. There is a moment of silence. Suddenly, a heavy thudding is heard on the stairs—the sound of a body dragging itself up each step. A head appears at the doorway. It seems to be crawling along the floor. It is followed by two overly muscular arms that drag the trunk in. The Cripple wears a pair of old shoes on his hands. The women scream and rush to cover their faces in front of the man. The Cripple looks over the space with a feverish eye. He tries to bow but his posture is twisted and ludicrous. He looks like a gargoyle.

CRIPPLE: Princess, honorable women, I greet you. Please excuse this intrusion if you can.

LELLA: Welcome, poor creature of God. You really frightened us. We thought a man was trying to get in. What brings you here without warning?

CRIPPLE: Although I am not worthy of such an honor, I have come to see you, light of the earth. I may be only half a man but I have always done my duty and I do not wish to frighten anyone. I am not worthy of this thread of life that binds my poor person.

LELLA: May God watch over you, courageous soul. You have greeted us, now speak your mind.

CRIPPLE: My life may seem of little value to others but it is my most precious possession. I offer it to you, Princess, and I tell you now: leave.

LELLA: Good man, have you been drinking?

CRIPPLE: No.

LELLA: Have you been fasting?

CRIPPLE: No.

LELLA: Have you taken any sort of drugs that makes you see and hear what does not exist?

CRIPPLE: No.

LELLA: Then I don't understand.

CRIPPLE: Pardon me, Princess, but there is nothing to understand except that you are in great danger. You must believe me.

LELLA: Sisters, what do you think?

VOICES OF WOMEN:
He is not whole but he is not crazy.
They say he never lies; he respects women and truth.
He is not fully a man but he is good and just.
He never lies.

LELLA: Very well... then I must listen to him... Nounou, give him something for his trouble.

CRIPPLE: No. I want nothing. You were always good to me; you never scorned me... you owe me nothing... just leave, quickly. I have heard little, but enough to know your life is threatened.

LELLA: Who is threatening me?

CRIPPLE: I do not know. This is all I know, may God have mercy.

LELLA: I thank you for your concern. You may leave now.

CRIPPLE: Farewell, Princess. I hope we will meet again... in better times.

LELLA: Farewell.

> *The deformed man exits, inching his trunk backwards. The sound of his thumping down the stairs is heard.*

LELLA: My heart is suddenly filled with sadness and questions concerning this misfortune. I've been told the birds are deserting the village. Is there to be an earthquake?

VOICES OF WOMEN:
We must sing...
Sing and dance...
Defy the malediction...
Chase our fears...
Be rid of dark ideas...

> *The Maboula awakes and sings her litany.*

MABOULA: *Berber ala dorrok.*

LELLA: Sisters, let's finish this couscous and have some desserts; then we will dance. What do you think of the dish?

VOICES OF WOMEN:
It must come straight from paradise.
Under the heavy fragrance of the sauce, you can taste the freshness of the butter that penetrates the smooth grain of the couscous.
The lamb is abundant and perfectly browned.
It's fit for a king.

The chick peas are wonderfully seasoned.
And the tomatoes, just the right note of sour.
We know we are in a fine house that serves only the best.
Lella, you're not eating...

LELLA: I admit I don't eat as much as I used to... but watching enjoy yourselves is a greater pleasure for me than eating. It reminds me of the old days we spent together.

BADIA: Lella, do you remember how we use to drive the dorm mistress crazy when we sang our own rendition of "Au clair de la lune?"

LELLA: Oh, yes! I had forgotten that.

BADIA: And how shocked the French girls were that we could massacre such a lovely little song for children?

LELLA: Yes, I remember.

AICHA: And do you remember our Jewish friends?

LELLA: Of course. I even remember their names: Vivi, Nanou and Poupée.

AICHA: We had a lot of fun together. The Jews and the Moslems, as they used to call us. We held each other's hands; we felt such solidarity. We used to dream of building a new world where justice reigned, remember? The French girls would laugh at us... I suspect they're still laughing.

LELLA: Please don't be bitter. Don't spoil these beautiful memories.

NOUNOU: Enough. It is time we got on with this meal. The Elders will be here soon and we still have to go to the cemetery to pay our respects.

ABLA: Nounou, you are a century old and your heart is serene.

We're still young and curious about the world. We are here to bring back memories as well as to mourn the Pilgrim, the *Hadj,* the saintly man who has left us.

NOUNOU: Mourn him, huh? I am sure your grief could be relieved with a little money.

HADDA: Nounou, you shouldn't talk like that, even though it might be true.

LELLA: Don't get upset, Nounou. You know you'll eventually have your way. It's useless to keep trying to appear so mean. We are enjoying a rare and precious moment together and your grumbling doesn't change that.

BADIA: Well said. Let's finish as we began, joyfully. The mourning period continues and we'll celebrate it our own way, by dancing for our beloved Princess.

> *One woman begins beating on the tambourine and is joined by other tambourines and the women's voices, crying and laughing in concert to the sharply marked rhythm. The music rises toward a crescendo. At last Lella gets up and enters into the dance. The rhythm becomes more precise and a voice, delicate and marvelous, rises high above the others, singing in French in a Tzigane style. At the end of the song, strains of "Au clair de la lune" emerge.*

PART II

It is early afternoon and the village is sleeping. Lella and Nounou are alone.

NOUNOU: Poor vulnerable child. And such a generous heart.

LELLA: Nounou, what's wrong? You seem so worried.

NOUNOU: May Allah be with us today.

LELLA: Stop courting misfortune. We have other things to do... What are you afraid of?

NOUNOU: The visit of the old women.

LELLA: *(laughing)* You know them better than I do, these old women. Why are you so afraid of them today?

NOUNOU: Because of the oracle. The Madwoman spoke. So did the Cripple. He is somewhat simple-minded, so I believe him.

LELLA: Here predictions always announce doom! Listen, I know these women who've invited themselves in this afternoon. I remember most of them. I know they're a little intrusive and sometimes shrewish but they're basically inoffensive.

NOUNOU: Time goes by... Things have changed...

LELLA: Time goes by for all of us.

NOUNOU: Some of them have changed a lot. They love you less since you married the foreigner. Some of them might even hate you.

LELLA: I never asked them to adore me! Is that coffee I smell?

NOUNOU: Oh, dear. Here I am chattering away while the coffee boils over. Come, child.

LELLA: Let's sit in the shade. Our first guest won't be here before midafternoon, I hope. I want the time to savor this coffee. *(Nounou serves the coffee.)* Mmm, the aroma of your coffee is really unique. I never found that over there.

NOUNOU: Listen to me now, you who talk without hearing what is said.

LELLA: You're the one who's talking, and loudly, too. Have you suddenly shed fifty years to be able to speak with such force?

NOUNOU: No, I am afraid.

LELLA: This coffee is perfect. Would you feel better if I told you I've never had any that was half as good elsewhere? It's true; you know just how to combine the strong coffee with the delicate flavor of the orange blossom and the sensuality of the sugar.

NOUNOU: What a time to drone on about the coffee! You must listen to me. Child of the child of my child, please.

> *There is a violent knocking on the door. Startled, Nounou jumps.*

LELLA: Don't worry; it's only our elderly guests. Your day isn't over yet.

> *Lella moves to the door to let in the women. She greets them cheer-fully and courteously. There are the usual embraces and exclama-tions. The women, who are dressed in somber colors, look like a group of keeners. Except for the traditional white veils that cover their faces, they are dressed in dark colors: black, navy, brown and indigo. Their attitude is strained as they exchange polite, ritual greetings.*

ALL:
Salem.
Salem.

> *As the guests enter, they take their places in a half-circle. Nounou enters and greets the group as Lella settles in her place. The*

Madwoman is also in the group, sitting at her previous place to the side of the old women. Conversation is superficial as the group waits for all the women to be seated. The women refuse to eat or drink from the tray that Nounou offers. This is a bad sign. Nounou bustles around, trying to mask her uselessness, for none will have coffee or tea. She is nervous, disturbed, on edge. She watches the group carefully. The muezzin's call to afternoon prayer is heard.

OLD WOMEN:
Life separates, as does death.
Twenty years already! Allah is great.
This is a blessed day. Praise be to God!
Allah is great, and Mohammed his prophet.

MABOULA: *Berber ala dorrok.*

OLD WOMEN:
Her again!
We don't need her.
What's she doing here anyway.

NOUNOU: She is our neighbor. She has been here since morning.

ANGRY WOMAN: If she's a neighbor, then she can go back where she came from.

LELLA: She won't disturb us. Let her be.

The Maboula continues her litany.

CHERIFA: Can't we shut her up?

ELDER: Then knock her out.

NOUNOU: No, we'd best leave her in peace. She's been very upset since last night and even more so since you have arrived, honorable ladies. *(She addresses the Elder.)* You are the Elder, which means that I have outlived my time, since I am older than you. Why do you wish of us on this eve of the Holy Day? You have refused to taste the salt of the house. It is too great an insult to ignore. It demands an explanation.

ELDER: Slave and daughter of slaves, who has given you permission to speak?

NOUNOU: I am long accustomed to taking permission, thanks to the goodness of this household that is your host. I have not to beg; I know I will die soon. It is a delivery that I have waited for too long not to recognize its coming. I will not bow to your arrogance. Have you as much as thanked the mistress of the house for receiving you?

ELDER: We can thank her directly without you butting in. You are nothing but a shadow. Remain in your place.

NOUNOU: May you be damned.

ELDER: We have much to discuss here. We will deal with your insolence later, decrepit witch.

LELLA: That's enough!

ELDER: She is not important. It is you we have come to see. Are you prepared to answer a few questions, questions born of a legitimate curiosity?

LELLA: If I had anything to hide, I wouldn't be there.

> *Nounou presses closer to Lella, as if to protect her. There is a heavy, threatening silence before the Elder speaks.*

ELDER: So, daughter of the saint, you are among us again.

LELLA: Yes, and my heart rejoices to be here.

ELDER: You have come back, after so many years away. Since you have left, the village children have become parents.

LELLA: I expect so.

ELDER: Back from so far away. From a country one cannot reach on foot... on the other side of the sea.

LELLA: That's true. Far away. But I've kept you all in my heart.

ELDER: Nor have we forgotten you.

OTHERS:
No; ah, no.
Never forgotten.
In our hearts.

LELLA: Dear Mothers, you knew me as a child. Do you recognize me now?

ELDER: Who could forget your jet-black hair, your round forehead, your eyes that are too big and your nose that is too small? And your mouth that says everything.

LELLA: That's a rather flattering portrait, venerable Mother. Have I always said everything?

NOUNOU: Be quiet! Do not say another word.

ELDER: We must admit that you have behaved as you should... at times.

NOUNOU: Princess, I tell you, do not speak. For the sake of all I've been for you and for the love of God, hold your tongue!

ELDER: However...

LELLA: Yes?

ELDER: I will let Zahra speak. She has a wicked tongue, a gift for words, especially in these matters.

ZAHRA: Woman of nobility, whose birth I witnessed, we have come because there has been talk... certain rumors have reached our ears.

OTHERS:
Of course we did not believe a word.
God forbid.
Never! It is unnatural.

LELLA: Mother Zahra, whose name means "Flower," who may be close to one hundred years old, what have you to say that is so terrible? You are generally more eloquent and your glib tongue has defended many a good cause.

ZAHRA: This will be the last, the last duty I fulfill for our people.

LELLA: Come to the point. The faster we deal with this, the sooner we'll drink together.

ZAHRA: It is true that my name is "Flower" and that I have seen four generations spring from my womb, like this old slave.

LELLA: Yes, go on.

ZAHRA: But never could I have been your mother. If I had been, if you had been my daughter, I would have smothered you early on, at the firsts signs of your disgraceful behavior.

LELLA: Those are very harsh words.

ZAHRA: They are nothing compared to the fury that rages in my heart on this day of anger.

OTHERS: *(in chorus)* On this day of anger.

ZAHRA: We have heard that you were married...

LELLA: Is that the terrible rumor? It is only natural to marry...

ZAHRA: To marry a man, yes.

LELLA: Forgive me if I want to laugh. Because I respect your white hair, I will not. But like you, your daughters and your daughter's daughters, I am married to a man.

ZAHRA: Ignominy!

OTHERS:
Dishonor! Oh, what shame! What a stigma!
Oh, what despair!
What grief!
What depravity, what disgusting behavior!
Disgrace and dishonor upon us!

LELLA: I have married a man for the sole purpose of living happily with him. Is that not simple and natural?

ZAHRA: Oh, I am suffocating. Air, I need air. Water. My heart is splitting.

> *One of the women goes to get a cup of water and tends to Zahra who has collapsed on the cushions.*

ELDER: Calm down, all of you. We must remain calm. We are here to discuss this matter. If we succumb to anger and resentment, we will not even hear what is said.

> *The Maboula stands and sways to her litany.*

LELLA: Maboula!

> *Suddenly the Maboula stops howling and stares, stupefied, at Lella.*

MABOULA: Lella, Princess, how wonderful! You have come back. I've been waiting for you for so long. Why did you leave, taking my senses with you?

LELLA: Come, sit beside me, right here, close to me.

Docile, as if hypnotized, the Maboula sits near Lella. She breaks out in a joyful contagious laughter.

ELDER: God sees us. God hears us. Sisters let peace come into your hearts. *(The women gradually quiet down.)* Let us go on... You, that they call Princess, what have you to say?

LELLA: I was speaking of my happiness and how natural this seems.

ELDER: Happiness, you say?

LELLA: Yes.

ELDER: What does that mean?

LELLA: Happiness is difficult to explain. It's... a joy for life... for sharing life with someone you love... very much.

ELDER: Love? Joy? What do these have to do with life? Life is misfortune and oppression, constraint, servility and despair.

LELLA: Venerable Mother, you talk like this because you have seen too many die. You ignore the pleasure, the joy, the sheer ecstasy that life offers, the simple wonder of children laughing.

ELDER: We do not speak the same language. You have abandoned our tongue and adopted the foreigners'. Zahra, talk to her if you can.

ZAHRA: It's very simple. For us, this is not a marriage. It is a betrayal, a desertion, a violation of our law...

LELLA: To live peacefully with a man is a betrayal, a violation?

OLD WOMEN: *(in chorus)*
What man?

The Madwoman is humming a love song.

ZAHRA: Shut her up once and for all!

NOUNOU: By what right have you set yourselves up as judges? For me there is only one supreme judge, who is looking at you now. Please, go right ahead. You have all the sacrificial lambs at your disposal.

ZAHRA: You shut up too, heathen old witch.

NOUNOU: No, I will not. To shut me up you will have to kill me.

LELLA: Please be quiet, Nounou, and let us get to the end of this.

NOUNOU: There is no good end that will come of this. Light of my life... be careful when they speak of betrayal. It is true, betrayal is all around us, veiled in black. Just look at them. Be on your guard.

LELLA: Mother, above all, let God into your heart. There, calm now. Come closer to me.

NOUNOU: These witches will have to pass over my dead body before they lay a hand on you. *(She sits at Lella's feet.)*

LELLA: Mother Zahra, you were speaking. Please continue.

ZAHRA: We asked you: What man?

LELLA: The father of my children.

ZAHRA: Are you talking about the Frenchman, the foreigner, the uncircumcised?

IN CHORUS: There, she said it! We heard. He is not circumcised. She said so.

ELDER: *(irritated)* Hush, let us go on.

IN CHORUS: Yes, let us go on.

ZAHRA: So you have married? This is true?

LELLA: And my marriage has been blessed with two children.

ZAHRA: Who is your husband?

LELLA: A man, gentle and kind.

ZAHRA: Can there be men outside of our people and our religion?

LELLA: I owe you the truth, Mother, even though you may find it painful. The answer is yes, outside of our beautiful country there are men, and it was meant to be so, since God has allowed other religions and other peoples to exist.

ZAHRA: Infidel! Woman of high rank turned woman of the streets!

LELLA: This is not the first time I've been insulted. It doesn't hurt me anymore since I know that I am right.

MABOULA: I'm thirsty.

ZAHRA: Get her out of here.

MABOULA: Is that you, Zahra? The old night witch. How many graves have you opened during your long life? How many people have fallen sick because of you, old witch?

LELLA: Go, drink. You'll find all you need in the house.

NOUNOU: She is not as mad as I thought. She is perfectly lucid now.

MABOULA: Oh yes, I am so thirsty. I'm so alive and thirsty. It's a good sign.

LELLA: Go get some water in the house.

MABOULA: But there is water here!

She moves to a jug of water and is about to pour it down her throat when one of the women rises and violently hits the jug, knocking it from her hands. The jug breaks and the water spills over the Maboula, who chokes in surprise and fear.

ONE OLD WOMAN: No one will drink until we have reached an agreement.

NOUNOU: It is a sin to refuse water to someone who is thirsty.

The terrified Maboula is crouched on the floor near Lella. She seems afraid she will be beaten and curls up, hoping she won't be noticed.

ZAHRA: Impudent slave, stop interrupting us. We have other sins to judge here, too great for you to understand or imagine.

IN CHORUS: Unworthy nurse, have you thought of the sins of this woman who has been your child through time?

NOUNOU: If she has sinned, she has also done much good in the world. You are the greater sinners because you have done nothing but harm.

ANGRY WOMAN: She is a sinner, a traitor, a whore.

IN CHORUS: May God forgive us.

ZAHRA: Yes, he sees all and hears all. We did not believed these despicable rumors, but today you have declared them true. You do not deny that you have fallen in the gutter?

ANGRY WOMAN: *(pointing to Nounou)* She is the first sinner, since she protected her and encouraged her vile acts. This old witch must be punished first.

LELLA: *(stands)* All of you here—mothers, grandmothers and

great-grandmothers—listen to me. We will never come to a reasonable agreement this way. Stop attacking this poor old nurse who is also my elder relative. If you wish to reproach me, speak to me. I am the only one responsible for my acts. I am listening.

IN CHORUS: She admits it. She is responsible. She said so.

ZAHRA: Odette, you may speak now.

CHERIFA: My name is no longer Odette. Odette the Christian, the infidel, died fifty years ago. I am now Cherifa, Allah's servant. Remember that.

IN CHORUS: Ah, well spoken, Cherifa.

ZAHRA: So, Cherifa, speak your mind.

CHERIFA: You who are called Princess, you claim to be married. But is it possible to speak of marriage in your case? To me this is blasphemous, disgusting.

LELLA: I am surprised to hear such harsh words coming from you. You who were brave enough to leave your own country to be with the man of your choice; you, who were long rejected by both communities.

CHERIFA: The comparison is insulting. I converted to Islam. And you, have you converted this man you live with?

Silence. Lella does not respond.

Yes or no?

IN CHORUS: Yes or no? No or yes? You must choose now. Answer.

LELLA: He is my husband, in the eyes of the law and in the eyes of God.

CHERIFA: Has he converted to Islam, yes or no?

LELLA: *(somewhat aggressive)* No!

CHERIFA: Then it is neither our law nor our God.

LELLA: Dear aunt, I cannot believe you're saying these things. When I was a child, you used to tell me wonderful stories about your life in France. Now you judge me more cruelly than the others. My pain is overwhelming.

CHERIFA: Why hasn't this foreigner from the other side of the sea embraced our religion?

LELLA: Because I didn't ask him to.

CHERIFA: Then your fault is greater than his. When do you expect to convert him?

LELLA: Never.

CHERIFA: Why?

LELLA: Because God is the same for all. Because both of us have God within us and we get along very well as it is.

CHERIFA: That's not true. Nothing can compare with the pure faith of Islam.

LELLA: Those who have met my husband say he is a good Moslem because his heart is pure and generous.

CHERIFA: We are not interested in the questionable opinions of travelers. We are interested in facts: you are the concubine of this infidel and your children are therefore bastards.

LELLA: They were conceived just as yours were.

CHERIFA: Your words are proof of how low you have fallen.

LELLA: Honorable women, what are your intentions? What have you come for?

CHERIFA: To hear what you have to say and to judge you accordingly.

IN CHORUS: To judge you, to judge you.

LELLA: Judge me? You? Judge me?

CHERIFA: As your father requested. He expressed this wish long before his death; it is the legacy he has left to the Elders. It is our honor and duty to judge you and, if necessary, to condemn you.

IN CHORUS: The last wishes of the dying are sacred.

Lella laughs is disbelief. Nounou and the Madwoman press closer to her.

LELLA: His last will and testament, complete with an inheritance, I suppose. You must execute his will to have access to his fortune?

ELDER: Daughter, you are mistaken. Our act is free of material concerns. Your saintly father left us his fortune and we have put it to good use already. This is why we must fulfill the promise we made at his death bed.

LELLA: *(surprised)* You have already spent his fortune?

ELDER: I said we have put it to good use. We old people have few needs and we have spent the money for the well-being of the community. You know our village is neglected by the government but we have made some improvements these past months. We are building a mosque. We have spent more for the glory of Islam than for ourselves.

LELLA: Did the entire village inherit this money?

ELDER: Don't be ridiculous. Only those of us who are worthy.

LELLA: Those of you?

ELDER: The Elders of the village.

LELLA: *(half curious, half amused)* And what about the young people? Did they inherit also?

ELDER: Certainly not. To begin with, they have not worked as much. And then... the faith of the young is inconstant. They find religion confining. We cannot trust them. We are close to the holy because we are free of material and personal concerns. But the young have no judgment. And then, they know you, admire you... some even adore you.

LELLA: But once you adored me.

ELDER: We adore only Allah, the merciful.

LELLA: Nounou had heard nothing of this inheritance, yet she is older than us all. She is part of your clan.

ELDER: Come now, an old whore who got pregnant to buy her freedom? She is not one of us.

LELLA: She is my mother, through centuries. I imagine there are other elders who were also excluded from the inheritance. The old man who was our caretaker, was he among you?

ELDER: That renegade, that outlaw who worships liquor? Never.

LELLA: And the Cripple?

ELDER: Half a man who walks on his haunches and before whom women do not even have to veil themselves? You cannot be serious.

LELLA: It is as I suspected. Only the pure have remained loyal to me. Excuse me now, for I am very thirsty and I am going to drink without waiting for your permission.

ELDER: No! After the verdict.

LELLA: Very well. Lets' finish up with this ridiculous game.

The Madwoman stands next to Lella who caresses her hair.

Speak up. Who is next? My conscience is clear.

IN CHORUS: It is you who must speak. Defend yourself.

LELLA: Have I known you all? Do you remember me?

KHADIJA: I brought you into the world. I remember as if it were yesterday. Your mother was young but she was too fat. She almost died at your birth.

LELLA: She did die not long after, undoubtedly struck by the fact that her life would never change, that she had to live forever with a man she had not chosen: my father. But you, dear Mother, let's talk about you. I remember you were well known for your beauty.

KHADIJA: God forgive me but I will not answer to that; I will not be moved by your flattery. I am here to judge you.

LELLA: And I remember how dignified you always were, despite your poverty.

KHADIJA: Do not try to trick me. Your generosity is a thing of the past. All I know today are the last wishes of your saintly father.

ELDER: Are we here to weep over old memories?

ANGRY WOMAN: No! We are here to learn the facts and to judge.

ELDER: That's enough! Now I will speak.

ANGRY WOMAN: No, it is my turn.

ELDER: Very well, if you can bring this to an end, speak.

LELLA: *(to the Angry Woman)* Who are you? Should I know you?

ANGRY WOMAN: I came to the village after you had left. I am old, ugly, greedy and mean, so you don't have a chance with me. We share no memories; I never knew you as a child nor your mother. It's simpler this way. I know only of the wishes of the *Hadj* and I kiss the ground he stepped on. *(She kisses the ground)*.

IN CHORUS: The ground he stepped on.

LELLA: Judging by your accent, you must come from the mountains toward the east.

ANGRY WOMAN: Wherever I come from, I am here now. Sisters, come closer, help me.

The circle tightens around the Angry Woman who faces Lella.

IN CHORUS: We are with you, with you.

ANGRY WOMAN: You who have come back, what have you to say?

LELLA: That I have come back because I wanted to and that I fear no one.

ANGRY WOMAN: You do not fear Allah?

LELLA: No, why should I, since I've done nothing wrong?

ANGRY WOMAN: You married a foreigner, an infidel. You have wronged us.

LELLA: I married a man for the peace that shines from his face and the goodness of his soul.

ANGRY WOMAN: Once again, will he convert?

LELLA: No.

IN CHORUS: No, she said no, did you hear? She said no.

ANGRY WOMAN: No conversion, no circumcision, is that correct?

LELLA: Yes.

ANGRY WOMAN: This is intolerable.

LELLA: I know foreigners have accepted circumcision to marry here, but customs lose their meaning elsewhere. *(Pause.)* Did you know, poor women who have never left your village and who cannot read; did you know that circumcision is a Semite ritual, that we Moslems share this with the Jews?

IN CHORUS: Blasphemy, more blasphemy.

LELLA: *(sadly)* Yes, more blasphemy. Did you also know, my poor ignorant sisters, that there were hundreds, even thousands of mixed marriages before; with circumcision and sometimes conversion, until the government realized our country was losing a lot of young women, especially the educated ones? Even worse, they were happy to leave! So it was decided: no more conversions, no more mixed marriages. All that is a little far from religious concerns, don't you think?

> There is a long pause and then a strange noise on the stairs. All heads turn to the doorway, where the head of the Cripple appears, followed by his shoed hands. He is out of breath and distraught.

CRIPPLE: Leave. Lella, Princess, you must leave now. Quick. I will stop them. They will not get past my body. Get out. Now.

LELLA: You have come back, man with half a body and a full honor.

CRIPPLE: No time to talk... Hurry. Leave at once.

LELLA: You look terrified.

CRIPPLE: I am. You are condemned, whatever you say, they will kill you. I have just discovered that is their promise. You must believe me... Go away.

ANGRY WOMAN: Get out, disgusting runt. How dare you? Throw him down the stairs.

CRIPPLE: Flee over my head and do not stop until you get to the other side of he sea...

LELLA: Man of good heart, don't worry. I know how to defend myself.

CRIPPLE: You do not stand a chance with them. Everything is stacked against you. I beg of you, Princess, listen to me.

LELLA: I hear you. I understand. Wait for me outside.

CRIPPLE: No, you leave first. I will protect you.

IN CHORUS: Get out half-man.

CRIPPLE: No one has ever wanted my life; I offer it to you today. Come. Your father has made slaves of these people, rich slaves that bow to his will.

ANGRY WOMAN: Push him down the stairs.

CRIPPLE: For the sake of those you love, go back to your new country.

> *Three women rise with determination, seize the Cripple and, with no hesitation, throw him down the stairs. As the Cripple topples down the stairs, he screams "Princess!" A final thud is heard and then silence. The three women return to their places.*

ANGRY WOMAN: Do you understand now? *(There is silence.)* So,

Princess... you were saying life in sin is beautiful?

LELLA: I cannot go on. What I have just seen revolts me so.

ANGRY WOMAN: So you have no more questions?

LELLA: *(aggressively)* None that you could possibly answer. When I first met the man who became my husband, I had a lot of questions, a lot of doubts myself.

ANGRY WOMAN: That did not stop you from straying down the wrong path.

LELLA: *(ignoring her)* I looked at the face of this foreigner and found only goodness. So I looked again.

ANGRY WOMAN: Without prejudice?

LELLA: Without the least prejudice. And after years of living together, we still love each other with the same wonder, the same delight.

NOUNOU: *(pleading)* Even a marriage outside our law becomes legitimate by the fruit it bears.

LELLA: Nounou, it's no use trying to reason with them.

ANGRY WOMAN: *(to Nounou)* Slave from before, slave forever, woman with an empty head and a overflowing mouth, who gave you permission to speak? Gag her; stop her from talking.

Footsteps are heard climbing the stairs. The Old Man appears.

OLD MAN: Honorable women, I beg of you...

ANGRY WOMAN: What does this pagan worshipper of the bottle want here?

OLD MAN: I beg of you, hear me out...

ANGRY WOMAN: We have nothing to hear from you and I am the one who is speaking. Vile alcoholic, traitor to Islam... Sisters, do you have the same hate I have in my heart for this monster? Shouldn't we strike him from the earth immediately? Let us be rid of him.

OLD MAN: *(continues courageously)* Humble women who have borne many children, listen to me. Do not undertake something that will plague you with guilt. You cannot possibly condemn this child.

> *At a signal from the Angry Woman, the group rises and stalks the Old Man. They throw him to the ground and sit on him, beating on his head with their fists.*

ELDER: Let us be rid of him!

IN CHORUS: Rid of him. Rid of him. *(They laugh fiendishly.)*

LELLA: Get off of him immediately! Leave him alone! I order you to let this old man go!

> *The Madwoman and Nounou move closer to Lella, to protect her and to seek protection. Unconscious, the Old Man is pitched into the stairwell. The group of elders returns to surround Lella and the three women clustered around her. Lella attempts to keep control of herself.*

NOUNOU: *(also trying to be controlled, she speaks in a low voice.)* That is enough. You have done enough for today. You will not touch another or you will have to pass through my dead body.

ANGRY WOMAN: That's easy enough. You are nonexistant; you have been but a shadow for so long that to be rid of you requires little effort.

NOUNOU: How can you have forgotten the good deeds of this child?

ANGRY WOMAN: I see no child here, only an old blabbering slave woman that we will put to rest once and for all.

> *The enraged women draw out heavy clubs from under their veils and move toward Lella's group. Lella moves from the clutching of her two disciples to shield them and confront the armed women.*

LELLA: Women of honor, let us talk again without anger.

> *Lella is thrust aside as the women descend on the helpless old nurse and the Madwoman. Lella tries to intervene but is held back by the raging blows of the attackers. The Nurse and the Madwoman are beaten to death and dragged offstage.*

ANGRY WOMAN: Good riddance to this filth.

ELDER: Lella, have you anything more to say to defend yourself?

LELLA: Mother, I have nothing more to say.

ELDER: Do you realize you are doomed? That you no longer have a past or a future?

LELLA: I have nothing more to say.

ELDER: Naive child. Then what is your last wish?

LELLA: I will not give it to you.

ELDER: For the last time, do you accept to convert this infidel husband?

LELLA: No, never. Do you want to see me on my knees, begging to you? Never!

ELDER: You are your mother's daughter. Live and die with honor, so she said.

LELLA: And you are daughters of none. You are, all of you, monsters without mothers, freaks, ogres.

ELDER: You had best remain silent.

IN CHORUS: You will soon be forever silent.

LELLA: You're armed with clubs to silence me forever? Are my words so powerful that you're afraid to face me with your bare hands?

IN CHORUS: Heathen! Whore! Repent!

LELLA: Never!

IN CHORUS: Repent or we will kill you as we have the others.

LELLA: Go ahead and try. I am leaving.

IN CHORUS: Watch out! She may escape.

LELLA: I am leaving and I see you as you are. I am no longer blinded by fond memories.

Proudly, she walks toward the stairs, followed by the group.

IN CHORUS: On your knees!

Lella continues walking toward the stairs.

LELLA: Never! Witches, servants of the Devil!

IN CHORUS: That is enough! Someone stop her!

LELLA: I am going far away from you to breathe fresh air, far from you poisoned souls, your rotting flesh.

IN CHORUS: Let us kill her slowly so that she is aware of her death.

LELLA: I am leaving. Thank you for ridding me of any illusions I had.

IN CHORUS: Stop her!

LELLA: I am alone but I am strong and alive. You are dead. You have been dead for ages.

IN CHORUS: Hit her! Kill her! Silence her!

> *They attack her. Struck by the first blows, she falls on her knees, but continues to move to the stairs.*

LELLA: Get your hands off me... filthy, greedy slaves.

IN CHORUS: Hit her! Kill her! Silence her!

> *Lella is battered and exhausted but relentless.*

LELLA: Till my last breath I tell you never, no, never, no, never... no... no...

> *Lella's voice fades away gradually as the others scream and beat on her until the stage is filled with the frenzy of the old women's death dance. They continue to spin, jump and shriek over Lella's dead body. Some fall on the ground while the others continue to shake. Suddenly, the male Elder enters.*

MALE ELDER: Women! That is enough!

> *All movement comes to a halt.*

You have done your duty. You may leave now.

> *The women help up those who have fallen, and all back out of the courtyard, bowing and kissing the male Elder's hand as they leave. Only the Elder and Lella's body remain on stage. He nods with satisfaction as the lights dim. The muezzin's call to evening prayer is heard.*

∽

ARABIC WORDS AND EXPRESSIONS

p.381 *Berber ala dorrok.*
Figuratively, "Rock your pain."

p.384 *Hadj*
One who has made the traditional pilgrimage to Mecca.

p.386 *Rabbi chef lina!*
"God has seen us!"

Rabbi kbir!
"God is great!"

El Hamdou lilleh!
"Praise be to God!"